MATERNAL, NEWBORN and CHILD HEALTH PROGRAMMES in INDIA

Thank you for choosing a SAGE product!
If you have any comment, observation or feedback,
I would like to personally hear from you.

Please write to me at **contactceo@sagepub.in**

Vivek Mehra, Managing Director and CEO, SAGE India.

Bulk Sales

SAGE India offers special discounts
for purchase of books in bulk.
We also make available special imprints
and excerpts from our books on demand.

For orders and enquiries, write to us at

Marketing Department
SAGE Publications India Pvt Ltd
B1/I-1, Mohan Cooperative Industrial Area
Mathura Road, Post Bag 7
New Delhi 110044, India

E-mail us at **marketing@sagepub.in**

Get to know more about SAGE

Be invited to SAGE events, get on our mailing list.
Write today to **marketing@sagepub.in**

This book is also available as an e-book.

MATERNAL, NEWBORN and CHILD HEALTH PROGRAMMES in INDIA

A Programme Science Approach

B.M. RAMESH
SHIVA S. HALLI
KRISHNAMURTHY JAYANNA
MOHAN H.L.

Los Angeles I London I New Delhi
Singapore I Washington DC I Melbourne

First published in 2018 by

 SAGE Publications India Pvt Ltd
B1/I-1 Mohan Cooperative Industrial Area
Mathura Road, New Delhi 110 044, India
www.sagepub.in

SAGE Publications Inc
2455 Teller Road
Thousand Oaks, California 91320, USA

SAGE Publications Ltd
1 Oliver's Yard, 55 City Road
London EC1Y 1SP, United Kingdom

SAGE Publications Asia-Pacific Pte Ltd
3 Church Street
#10-04 Samsung Hub
Singapore 049483

Published by Vivek Mehra for SAGE Publications India Pvt Ltd, typeset in 10.5/13 pt Sabon by Zaza Eunice, Hosur, Tamil Nadu, India and printed at Chaman Enterprises, New Delhi.

Library of Congress Cataloging-in-Publication Data

Names: Ramesh, B.M., author. | Halli, Shivalingappa S., author. |
    Jayanna, Krishnamurthy, author. | Mohan H.L., author.
Title: Maternal, newborn, and child health programmes in India: a programme
    science approach / B.M. Ramesh, Shiva S. Halli, Krishnamurthy Jayanna, and
    Mohan H.L.
Description: New Delhi, India; Thousand Oaks, California, USA: SAGE
    Publications, 2018. | Includes bibliographical references and index.
Identifiers: LCCN 2018008431| ISBN 9789352807048 (hb) | ISBN 9789352807055
    (e-pub) | ISBN 9789352807062 (e book)
Subjects: | MESH: Maternal-Child Health Services | Child Health Services |
    Program Development | Developing Countries | India
Classification: LCC RG965.I4 | NLM WA 310 JI4 | DDC 362.198200954–dc23 LC record
available at https://lccn.loc.gov/2018008431

ISBN: 978-93-528-0704-8 (HB)

SAGE Team: Rajesh Dey, Alekha Chandra Jena, Shaonli Deb and Ritu Chopra

All figures/tables/graphs used in this book are conceptualized during the authors' work unless otherwise specified.

CONTENTS

LIST OF TABLES

LIST OF FIGURES

LIST OF ABBREVIATIONS

AAA	ANMs, ASHAs and AWWs
AHS	Annual Health Survey
AMMA	Assess, Manage, Measure, Advocate
AMTSL	active management of the third stage of labour
ANC	antenatal care
ANMs	auxiliary nurse midwives
ARSs	Aarogya Raksha Samitis
ASHAs	accredited social health activists
AWWs	Anganwadi workers
AYUSH	Ayurveda, Yoga and Naturopathy, Unani, Siddha and Homoeopathy
BCSs	block community supervisors
BEmONC	basic emergency obstetric and newborn care
BMGF	Bill & Melinda Gates Foundation
BMV	block monitoring visit
BP	blood pressure
BPHC	block primary health centre
BPL	below poverty line
BPMs	block programme managers
CBR	crude birth rate
CBTSs	community behaviour tracking surveys
CDL	community demands list
CEmONC	comprehensive emergency obstetric and new-born care
CHCs	community health centres
CMO	chief medical officer
CMS	chief medical superintendents
CNA	community needs assessment
CPGs	clinical practice guidelines
CRPs	community resources persons

CRS	civil registration system
CSSM	Child Survival and Safe Motherhood
DAPCUs	District AIDS Prevention and Control Units
DDW	district drug warehouse
DFWO	district family welfare officer
DEO	data entry operator
DHs	district hospitals
DHFW	Directorate of Health and Family Welfare
DHO	district health officer/district health and family welfare officer
DHS	district health society
DLHS	district level household survey
DPs	development partners
DPM	district programme managers
DPMU	district programme management unit
DPS	district programme specialist
DRCs	district recruitment committees
DRHO	district reproductive health officer
DTC	district training centre
EAG	Empowered Action Group
EDD	expected date of delivery
EDS	equipment, drugs and supplies
EmONC	emergency obstetric and newborn care
EMRI	Emergency Management and Research Institute
ESIC	Employees' State Insurance Corporation
ETTs	enumeration and tracking tools
FHR	foetal heart rate
FOGSI	Federation of Obstetric and Gynaecological Societies of India
FFC	family focused communication
F-IMNCI	facility-based integrated management of neonatal and childhood illness
FLWs	front-line workers
FP	family planning
FRUs	first referral units

GIS	geographic information system
GoK	Government of Karnataka
GoUP	Government of Uttar Pradesh
Hb	haemoglobin
HBFFC	home-based family-focused counselling
HBNC	home-based newborn care
HBMNC	home-based maternal and newborn care
HMIS	health management information system
HPDs	high-priority districts
HRIS	human resource information system
ICDS	Integrated Child Development Services
ICO	India Country Office
ICT	information and communication technology
IDIs	in-depth interviews
IEC	information, education and communication
IFA	iron–folic acid
IHAT	India Health Action Trust
IIPS	International Institute for Population Sciences
IM	intramuscular
IMCI	integrated management of childhood illness
IMNCI	integrated management of neonatal and child-hood illness
IMR	infant mortality rate
ISDP	integrated skills development programme
IUCD	intrauterine contraceptive device
IV	intravenous
IVR	interactive voice response
IYCF	infant and young child feeding
JHAs	junior health assistants
jhpiego	Johns Hopkins Program for International Education in Gynecology and Obstetrics
JSY	Janani Suraksha Yojana
JSSK	Janani Shishu Suraksha Karyakram
KAP	knowledge, attitude and practices
KHPT	Karnataka Health Promotion Trust

KHSDRP	Karnataka Health Systems Development Reform Project
KMC	kangaroo mother care
KPI	key performance indicator
KSAPS	Karnataka State AIDS Prevention Society
KDWLS	Karnataka Drug Warehousing and Logistics Society
LBW	low birth weight
LHVs	lady health visitors
LMP	last menstrual period
LMIS	logistics management information system
LSAS	life-saving anaesthetic skill
M&E	monitoring and evaluation
MCH	Maternal and Child Health
MCTS	mother and child tracking system
MDGs	Millennium Development Goals
MHW	male health worker
MIS	management information system
MK	Madilu Kit
MMR	maternal mortality rate
MNCH	maternal, newborn and child health
MNH	maternal and newborn health
MoHFW	Ministry of Health & Family Welfare
MOs	medical officers
MOIC	medical officer in-charge
MPR	monthly performance review
MWCD	Ministry of Women & Child Development
NBSUs	newborn stabilization units
NFHS	National Family Health Survey
NHM	National Health Mission
NHSRC	National Health Systems Resource Centre
NIC	National Informatics Centre
NMs	nurse mentors
NNF	National Neonatology Forum
NPCC	National Programme Coordination Committee
NRCs	nutrition rehabilitation centres

NRHM	National Rural Health Mission
NRU	National RMNCH+A Unit
NSSK	Navjaat Shishu Suraksha Karyakram
OBG	obstetrics and gynaecology
OCPs	oral contraceptive pills
ORS	oral rehydration salts
ORT	oral rehydration therapy
OSCEs	objectively structured clinical examinations
OT	operation theatre
PAC	post-abortion care
PHCs	primary health centres
PI	performance improvement
PIH	pregnancy-induced hypertension
PIPs	programme implementation plans
PNC	postnatal care
PPE	personal protective equipment
PPH	postpartum haemorrhage
PPIUCD	postpartum intrauterine contraceptive devices
PPIUD	postpartum intrauterine device
PPPs	public–private partnerships
PPTCT	prevention of parent-to-child transmission
PQI	performance and quality improvement
PROM	premature rupture of the membranes
PS	programme science
QIC	quality improvement committee
RAA	Remote Area Allowance
RCH	reproductive and child health
RFS	rolling facility survey
RHS	Reproductive Health Survey
RKSs	Rogi Kalyan Samitis
RMNCH+A	reproductive, maternal, newborn, child and adolescent health
RP	resource person
RTIs	respiratory tract infections
SBA	safe birth attendant
SCMT	supportive community monitoring tool

SCs	subcentres
SDGs	sustainable development goals
SEARCH	Society for Education, Action and Research in Community Health
SHG	self-help group
SIHFW	State Institute of Health & Family Welfare
SJMC	St. John's Medical College Hospital
SLP	state lead partner
SNCUs	special newborn care units
SOP	standard operating procedure
SPMU	state project management unit
SRS	Sample Registration System
SSLC	secondary school-leaving certificate
STIs	sexually transmitted infections
TFR	total fertility rate
THs	taluk hospitals
TL	tubal ligation
TRIPS	Trade-Related Aspects of Intellectual Property Rights
TOT	training of the trainer
TSU	technical support unit
TT	tetanus toxoid
U/Alb	urine albumin
U5MR	under-five mortality rate
UoM	University of Manitoba
UP	Uttar Pradesh
VHIR	Village Health Index Register
VHSCs	village health and sanitation committees
VHSNCs	village health and sanitation nutrition committees
VHNDs	village health and nutrition days
WIFS	weekly iron and folic acid supplementation

ACKNOWLEDGEMENTS

The material presented in this book is based on our many years of working in the area of maternal and child health both in Karnataka and Uttar Pradesh in the form of providing technical support to the respective state governments to implement their maternal, neonatal and child health programmes. The funding was provided by the Bill & Melinda Gates Foundation for the technical support units, and without it, we would not have taken up these tasks and this publication. The views expressed herein are those of the authors and do not necessarily reflect the official policy or position of the Bill & Melinda Gates Foundation. The two technical support units in the two states involved many leaders, especially from the University of Manitoba, and without naming them, we would like to sincerely acknowledge their contributions. Similarly, thousands of people work on the ground and are pillars of these technical units, including community members, front-line workers, providers, administrators and project staff of Karnataka Health Promotion Trust and India Health Action Trust and their consortium partners namely Intrahealth International, St John's National Academy of Health Sciences, Karuna Trust, Engender Health and John Snow International. We are also grateful to them. Of course, the technical support units would not have existed without the support and cordial working relationships, especially with the ministries of health of the two states at all levels and at the national level. We have no words to express our gratitude.

We are also grateful to many people who helped us to put together this book, most notably, Dr Ravi Kanth M. Similarly, Karnataka Health Promotion Trust staff helped us to develop figures and illustrations presented in the book. Of course, we would like to thank the staff at SAGE Publications for guiding us through the process.

ACKNOWLEDGMENTS

INTRODUCTION

The progress of any country is dependent on its today's children. Because children are the future of any society, and their mothers are guardians of that future, quality health care for mothers and children leads to many positive outcomes. Mothers are seen more as caregivers and homemakers and their value is generally underestimated by society. But mothers are the ones who transmit the cultural history of communities and their families, and pass on social norms and traditions. As Amartya Sen writes in his book *Development as Freedom*, mothers have the power to influence the early behaviour of a child and establish lifestyle patterns that not only define the child's future development and health but also ultimately shape societies. Because of this, society must value the health of mothers and children as an end in itself and not merely treat it as a contribution to the capital of the nation.[1]

Healthy children form the core of human capital of any country. If health is not taken care of, illnesses and malnutrition reduce the cognitive development of a child and lead to suboptimal intellectual performance,[2] negatively affect school enrolment and attendance[3] and impair final educational achievement. As many studies show, intrauterine growth retardation and malnutrition during early childhood will have long-term negative effects on a child's body size and strength,[4] with negative impact on productivity in adulthood. In addition, a maternal death would lead

[1] A. Sen, *Development as Freedom* (New York, NY: Anchor Books, 1999).

[2] A. Bhargava, 'Nutrition, Health and Economic Development: Some Policy Priorities', *Food and Nutrition Bulletin* 22, no. 2(2001): 173–177.

[3] P. Glewwe, H. G. Jacoby, and E. M. King, 'Early Childhood Nutrition and Academic Achievement: A Longitudinal Analysis', *Journal of Public Economics* 81, no. 3(2001): 345–368.

[4] R. Martorell, U. Ramakrishnan, D. G. Schroeder, P. Melgar, and L. Neufeld, 'Intrauterine Growth Retardation, Body Size, Body Composition

to loss of a member of a society whose presence and labour are essential to cohesion of families and communities. Healthy mothers are more available for social interaction and creation of social capital, which are prerequisites of a well-functioning society.

Maternal and child health (MCH) care is also a prerequisite for equity. Motherhood and childhood are periods of particularly high vulnerability, and mothers and children require special care and assistance during those times.[5] Illnesses among mothers and children, particularly those that occur as major obstetric complications, are mostly unpredictable and can lead to catastrophic expenditures. Studies show that this pushes many households into poverty.[6] The fear of unaffordable expenditures is often a deterrent for the timely uptake of health care services. In short, not many other inequities that exist in our society are as detrimental as those that affect the health and survival of women and children. Therefore, for governments that take the development of the poor and the vulnerable seriously and aim to address the inequality and redistribution of wealth, it is a logical starting point to improve the living conditions and access to health care for mothers and children. Indeed, improving the health of mothers and children is central to the world's push to reduce poverty and inequality.

Initiatives to Address Maternal and Child Health in India

Given the importance of MCH for a country's progress, India has a long history of health initiatives that address the needs of

and Physical Performance in Adolescence', *European Journal of Clinical Nutrition* 52, Suppl. 1 (1998): S43–S52.

[5] H. E. Reed, M. A. Koblinsky, and W. H. Mosley, *The Consequences of Maternal Morbidity and Maternal Mortality: Report of a Workshop* (Washington, DC: National Academy Press, 1998).

[6] J. Borghi, K. Hanson, C. A. Acquah, G. Ekanmian, V. Filippi, C. Ronsmans et al., 'Costs of Near-miss Obstetric Complications for Women and Their Families in Benin and Ghana', *Health, Policy and Planning* 18, no. 4(2003): 383–390.

MCH. Reproductive health services in India were first initiated in the early 1900s with training of rural midwives and birth attendants to improve maternity services. This was not done by the government of the time but by the Indian Red Cross Society. However, in 1931, the Madras State established a separate Maternal Welfare Section as part of the Directorate of Health Services. In 1946, MCH services were integrated within General Health Services but the actual implementation happened only after 1955. There was also pressure from the United Nations (UN) agencies, such as the World Health Organization (WHO) and United Nations International Children's Emergency Fund (UNICEF), to expand MCH services, especially in rural areas. Eventually, after 1962, MCH services were integrated with the primary health centres (PHCs), and an auxiliary nurse midwife (ANM) was allocated per 10,000 population in the rural areas. More importantly, a national policy and a children's board were established in 1974.

A significant development took place in 1992 when the political system was decentralized through the enhancement of the Panchayat Raj Act. According to this Act, primary health care and basic amenities to people became the responsibility of the Panchayats. An important feature of the Act was that women were politically empowered through reservation of one-third seats in Panchayats. Similarly, at the International Conference on Population and Development in 1994, women's groups successfully argued that population policies should include programmes for women's development, women's rights and women's reproductive health, among others. Consequently, the Government of India (GoI) began to implement programmes for education of girls, gender equity, equality and empowerment of women, universal access to reproductive health and reproductive rights. Thereafter, in 1997, the GoI launched official reproductive and child health (RCH) programmes, including MCH services, immunization services for children, treatment of reproductive tract infections (RTIs) and sexually transmitted diseases (STDs) as well as special services for adolescent girls and boys. (For a more detailed review of the GoI programmes for RCH, please refer to Srinivasan et al.).[7]

Another significant move was the launch of National Rural Health Mission (NRHM) in April 2005, a flagship programme by the GoI, to tackle the high rate of maternal, neonatal and child morbidity and mortality among India's rural populations. More recently, the GoI named the programme National Health Mission (NHM) to also include coverage of the urban poor. Through the NHM, the GoI initiated programmes such as the Janani Suraksha Yojana (JSY) in 2005, which provides conditional cash transfers to incentivize women to give birth in a health facility rather than at home.[8] Key aspects of the NHM are its enormous scale, its focus on extending services to the poor and its inherent flexibility for introducing innovative approaches for improving health-system responses to improve reproductive, maternal, newborn, child and adolescent health (RMNCH+A) outcomes.

In their published document 'A Strategic Approach to Reproductive, Maternal, Neonatal, Child and Adolescent Health (RNMCH+A) in India' (2013), the GoI recognizes that to improve RMNCH+A outcomes, these thematic components cannot be addressed in isolation but should be approached as a whole. This renewed the GoI's campaign to improve RMNCH+A outcomes across India and led to the development of a 5×5 matrix for addressing RMNCH+A. Additionally, the GoI and the NHM released the Maternal and Newborn Health Toolkit (2013) to provide guidance and standardization in the provision of quality maternal and newborn health services across the states as they address the 5×5 matrix.

[7] K. Srinivasan, C. Shekhar, and P. Arokiasamy, 'Reviewing Reproductive and Child Health Programmes in India', *Economic and Political Weekly* July 14(2007): 2931–2939.

[8] Y. Lim, J. Y. Kim, M. Rich, S. Stulac, J. B. Niyonzima, M. C. Smith Fawzi et al., 'Improving Prevention of Mother-to-Child Transmission of HIV Care and Related Services in Eastern Rwanda', *PLoS Med* 7, no. 7 (2010): e1000302.

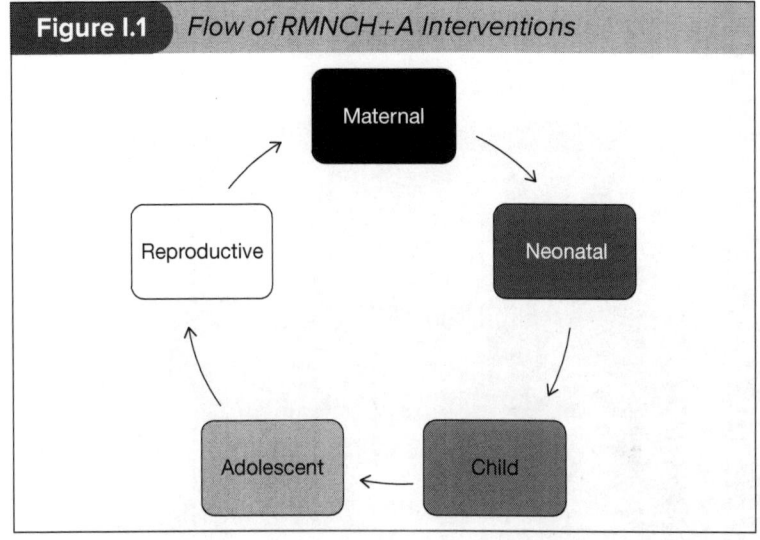

Figure I.1 *Flow of RMNCH+A Interventions*

The GoI identified five primary bottlenecks to improving coverage of key RMNCH+A intervention along a continuum of care:

1. Availability
2. Access
3. Utilization
4. Coverage
5. Quality of services

Moreover, private sector participation with government programmes in RMNCH+A services remains inadequate because of varied competencies, lack of financial incentives and little use of data for decision-making. Therefore, a RMNCH+A strategic roadmap, titled 'A Strategic Approach to RMNCH+A in India', has been designed by the GoI to focus on the life-cycle approach from pregnancy to childbirth to adolescent age groups in the most underserved districts in each state of the country. The effectiveness of high-impact RMNCH+A interventions, described as

Figure I.2 *5 x 5 Matrix for RMNCH+A by the GoI*

5 X 5 Matrix for High Impact RMNCH+A Interventions
To be Implemented with High Coverage and High Quality

Reproductive Health

- Focus on spacing methods, particularly PPIUCD at high case load facilities
- Focus on interval IUCD at all facilities including subcentres on fixed days
- Home delivery of Contraceptives (HDC) and Ensuring Spacing at Birth (ESB) through ASHAs
- Ensuring access to Pregnancy Testing Kits (PTK- "Nischay Kits") and strengthening comprehensive abortion care services.
- Maintaining quality sterilization services

Maternal Health

- Use MCTS to ensure early registration of pregnancy and full ANC
- Detect high risk pregnancies and line list including severely anemic mothers and ensure appropriate management.
- Equip Delivery points with highly trained HR and ensure equitable access to EmOC services through FRUs; Add MCH wings as per need
- Review maternal, infant and child deaths for corrective actions
- Identify villages with high numbers of home deliveries and distribute Misoprostol to selected women in 8th month of pregnancy for consumption during 3rd stage of labour; Incentivize ANMs for home deliveries

Newborn Health

- Early initiation and exclusive breastfeeding
- Home based newborn care through ASHA
- Essential Newborn Care and resuscitation services at all delivery points
- Special Newborn Care Units with highly trained human resource and other infra structure
- Community level use of Gentamycin by ANM

Child Health

- Complementary feeding, IFA supplementation and focus on nutrition
- Diarrhoea management at community level using ORS and Zinc
- Management of pneumonia
- Full immunization coverage
- Rashtriya Bal Swasthya Karyakram (RBSK): screening of children for 4Ds' (birth defects, development delays, deficiencies and disease) and its management

Adolescent Health

- Address teenage pregnancy and increase contraceptive prevalence in adolescents
- Introduce Community based services through peer educators
- Strengthen ARSH clinics
- Roll out National Iron Plus Initiative including weekly IFA supplementation
- Promote Menstrual Hygiene

Health Systems Strengthening

- Case load based deployment of HR at all levels
- Ambulances, drugs, diagnostics, reproductive health commodities
- Health Education, Demand Promotion & behaviour change communication
- Supportive supervision and use of data for monitoring and review, including scorecards based on HMIS
- Public grievances redressal mechanism; client satisfaction and patient safety through all round quality assurance

Cross Cutting Interventions

- Bring down out of pocket expenses by ensuring JSSK, RBSK and other free entitlements
- ASHAs & Nurses to provide specialized and quality care to pregnant women and children
- Address social determinants of health through convergence
- Focus on un-served and underserved villages, urban slums and blocks
- Introduce difficult area and performance based incentives

Source: GoI document on RMNCH+A.
Disclaimer: This image is for representation purpose only.

a continuum of care, would be determined by the coverage of quality services achieved among the affected section of the population as also the availability, acceptability, actual utilization of services and quality of services delivered. Currently, RMNCH+A services are being implemented across the country with further intensification of efforts in 184 high-priority districts (HPDs) in 29 states with technical support provided by the development partners (DPs). Moreover, the states are mandated to allocate at least 30% higher resources (within the overall state resource envelope under NRHM) to the HPDs.

These initiatives by the GoI also corresponded with the global movement that focused on the health needs of mother and child as the health indicators pointed to a pressing need for interventions that could be facilitated by knowledge sharing through global partnerships. Most significant of these initiatives happened in September 2000. Building upon a decade of major UN conferences and summits, world leaders came together at UN Headquarters in New York to adopt the UN Millennium Declaration, committing their nations to a new global partnership to setting out a series of time-bound targets with a deadline of 2015. These targets have come to be known as the Millennium Development Goals (MDGs). Among the MDGs, Goal 4 refers to reducing infant and child mortality and Goal 5 refers to improving the maternal health. The UN Millennium Campaign, started in 2002, supported and inspired people from around the world to take action in support of the MDGs.

An MDG Summit was held in 2010 and it concluded with the adoption of a global action plan—Keeping the Promise: United to Achieve the Millennium Development Goals—and the announcement of a number of initiatives. In a major push to accelerate progress on MCH, a number of heads of states and governments from developed and developing countries, along with the private sector, foundations, international organizations, civil society and research organizations, pledged over US$40 billion in resources over the next five years. Moreover, in September

2013, the Secretary General hosted a high-level forum to catalyse and accelerate further action to achieve the MDGs and enrich the deliberations of the General Assembly and beyond. The forum focused on concrete examples of scaling up success and identifying further opportunities.

India is a signatory to the Millennium Declaration adopted at the UN General Assembly in September 2000, and has consistently reaffirmed its commitment towards the eight development goals. The targets of the MDGs converged with India's own development goals to reduce poverty and other areas of deprivation. India's MDG framework was based on UNDG's MDG 2003 framework, and it included all the 8 goals and 12 out of the 18 targets which were relevant for India. The MDG framework of the country was contextualized through a concordance with the existing official indicators of corresponding dimensions in the national statistical system. This process witnessed dropping some targets and indicators, which were not relevant for India or due to non-availability of sufficiently reliable data and modifying/including some indicators found better suited to the Indian context.[9]

Situational Analysis of Maternal and Child Health in India

As a result of all these efforts and the import of MDGs in public health, the global maternal mortality rate (MMR) declined dramatically between 1990 and 2015, from 385 maternal deaths per 100,000 live births in 1995 to 216 in 2015. Despite this 44% decline, the MDG target of reducing the MMR by three-quarters was not met. In 2015, 109 of the 228 countries in the world for whom the maternal mortality data was available had a MMR

[9] Ministry of Statistics and Programme Implementation, *Millennium Development Goals: India Country Report 2015* (New Delhi: Social Statistics Division, Government of India, 2015).

of over 70 per 100,000 live births.[10] With a MMR of 174, India ranked 74th among countries with the highest MMR. In 2015, the global under-five mortality rate (U5MR) was less than half the rate in 1990, falling just short of the MDG target of a two-thirds reduction.

At this juncture, the UNDP released country reports that assessed the achievements of the MDGs for each country, including India. The report detailed how India witnessed significant progress towards the MDGs, with some targets met ahead of the 2015 deadline. However, the progress has been inconsistent. The following is the summary of the progress related to Goal 4 and Goal 5 as mentioned in the country report released by UNDP in 2015:[11]

Goal 4. Reduce Child Mortality: The fourth Millennium Development Goal aims to reduce mortality among children under five by two-thirds. India's Under Five Mortality (U5MR) declined from 125 per 1,000 live births in 1990 to 49 per 1,000 live births in 2013. The MDG target is of 42 per 1000, which suggests that India is moderately on track, largely due to the sharp decline in recent years. Child survival in India needs sharper focus. This includes better managing neonatal and childhood illnesses and improving child survival, particularly among vulnerable communities. Survival risk remains a key challenge for the disadvantaged who have little access to reproductive and child health services. Major states in the heartland of India are likely to fall significantly short of these targets. Infant Mortality Rate (IMR) is lowest in Kerala (12) and highest for Madhya Pradesh (54). The key to significant progress in reducing U5MR and infant mortality rates rests with reducing neonatal deaths, that is, infant deaths that occur within a year of birth at a fast pace. The large scale of under-nutrition in expectant mothers and children poses a critical development challenge for India. On a positive note, various Ministries under the Government of

---

[10] World Bank, 2015. Available at: http://data.worldbank.org/indicator/ (accessed on 2 October 2017).

[11] Ministry of Statistics and Programme Implementation, *Millennium Development Goals: India Country Report 2015*.

India are implementing child centric policies and programmes which are vigorously attending the issues related to child health. This includes the National Policy on Children (2013); National Policy on Early Childhood Care and Education; Integrated Child Development Services (ICDS) and other initiatives focusing on holistic child development.

Goal 5. Improve Maternal Health: From a Maternal Mortality Rate (MMR) of 437 per 100,000 live births in 1990–91, India is required to reduce MMR to 109 per 100,000 live births by 2015. Between 1990 and 2006, there has been some improvement in the MMR, which has declined to 167 per 100,000 live births in 2009. However, despite this, India's progress on this goal has been slow and off track. Safe motherhood depends on the delivery by trained personnel, particularly through institutional facilities. Delivery in institutional facilities has risen from 26 percent in 1992–93 to 72 percent in 2009. Consequently, deliveries by skilled personnel have increased at the same pace, from 33 percent to 76.2 percent in the same period. One contributing factor has been the introduction of a conditional cash transfer scheme, Janani Suraksha Yojana which improved the delivery of babies in hospitals and nursing homes to 72 per cent in 2009. However, the quality of maternal care remains a concern.[12]

More detailed statistics related to MCH give a nuanced picture of where the country stood in relation to MCH.[13] For instance, according to the Ministry of Health and Family Welfare (MoHFW), approximately 2.6 crore babies are born in the country annually, out of which 7.3 lakh die within the first 30 days of their lives. Also, about 13% of India's population is comprised of children below six years of age, and among them an estimated 12.7 lakh die annually. Similarly, around 45,000 women die

---

[12] UNDP, 2015. Available at: http://www.in.undp.org/content/india/en/home/post-2015/mdgoverview.html (accessed on 5 November 2017).

[13] For detailed review, please see Priyanka Shah, 'MDGs to SDGs: Reproductive, Maternal, Newborn and Child Health in India: What Needs to Be Done in the SDG Era?', *Health Express* (New Delhi: Observer Research Foundation, 2016).

annually during pregnancy, and most of these deaths are from preventable causes.[14]

While the U5MR in 1990 was around 125 deaths per 1,000 live births, the Sample Registration System (SRS) 2014 revealed that the figures had dropped to 45 deaths per 1,000 live births. However, the survey found that the rural–urban and gender divides exist in the data, which showed that rural areas recorded U5MR at 51 deaths as compared to 28 deaths per 1,000 live births in urban regions. Moreover, when one looks at gender, at the national level, U5MR is higher for females (49) than that of males (42). There was a greater gap between male and female in rural areas than in urban areas. Also, there were inter- and intra-state variations: while states such as Kerala showed U5MR to be 13, states such as Assam (66) and Madhya Pradesh (65) registered one of the highest rates in India.[15] Infectious diseases such as pneumonia, diarrhoea, measles and other neonatal causes result in one-third of the under-five deaths among children in India.[16]

Another important indicator of child health is the IMR. India did not make significant progress when it came to IMR. From 80 deaths per 1,000 live births in 1990, it went down to 39 by 2014. However, the target was to reach 27 by 2015. The country also witnessed high neonatal mortality rates. As with other indicators, IMR in rural areas was observed to be much higher

[14] National Health Mission, 'Child Health: Background, Ministry of Health & Family Welfare', Government of India. Available at: http://nrhm. gov.in/nrhmcomponents/rmnch-a/child-health-immunization/child-health/ background.html (accessed on 5 November 2017); PTI, '5 Women in India Die Every Hour Due to Childbirth: WHO', *The Indian Express*, 16 June 2016. Available at: http://indianexpress.com/article/lifestyle/health/5-women-in-india-dieevery-hour-during-childbirth-who-2856975/ (accessed on 10 September 2016).

[15] C. Kumar, P. K. Singh, and R. K. Rai, 'Under-Five Mortality in High Focus States in India: A District Level Geospatial Analysis', *PLOS ONE* 7, no. 5 (2012): e37515.

[16] Ministry of Health and Family Welfare, *A Strategic Approach to RMNCH+A in India* (New Delhi: Government of India, 2013).

than in urban areas.[17] Further, IMR was noticed to be higher among female babies than male, and the gender gap was highest in Rajasthan. The shortage of trained medical personnel and poor health infrastructure in rural areas has been linked to higher neonatal deaths in the country.[18] Malnutrition is another contributing factor to infant and child mortality. Other reasons such as improper breastfeeding practices, lack of proper supplementary feeding and insufficient quantities of breastmilk (due to poor nutrition of the mother) lead to severe malnutrition in children.

MMR is another important health indicator because it gives an insight into the maternal health situation in a country and can also be used as a proxy indicator for the quality of the health care system. Based on MDGs, MMR was expected to reach the level of 109 maternal deaths per 100,000 live births by 2015. While the target has been missed by a huge margin, the data shows that there has been over a 50% decline in the last two decades. As with IMR, MMR varies from state to state based on performances—from 61 in Kerala to 300 in Assam. What is alarming is that around 67% of the total maternal deaths in India occur in only four states: Bihar, Uttar Pradesh, Madhya Pradesh and Rajasthan. Moreover, the data shows that in terms of age groups, women between ages 20 and 29 years constitute 68% of total maternal deaths.[19] According to a report by the MoHFW, postpartum haemorrhage, sepsis due to infection, unsafe abortions, anaemia and malaria are the top medical causes of maternal deaths in India. Additionally, roughly 54% of pregnant women in India suffer from anaemia, a condition largely caused by dietary deficiency.[20]

---

[17] SRS Statistical Report 2014, Government of India.

[18] R. P. Upadhyay, Chinnakal P., Odukoys, O., Yadav, K., Sinha, S., Rizwan, S. A., Daral, S., Chellaiyan, V. G. and Silan, V. 'High Neonatal Mortality Rates in Rural India: What Options to Explore?' ISRN Pediatrics September 16(2012): 1–10.

[19] Ministry of Statistics and Implementation, Millennium Development Goals: India Country Report (New York, NY: UNDP, 2015).

[20] World Bank, Prevalence of Anaemia Among Pregnant Women (Washington, DC: World Bank, 2016).

Another important indicator related to maternal health is the proportion of births attended by skilled health personnel. It was expected that the country would achieve the target of 100% by 2015. While the country did not reach the target, the data shows that the proportion of live births attended by skilled health personnel increased from 34% in 1993 to 87 in 2015.[21] It is remarkable to note that states such as Kerala, Goa and Tamil Nadu achieved 99% coverage. On the other hand, states such as Nagaland, Jharkhand and Bihar are still lagging behind with around 50% coverage. There are various reasons why women do not access health facility for delivery: high costs, long distances, lack of transportation or purely out of preference. This points to the important role a skilled birth attendant can play in safe delivery.[22]

Challenges to maternal, newborn and child health programmes

To understand why MDG targets for health were not reached, one has to look at the challenges faced by the MCH programmes in India. For instance, Srinivasan et al. have attempted to assess the impact of RCH approach to programme implementation using National Family Health Surveys (NFHSs).[23] Their analyses indicate that post RCH approach there is a slowdown in progress. More specifically, it is noted that in 25 out of 29 MCH and Family Planning indicators, pace of improvement during the period 1998 to 2005–2006 is slower than the pace of improvement during the

---

[21] A. L. Montgomery, Fadel, S., Kumar, R., Bondy, S., Moineddin, R. and Jha, P. 'The Effect of Health-Facility Admission and Skilled Birth Attendant Coverage on Maternal Survival in India: A Case Control Analysis', *PLOS ONE* 9, no. 6 (2014): e95696.

[22] R. Khanna, 'MDG 5 in India: Whither Reproductive and Sexual Rights?' Common Health, RUWSEC and SAHAJ, 2013, 2016. Available at: http://www.commonhealth.in/pdf/MDG-5-in-India-Whither-reproductiveand-sexual-rights.pdf (accessed on 3 December 2016).

[23] Srinivasan, Shekhar, and Arokiasamy, 'Reviewing Reproductive and Child Health Programmes in India'.

periods 1992–1993 and 1998–1999. Further, they argue that this is in spite of substantial increase in both at an aggregate level expenditure and on a per capita basis. The authors question the very fact of decentralization and integrative approach and argue that there is no synergy between different programmes. For them, the RCH umbrella is leaking!

The authors also assess the decentralization approach by extensively analysing the District Level Health (RCH) Surveys (DLHSs). Their conclusion is that the states have a significantly larger effect than the districts on the RCH indicators such as antenatal care (ANC), institutional deliveries, treatment of any delivery complications, awareness of RTIs and oral rehydration therapy. In other words, decentralization and integrated approaches to MCH services will not be effective to increase programme efficiency and effectiveness. However, they do notice that active involvement of communities through front-line workers (FLWs) and careful integration of different health services with well-trained health workers resulted in success at least in some states.[24] Indeed, based on evidences such as these, the community interventions are designed specifically to enhance participation of community-level structures in supporting and monitoring the utilization and coverage of MCH services using a continuum of care approach through building the capacity of community-based FLWs. (Case studies related to this that are based in northern Karnataka and the HPDs of Uttar Pradesh are discussed in this book.)

Similarly, Priyanka Shah takes stock of the situation in her paper titled 'MDGs to SDGs: Reproductive, Maternal, Newborn and Child Health in India'. Along with describing the MCH situation in India, she details the various challenges that one encounters while making the health system equitable and efficient. The following are some of the challenges MCH programmes encounter in India, based on the available evidence:[25]

[24] Ibid.
[25] Shah, 'MDGs to SDGs: Reproductive, Maternal, Newborn and Child Health in India'.

- Less than 20% of the community health centres (CHCs) and PHCs in the country have the means to provide basic newborn care services, research conducted by the Neonatal Health Research Initiatives found. Studies show that 62% of government hospitals lack gynaecologists and 22% of subcentres are short of auxiliary nurse midwives. Further, 80% of public hospitals attend to twice the number of patients they were intended for, indicating grave shortage in health facilities.[26] The situation is far worse in rural areas where most of the vulnerable populations reside. A precondition for the success of any programme meant to improve health care facilities is, foremost, to have enough trained medical staff to deliver the services. Since India has a massive shortage of medical staff, it becomes increasingly difficult for citizens to access health care facilities.

- The lack of timely and quality data in health outcomes tends to paint a distorted picture, and can potentially impact decision-making and tracking progress. For instance, basic health indicators are not available beyond the state level and disaggregate data across caste, region and gender do not exist for most of the core indicators.[27]

- High maternal mortality can be attributed to medical, socio-economic and health system-related problems. Women, especially in rural areas, prefer to give birth at home as opposed to government hospitals as they fear mistreatment by hospital staff.[28] With increasing reports of obstetric violence in public hospitals, it is important that the NHM hospital-care evaluations take into account quality

[26] Upadhyay et al., 'High Neonatal Mortality Rates in Rural India', *ISRN Pediatrics* (2012); P. Mittal and V. Singh, 'Understaffed, Underserved: Human Problems of India's Public-Health System', *IndiaSpend*, 7 September 2016.

[27] O. C. Kurian, 'Health Data Should Leave No Indian Behind', *The Wire*, 8 July 2015.

[28] S. Chattopadhyay, '"I Can't Take It Anymore": Sights and Awful Sounds from the Labour Room of an Indian Public Hospital', *Scroll.in*, 31 May 2015.

of staff behaviour. Disrespect, violence, mistreatment and neglect during childbirth are violations of fundamental human rights of women, and thus it is the responsibility of the state to ensure that women using these facilities feel safe and secure.

- WHO has pointed to lack of coordination among different stakeholders and sectors that impact health. Water, sanitation, education and nutrition, all have direct or indirect consequences on health and it is important for all sectors to work together to achieve progress.[29]
- The Health Management Information System (HMIS)—The HMIS which was set up to oversee the NHM and which collects data from 1.8 lakh health facilities has been riddled with problems relating to poor quality and inaccurate records. The HMIS needs to be reformed and gaps in quality and efficiency of hospitals identified. Taking quality of hospital care into account will improve policy decisions and distribution of resources.[30]
- A robust monitoring and evaluation (M&E) system is essential for tracking progress towards sustainable development goals (SDGs). The current statistical system does not provide quality and timely data. Further, lack of disaggregate data across religion, caste and other important variables may impede the ability of policymakers to frame policies that are sensitive to the socio-economic differences in population.

The aforementioned critical barriers to and gaps in the availability, accessibility, quality, utilization and coverage of maternal, newborn and child health (MNCH) services can be put into three levels:

Community level: This level includes community health workers and outreach workers. It utilizes resources such as volunteers'

---

[29] Ministry of Health and Family Welfare, *The Transition from MDGs to SDGs in India* (New Delhi: Government of India, 2016).

[30] Shah, 'Reproductive, Maternal, Newborn and Child Health in India'.

time, local knowledge and community confidence and trust as channels for delivery of interventions generally related to safe motherhood, nutrition, and simple prevention and treatments. Many programmes have attempted to construct links between community-based health care resources and households for a range of health programmes. These programmes do not substitute for a health system, but provide a channel for reaching families with information and resources. Community health workers not only promote healthy behaviours and preventive action but can also mobilize demand for appropriate services at other levels. The success of community health efforts depends critically on the context, including level of development of infrastructure, services and socio-economic resources.

Facility level: This level of care includes professionals. The basic idea is that a certain range of health care services must act as an interface between families and community programmes on the one hand and tertiary hospitals and national health policies on the other. There has been substantial convergence in the content of general first-level primary health care over time: maternity-related care (for instance, prenatal care, skilled birth attendance and family planning), interventions to address childhood diseases (such as vaccine-preventable diseases, acute respiratory infections and diarrhoea) and prevention and treatment of major infectious diseases.

Health systems level: Health system encompasses the management and delivery of quality and safe health services so that people receive a continuum of health promotion, disease prevention, diagnosis, treatment, disease management, rehabilitation and palliative care services through the different levels and sites of care within the health system and, according to their needs, throughout the life course. Health system stands for all the activities whose primary purpose is to promote, restore and/or maintain health and the people, institutions and resources arranged together in accordance with established policies to improve the health of the population they serve, while responding to people's

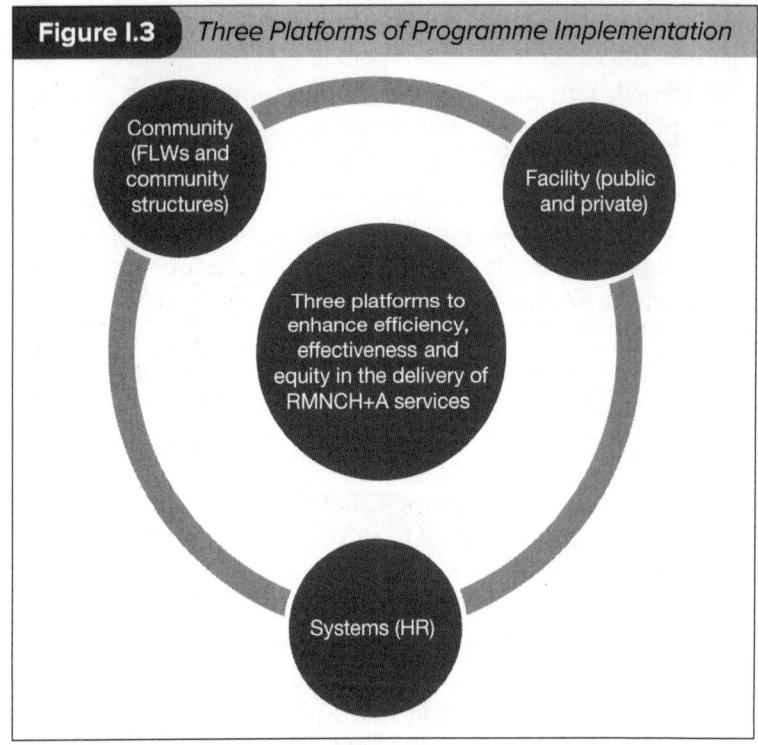

Figure I.3 *Three Platforms of Programme Implementation*

legitimate expectations and protecting them against the cost of ill health through a variety of activities whose primary intent is to improve health.

In order to improve MCH, it is important to leverage three platforms for enhancing the efficiency, effectiveness and equity of RMNCH+A services: community, facility and systems.

Sustainable development goals and health

The MDGs played a major role in focusing global attention and resources towards basic development issues. They no doubt have been among the most successful initiatives undertaken on a global scale. Given that many countries did not reach MDGs as intended, on 25 September 2015, the UN General Assembly adopted a resolution for the 2030 agenda for sustainable development, including a goal to ensure healthy lives and promote well-being for all at all ages. Taking the momentum forward in the post-2015 era, the SDGs aim to complete the work started by the MDGs, and build on them in a more holistic manner.

The SDG Goal 3 aims to 'ensure healthy lives and promote well-being for all at all ages'. It includes reduction in maternal mortality, ending newborn and child deaths due to preventable causes and combating diseases such as human immunodeficiency virus (HIV), tuberculosis (TB) and malaria, among others. The 13 specific targets for Goal 3 included:

- By 2030, reduce the global MMR to less than 70 per 100,000 live births.
- By 2030, end preventable deaths of newborns and children under 5 years of age, with all countries aiming to reduce neonatal mortality to at least as low as 12 per 1,000 live births and under-five mortality to at least as low as 25 per 1,000 live births.
- By 2030, end the epidemics of AIDS, TB, malaria and neglected tropical diseases and combat hepatitis, water-borne diseases and other communicable diseases.
- By 2030, reduce by one-third premature mortality from non-communicable diseases through prevention and treatment and promote mental health and well-being.
- Strengthen the prevention and treatment of substance abuse, including narcotic drug abuse and harmful use of alcohol.
- By 2020, halve the number of global deaths and injuries from road traffic accidents.
- By 2030, ensure universal access to sexual and reproductive health care services (including for family planning),

information and education, and the integration of reproductive health into national strategies and programmes.

- Achieve universal health coverage, including financial risk
protection, access to quality essential health care services
and safe, effective, quality and affordable essential medicines and vaccines for all.

- By 2030, substantially reduce the number of deaths and
illnesses from hazardous chemicals and air, water and soil
pollution and contamination.

- Strengthen the implementation of the World Health
Organization Framework Convention on Tobacco Control
in all countries, as appropriate.

- Support the research and development of vaccines and
medicines for the communicable and non-communicable
diseases that primarily affect developing countries, provide access to affordable essential medicines and vaccines,
in accordance with the Doha Declaration on the TRIPS
Agreement and Public Health, which affirms the right of
developing countries to use to the full the provisions in the
TRIPS Agreement (Agreement on Trade-Related Aspects
of Intellectual Property Rights) regarding flexibilities to
protect public health and, in particular, provide access to
medicines for all.

- Substantially increase health financing and the recruitment,
development, training and retention of the health workforce in developing countries, especially in least-developed
countries and small-island developing states.

- Strengthen the capacity of all countries, in particular
developing countries, for early warning, risk reduction and
management of national and global health risks.

The sustainable development encompasses the achievement of
three interconnected objectives, that is, economic development,
social inclusion and environmental sustainability, which are
necessary for the well-being of individuals and societies. SDGs,
enabled by the integration of economic growth, social justice

and environmental stewardship, are an important global guiding principle and operational standard.

However, there are a number of challenges for achieving SDGs, such as lack of effective leadership, coordinated partnerships, investments, implementation and indicators with effective data collection. Leadership is essential for progress in relation to policy change, legislation, investment, implementation, advocacy and popular representation. SDGs demand an increasing interface with global governance for health among those institutions and processes that directly and indirectly impact on health in the context of globalized trade, security, migration and environment.[31]

To adopt a universal post-2015 development agenda with sustainable development at its core, a country like India needs to recognize the profound transformation required to address the emerging challenges of sustainable development. These include economic shifts to sustainable patterns of production and consumption, effective governance and renewed partnerships and novel means of implementation. Another set of challenges is lack of social inclusion, widespread regional disparities and urban–rural gaps and gender inequality. A key challenge is to adopt a meaningful standard of basic needs country, that is, access to safe and sustainable water and sanitation, adequate nutrition, primary health services and basic infrastructure including electricity, roads and connectivity to the information network.[32] It also entails new ways of implementing programmes and new ways of monitoring and evaluating interventions needed for MCH.

One such innovative approach to public health initiatives is programme science (PS). It has the capacity to address the challenges facing the implementation of public health programmes in India and have the potential to deliver results of quality and efficiency.

---

[31] Z. Singh, 'Sustainable Development Goals: Challenges and Opportunities', *Indian Journal of Public Health* 60, no. 4(2016): 247–250.
[32] Ibid.

Programme Science: Theory and Approach

PS is a relatively new term that describes the systematic application of scientific knowledge to improve the design, implementation and evaluation of programmes. PS is becoming increasingly important for advancing the response to various public-health initiatives. The endpoint of PS is the population-level impact on incidence of infections by optimizing the choice of right strategy for the right populations, at the appropriate time, by doing the right things the right way and by ensuring appropriate scale and efficiency.[33]

In 2010, three global meetings were held on programme science for the development of a programme science consortium. The participants included London School of Hygiene and Tropical Medicine, University College (London), Imperial College, Johns Hopkins University, University of Washington, Family Health International and University of Manitoba. Programme and policy leaders from the World Bank, the Global Fund, Joint United Nations Programme on HIV/AIDS (UNAIDS), US Agency for International Development (USAID)/President's Emergency Plan for AIDS Relief (PEPFAR) and the Gates Foundation were present as well. Country Programme leaders from India, Kenya, Nigeria, the United States of America and Canada also participated in these meetings. Two complementary grants for the PS initiative were provided by the World Bank (US$2.2 million) and the Bill & Melinda Gates Foundation (US$5 million).

The key focus of these meetings was on increasing focus on prevention globally and at the country level. A few questions the consortium tried to address: What drives the epidemics in different countries and at the local level? What is the right mix of interventions? The group agreed that resource allocation must be strategic to achieve impact efficiently. However, the challenge

---

[33] S. O. Aral and J. F. Blanchard, 'The Program Science Initiative: Improving the Planning, Implementation and Evaluation of HIV/STI Prevention Programs', *Sexually Transmitted Infection* 88, no. 3(2012): 157–159.

was to convert scientific discovery into impact and to convert efficacious interventions at the individual level into programmes that will have an impact on the epidemic at a population level.

Interest in this topic springs from the recognition that traditional research methods, which typically feature narrow problem definitions and linear analytic representations are by themselves insufficient to adequately address the full complexity of our most pressing population health challenges. The concept tries to close the gap between science and programmes and recognizes the 'systems' nature of transmission. Systems science perspectives involve taking into account the big picture in all its complexity (a system view) while also taking into account the important relationships between components of a system and changes in the system over time. Systems science offers a complementary approach, capable of addressing more complex and interactive phenomena while also attending to the practical constraints and opportunities that shape the social, physical and organizational settings in which responses to those health challenges will occur.

PS, which is derived from systems science, extends beyond implementation research to also consider entire programmes involving combinations of interventions for a particular population in a specific context. Various research methods are used to address questions related to holistic aspects of a programme including the following:

- Strategic planning: Who should be targeted on the basis of the particular context of the programme? When? For how long?
- Programme implementation: What is the optimal mix of interventions? How can synergy across interventions be maximized?
- Programme management: How can effective interventions be sustained? How should the programme be modified as new knowledge emerges during implementation? What quality improvement processes are important?

PS typically involves an ongoing process of engagement between researchers, policymakers, programme planners, FLWs and communities through which research is embedded into the design, implementation and continuous improvement of the overall programme. Because the focus is on how an entire programme impacts a population, PS typically involves consideration of overall health systems. Development and linkage of population-level databases (such as electronic health records) that provide information on testing and diagnosis of health problems, treatments prescribed, health-related outcomes and health-service usage can be important tools in PS.

PS is different from implementation science that focuses on identifying and scaling up a single 'evidence-based' intervention whereas PS is concerned with the totality of a programme, including an appraisal of the epidemic transmission dynamics, setting appropriate prevention objectives by sub-population, selecting and combining interventions and allocating resources between interventions accordingly. PS is also different from translational research, which focuses on how to get scientific 'evidence into practice'. The process tends to focus on single interventions and a unidirectional process of knowledge translation. However, in PS, in addition to focusing on multiple interventions and their interfaces at the population level, it emphasizes 'getting research out of practice' and formulating new hypotheses. Moreover, PS differs from operations research because operations research focuses on how to optimize the implementation of a particular intervention, not on strategic planning to achieve maximum population-level impact. In addition to optimizing implementation, PS focuses on population impact, which depends on population focus, selection of interventions and interactions between interventions.

PS aims at integrating science into all aspects of programme cycle such as goal setting, deciding strategic priorities, design and planning, implementation, monitoring and evaluation. Believing that the public-health programme management is a dynamic process requiring continuous iterations between programme and science, it equips the programme managers to function like scientists that are embedded within the programmes.

This concept and approach has gained significance in the last decade in the areas of infectious diseases, particularly HIV-prevention projects, as well as in the area of MNCH. In the MNCH programmes, it provides approach, tools and framework for the programme managers to identify gaps, develop and test scalable solutions and finally support the primary stakeholder (government) to scale up the solutions; the focus is continuously retained on the outcomes and critical pathways and processes towards achieving the outcomes.

PS is operationalized as a three-pronged approach, which can be delineated as follows:

Epidemiological appraisal and strategic planning: This is the first and a critical phase of PS approach. It starts with the hypothesis that improving availability, accessibility, quality, utilization and coverage of critical MNCH services can reduce mortalities in the population thus compelling the programme managers to first define the critical services package and later understand the gaps in the availability/accessibility, quality, utilization and coverage in the region. Strategic planning helps the managers to locate the levels of change that can address the gaps efficiently and effectively, thus paving way for designing specific intervention solutions.

Effectiveness and programme implementation: This calls for developing implementation plans and approaches that are informed by evidence and that are context sensitive. An intervention that is effective in a particular context may not be so in others. The population dynamics, health systems capacities and other contextual factors compel programme managers to use or develop an implementation model that can effectively and efficiently improve the coverage and quality of the intervention.

The PS approach advocates for developing such implementation models or solution levers and for studying the mechanisms and processes involved and the efficiency of the models in terms of costs, scalability and integration into the existing health systems.

Monitoring, evaluation and programme management: While developing effective interventions and designing efficient implementation plans are crucial, they are incomplete without a programme-management machinery that is guided by a strong M&E system. Innovative, integrated and simple M&E systems to make high-quality data available to the programme managers in a timely manner calls for in-depth exploration. The programme managers require data related to critical processes, outputs and outcomes which need to be considered. The capacities of health systems to gather, analyse, interpret and use data requires planning of capacity-building efforts within the programme-management plans.

Operationalizing programme science approach

As elucidated earlier, PS hypothesizes that ensuring availability, accessibility, quality, utilization and coverage of critical MNCH services improves outcomes. Thus, it calls for the following steps:

- Define the critical MNCH services package
- Identify gaps and barriers in each of these areas through appropriate assessment methods
- Develop tools, processes and interventions to address the gaps
- Develop implementation plans and pilot and scale up the interventions across the populations

It is important to leverage three platforms for enhancing the efficiency, effectiveness and equity of RMNCH+A services: community, facility and systems.

In short, PS approach entails optimization of the choice of the right strategy for the right populations at the appropriate time, implementation of the right things the right way, achievement of appropriate scale and efficiency, prioritization of key populations (responsible for spread) and prioritization of optimal intervention packages.

There is a valuable opportunity to achieve the SDGs collectively by using innovative approaches such as PS approach. It is an opportunity for the public health practitioners to highlight the interdependence of health and education, population and governance and view MCH as a precondition for social sustainability and progress. Use of innovative approaches such as PS offers an unprecedented opportunity. PS approach helps identify synergies and integrate these interventions across the continuum of care. Despite existing plethora of knowledge, there is a lack of consensus on how best to move forward in a coordinated manner so as to achieve progress towards SDGs. The specific objective of this book is to serve as a first step towards developing a strategy to design the RMNCH packages of interventions at each level of the health system across the continuum of care, facilitating the scaling up of these interventions and identifying innovations that enhance the core packages of interventions.

Objectives and Organization of the Handbook

The objective of this handbook is to enhance the available literature on the application of PS to improve the delivery of critical MNCH services in India, with illustrations from technical support to governments of Karnataka and Uttar Pradesh.

The book lays out interventions that are prioritized according to the following criteria:

- Interventions expected to have a significant impact on maternal, newborn and child survival and addressing therein the main causes of their mortality

- Interventions suitable for implementation in low-resource settings
- Interventions delivered throughout the health sector—from the community level up to the first referral level of health-service provision

The handbook is organized into four chapters.

Chapter 1 deals with assessments, gap analysis and technical interventions. To gather evidence of gaps at the district level, the book proposes a series of assessments that have to be undertaken, including analyses of secondary data and collection of primary data, both qualitative and quantitative. The chapter describes what methodology needs to be followed and what tools need to be developed and tested in this process, so that these tools and methods can be adapted for use across the state and the country. The assessment methodology proposed in this chapter is meant to assist states, and particularly their district health-management teams, in strengthening the health systems. It places emphasis on understanding existing and functional structures and managerial processes in a district, which enable the provision of essential health care to the population. Through the assessment process, one identifies and describes the health status of the community; factors in the community that contribute to health challenges; and existing community assets and resources that can be mobilized to improve the health status of the community. The chapter also details clearly the assessments that would lead to the documentation of current systems and policies by study of actual systems in the field, identification of gaps and issues, followed by provision of recommendations. The assessments suggested cover both the demand side (community) and the supply side (health care provider) perspectives. The chapter describes various surveys that can be used to assess the costs, utilization and barriers to use of ANC services, postnatal care (PNC) services, newborn and child care services. Moreover, the strengths and weaknesses of each of these methods are detailed in the relevant section. The chapter also suggests various secondary data sources that can be used and the strengths and limitations of each data source is accounted for as well for assessing differences in findings between sources. It also provides an overview of how to develop an implementation design for RMNCH+A intervention: it outlines the intervention theory and approach; technical interventions, solution categories and individual solution levers; project framework and, for each solution category, the background and rationale, hypotheses, objectives, intervention approach and strategy and key activities.

Chapter 2 deals with nurse mentoring. It describes a model of nurse-mentoring process based on the 'learning by doing' theory of learning and emphasizes learning on the job while handling issues related to MCH. To address many of the quality gaps in public health facilities, the chapter recommends on-site mentoring in clinical care and service delivery could be used to improve the quality of services and continuity of care. The chapter describes in detail the following:

1. Hiring mentors: This describes the qualifications of these health care providers. Other considerations that are discussed include factors that needed to be taken into account in the decision-making process to use nurses as mentors.
2. Training nurse mentors: This aspect is focused on the process of developing the training course material and training the nurse mentors.
3. Mentor visits: This covers the number of PHCs the mentors can visit, the timeframe for conducting these visits and the time duration of each visit, among other things.
4. Monitoring mentoring intervention: The focus here is on developing a management structure and management process to oversee implementation of the mentoring intervention. It describes how overall guidance and support can come from a core technical team consisting of the technical lead, QI specialist and clinical consultant. It also describes how project consultants can also periodically conduct site visits and offer advice.

Chapter 3 deals with interventions for front-line workers (FLWs) and community. As there is not enough awareness in the community on healthy RMNCH+A practices, and available services, and there is a lack in population-based coverage for these interventions, one of the many strategies the chapter recommends is the introduction of community resources persons (CRPs). It describes how the CRPs can support the FLWs particularly accredited social health activists (ASHAs) to increase the efficiency, effectiveness and equity to facilitate changes in community norms, knowledge and behaviours, to enhance positive health-seeking practices and to provide the necessary linkages to preventive and treatment services. It shows how there is an urgent need for innovative, field-tested and user-friendly set of tools and job-aids that equip FLWs with competencies to improve the coverage for routine MNCH services; help in better communication with families about the importance of availing MNCH services and adopting healthy practices for pregnant women and newborns and help them screen, identify and refer danger signs, especially during the critical postnatal period. Suggestions are also provided on how to develop and pretest tools and training modules through collaborative efforts where the technical experts and the FLWs discuss and critically evaluate the relevance, applicability and usefulness of the interventions and the tools. The chapter also focuses on community engagement as it is essential to ensure that achievements are sustainable beyond the duration of projects and programmes. How to involve communities in the identification of RMNCH problems as well as in the planning, financing and implementation of solutions is also detailed, along with how community systems can be funded, built and administered at grassroots levels, thereby creating a degree of community ownership of women and children's health and a potential for sustainability. To involve communities in the creation of accountability mechanisms and quality assurance, the chapter discusses how community scorecards and other social auditing mechanisms will allow communities to provide feedback to health administrators as to the performance of local health facilities. Thus, the chapter foregrounds the importance of community monitoring process under NRHM and shows how efforts can be made to educate and capacitate community members to assess, review and suggest recommendations in the implementation of health programmes, which will enhance participation of people in planning, implementing, monitoring and evaluating public health programmes.

Chapter 4 deals with data management. The lack of quality vital statistics data points to the urgent need for investment in building country-vital registration and health-information systems. The chapter focuses on the framework for accountability and in enhancing the government's capacity to monitor and evaluate the results. Furthermore, data quality in terms of completeness, timeliness and accuracy of reporting is often problematic. The availability of these data is not consistent across or within states. Lack of data constitutes a major gap for maternal mortality because the measurement of maternal deaths, regardless of data source, is complex and often inaccurate. The chapter shows how to improve measurement of the core indicators and how to strengthen country-health information systems. The chapter recommends steps to achieve this goal, including (a) development of a harmonized programme of health surveys to collect data; (b) investment in building a complete and universal registration of vital events, including births, deaths and certification of cause of death; (c) investment in health facility and administrative data-recording systems to improve data quality and monitoring efforts; (d) evaluation of current initiatives to explore the potential of information and communication technologies to improve the speed and accuracy of reporting, particularly at community level, and scaling up where there is evidence of their effectiveness and (e) support to build country capacity to monitor, review and act on data. The chapter also discusses various tools and covers topics such as assessment of data quality, triangulation and reconciliation of data from different sources as well as the use of data for monitoring purposes and strengthening reporting mechanisms at all levels of the health system.

The handbook ends with brief recommendations to improve future MNCH programmes.

1

Assessments and Interventions

An important component of any RMNCH programme is to promote evidence-based decision-making at the district level in accordance with state and national guidelines. Evidence-based planning leads to increased availability and accessibility of quality services and ultimately to increased utilization of health services and improved health outcomes. For this, one has to know the existing gaps at multiple levels of service delivery as well as systems to customize the interventions to address the gaps. To gather evidence of gaps at the district level, a series of assessments have to be undertaken, including analyses of secondary data and collection of primary data, both qualitative and quantitative. Validated methods need to be followed and tools need to be developed and tested in this process, and these can be adapted for use across the state and the country.

Anchored by the RMNCH+A road map discussed in the Introduction, in this chapter a conceptual framework is suggested to isolate and identify service gaps at the facility level, community level and health systems level. This framework is guided by the foundational principle of reducing maternal and neonatal mortality, the positive consequences of which flow into all areas of the RMNCH+A life cycle.

Gap analysis is done for multiple reasons. The most important objectives of gap analysis are:

- **Designing relevant critical interventions:** To focus attention of the programme design on specific gaps in the delivery of a particular intervention or a set of interventions and bridge these gaps with location-specific solution levers. Specific gaps can be around the aspects of availability and accessibility, quality, utilization and coverage of RMNCH services and interventions.
- **Support programme implementations plans:** To enable programme implementation plans (PIPs) of National Health Mission (NHM) at village, block, district and state levels to identify the gaps and constraints to improve services with regard to access, demand and quality of health care.
- **Evaluation of interventions:** For the purpose of monitoring and evaluating the progress and results about various components of RMNCH+A, there is a need to establish a baseline from various sources. Conducting gap analysis at various levels with assessments using standardized tools can inform evaluation plans.

Availability and accessibility pertains to trained and skilled human resources, infrastructure, drugs, equipment and supplies related to critical RMNCH services and is applicable to both public and private sector. National guidelines stipulate availability of skilled birth-attendant services in all subcentres (SCs) and primary health centres (PHCs), basic emergency obstetric and neonatal services (BEmONC) in 24×7 PHCs and community health centres, comprehensive emergency obstetric and neonatal services (CEmONC) in first referral units at block and district levels. UN/WHO also suggests that policies and plans should ensure availability of at least one BEmONC facility for every lakh population and one CEmONC facility for every five-lakh population. What availability and accessibility barriers are faced by populations become the first step to understand and improve services from a supply side perspective.

Quality of services is informed by many facets that should be a part of the assessments. Do the providers have required readiness to provide the services for the level of care (provider readiness)? This means whether the providers have the required knowledge and skills pertaining to the interventions and if they are practising in line with standards of care. Provider preparedness without adequate facility readiness is not good enough. Are facilities adequately ready to ensure uninterrupted and timely availability of drugs and equipment? Do facilities have appropriate referral linkages with higher facilities and community to ensure continuity of care? Are infection-control systems in place as per the standards? Similarly, the clients have their rights and perceptions about quality of care that will influence utilization of services. Clients expect respectful and safe care in a timely manner, security during stay at facilities, clean and hygienic space, nutritious food and safe drinking water and the like become important parameters that may have to be given due consideration when it comes to holistic quality assessments using a wide variety of methodologies and tools.

Coverage gaps can provide critical piece of information to policymakers and planners about not only the community level gaps but also gaps related to facilities and systems as well. For example, poor coverage can be due to inadequate availability of front-line workers (FLWs) and facilities, because of inadequate skills, process and tools (quality) or because of neglect of a particular geography or population group from planning (health systems). Some important questions need to be asked in order to plug gaps in utilization and coverage of services. When supply side of health systems can ensure optimal availability, accessibility and quality of RMNCH services, does that lead to proportionate increase in utilization of services? Whether improved utilization is getting reflected in population-level coverage of RMNCH services? Are there inequities in utilization and coverage by certain population groups versus the rest? If yes, what are the reasons? Are there cultural and contextual connotations to inequities? Are there specific community norms, systems, beliefs and traditions that are influencing the coverage? Are some population groups and geographies more vulnerable than the rest?

Levels of Gap Analyses

The programme science (PS) framework helps to frame gap assessments and analysis in a structured and systematic way with a focus on end outcomes. This chapter summarizes the typical questions that will be answered through this gap analysis at each level and the suggested methodology that is appropriate for each level. The gap analysis at each level is described in more detail in the following sections. In this section, we focus on the assessments done at three levels:

1. Facility level
2. Community level
3. Health system level

Facility-level assessments

Facility-level assessments (also referred to as facility mapping) are necessitated by the absence of a comprehensive profile of the public and private facilities at the district level, including details on service delivery. Such a profile is a fundamental tool for the preparation of district project-implementation plans. The specific objectives of the facility gap analysis are:

- To map the availability and accessibility of reproductive, maternal, newborn and child health (RMNCH) services in public and private sector as per population and geography
- To identify gaps in infrastructure, staffing, equipment, drugs and supplies related to the provision of RMNCH services

More specifically the facility-level gap analysis tries to answer the following questions:

- Are the functional delivery points (including skilled birth attendant (SBA), BEmONC and CEmONC-level facilities) equitably distributed across populations and geographies in the district?

- Is the availability of C-section, blood storage units/blood bank and newborn-care facilities equitably distributed across populations and geographies in the district?
- Do these delivery points in the district have adequate infrastructure, skilled human resources, capacity, equipment and commodities, emergency transportation, infection-control measures and funds to provide each of the strategic RMNCH interventions with quality?
- Are recommended protocols and guidelines being followed for management of specific conditions?
- What have been the caseloads in these facilities?

It is important that all the public health facilities and all private facilities providing RMNCH + A services in a district be covered in this mapping. The GoI has suggested that the gap analysis should aim at collection of primary data from the designated 'delivery points', including all first referral units (FRUs), the district hospital (including special newborn care units [SNCUs] and nutrition rehabilitation centres [NRCs]), newborn sick units and all NRCs (if located at subdistrict level), regarding availability, accessibility, quality and utilization of each of the aforementioned RMNCH interventions.

This approach provides the necessary information to identify the potential facilities where RMNCH services, including delivery services, can be activated to meet the population and geographic need for these services.

The following aspects could be part of the mapping:

1. **Human resources:** Whether the required type and number of staff are regularly available to deliver the services in the facility.
2. **Infrastructure:** Whether the designated facilities have adequate space, electricity and water supply, communication facilities, toilet and other facilities for effective delivery of intended services.
3. **Equipment and commodities:** Whether the facility has adequate type and number of equipment to provide the

specific RMNCH services along with a regular supply and stock of essential drugs and commodities related to these services.

4. **Infection control:** Whether the facility has adequate infection control measures, including hygiene and sanitation.

5. **Emergency transportation:** Whether the facility has access to emergency transportation to move patients to the nearest referral facility quickly.

6. **Capacity:** Whether the staff delivering the specific services has received relevant trainings on topics such as SBA, Navjaat Shishu Suraksha Karyakram (NSSK), facility-based integrated management of neonatal and childhood illness (F-IMNCI), postpartum intrauterine contraceptive device (PPIUCD), BEmONC, CEmONC and Minilap, and whether the concerned staff is provided with supportive supervision.

7. **Funds:** Including the facility untied funds to manage the ad hoc requirements.

Additionally, the distribution of the designated and 'fully functional' delivery points, FRUs, SNCUs, newborn stabilization units (NBSUs) and NRCs can be assessed by plotting the location of these facilities on a GIS map, along with the designated areas and populations covered by each such facility. This will help in understanding whether these facilities are equally accessible across geographies and populations within the district. Needless to say, inequitable distribution of service provision will result in inequitable utilization and thus, resulting in uneven health outcomes.

One also needs to understand the service-provider competencies in providing quality care in the health system, from both a technical (provider knowledge, competence in service delivery) perspective and client satisfaction perspective. The main objectives of quality assessment are:

- To understand the provider readiness, that is, gaps in the knowledge, skills and practice of care providers involved in

RMNCH service delivery in the public and private sector in the districts

- To understand gaps in facility readiness in relation to critical systems such as supply chain, infection control, referral linkages and documentation
- To determine client satisfaction of RMNCH services

Also statistical information such as caseloads, the number of deliveries conducted and number of cases treated for complications for each facility and case fatality rates for complications should be analysed using the health management information system (HMIS) data or the data from the case sheets and registers to understand if quality and utilization are proportionate to availability of services.

Community-level assessments

The term 'community' here refers to the populations covered by the health SC along with the associated FLWs such as the auxiliary nurse midwives (ANMs), accredited social health activists (ASHAs) and Anganwadi workers (AWWs). Several of the strategic RMNCH interventions are envisaged to be provided by these FLWs to the populations through community outreach. These include:

1. **Reproductive health care services** such as family planning (including intrauterine contraceptive device (IUCD) insertion, oral contraceptive pills (OCPs) and condoms), prevention and management of sexually transmitted infections (STIs), weekly iron–folic acid (IFA) supplementation, information and counselling on sexual reproductive health and family planning, community-based promotion and delivery of contraceptives and menstrual hygiene.
2. **Antenatal care (ANC) services** including full ANC package and prevention of parent-to-child transmission (PPTCT) services with quality as assessed by monitoring of pregnant mother (weight gain, pallor, haemoglobin (Hb), fundal

examination and BP monitoring), counselling on preparation for newborn care, breastfeeding and birth preparedness, complication readiness, demand generation for pregnancy care and institutional delivery (Janani Suraksha Yojana [JSY] and Janani Shishu Suraksha Karyakram [JSSK]).

3. **Postnatal visit as recommended for postnatal care (PNC) services** such as assessment for early detection of birth defects and management of illnesses in mother and newborn, immunization, home-based newborn care, including hygiene and sanitation, thermal care, exclusive breastfeeding, antibiotic for suspected case of newborn sepsis and prompt referral.

4. **Special attention to home- and facility-based newborn care** through assessment classification, treatment, counselling and referral, if required.

5. **Child-health care services** such as first-level assessment and care for newborn and childhood illnesses, immunization and micronutrient supplementation, infant and young child feeding (IYCF) including hygiene, exclusive breastfeeding and complementary feeding, use of oral rehydration salts (ORS) and zinc for diarrhoea, sanitation and antibiotic for pneumonia.

During the district gap analysis, primary data on each of these interventions can be collected from a sample of health SCs and related front line workers on the following aspects of service delivery:

1. **Capacity:** Whether the FLWs are adequately trained and provided with the necessary tools and methods (microplanning, BCC materials, tracking tools, planning tools and so on) for each of the designated quality services and whether they are provided with adequate supportive supervision. Under this section, gap analysis can also analyse if the ANMs positioned at delivery points have received SBA and NSSK training, if all the ASHAs are trained in home-based newborn care (HBNC) and the number of AWWs trained in IYCF and integrated management of neonatal and childhood illnesses (IMNCI).

2. **Commodities and supplies:** Whether the FLWs receive timely and adequate supply of commodities necessary for the provision of these services including vaccines, contraceptives, drugs and equipment.
3. **Community outreach:** Regularity with which the home visits, village health and nutrition days (VHNDs) and immunization days are organized and the extent of populations 'not-covered' by these activities, not only in terms of number of session but in quality of all components being provided during these outreach activities.
4. **Incentives:** Regularity with which the incentives for the providers and beneficiaries are received.
5. **Formation and functioning of community structures:** Whether the village health and sanitation nutrition committees (VHSNCs) are formed as per guidelines and are functioning appropriately to promote healthy outcomes.

Additionally, the distribution of the 'in-position' FLWs can be assessed by plotting their availability by location on a map, along with the designated areas and populations covered by each SC. This will be used to understand whether these FLWs are equally available/accessible across geographies and populations within the district.

Finally, the population-based utilization and coverage statistics for each of the RMNCH interventions has to be compiled for the district, based on the available survey data, to compare against the state targets. The indicators for which district specific data is not available, triangulation from available state level data can be used along with an assumed deviation for the district (plus or minus) from the state average. Some of the indicators that impact on neonatal and maternal mortality include the following:

1. Percentage of adolescent girls and boys (15–19 years) with anaemia (AHS,[1] NFHS)

---

[1] AHS: Annual Health Survey, particularly in the Empowered Action Group (EAG) states.

2. Percentage of total fertility contributed by adolescents (15–19 years) (AHS, NFHS)
3. Percentage of all births in government and accredited private institutions (AHS, SRS)[2]
4. Percentage of pregnant women receiving ANC (AHS, CES)[3]
5. Percentage of mothers and newborns receiving PNC (AHS, CES)
6. Percentage of deliveries conducted by skilled birth attendants (AHS, CES)
7. Child sex ratio in the 0–6 years age group (Census 2011)
8. Exclusive breastfeeding rate (AHS, CES)
9. Prevalence of under-five children who are underweight (AHS, NFHS)
10. Coverage of three doses of combined diphtheria–tetanus–pertussis (DTP3) (12–23 months) (AHS, CES)
11. Use of oral rehydration salts (ORS) in under-five children with diarrhoea (AHS, CES)
12. Unmet need for family planning methods among eligible couples, married and unmarried (AHS, district level household survey [DLHS])
13. Unmet need for modern family planning methods among eligible couples (AHS, DLHS)
14. Prevalence of anaemia among women aged 15–49 years

Community-level assessments are incomplete without assessing the barriers and facilitators for optimal coverage of RMNCH services. Particularly, community- and family-level norms and traditions, behaviours and practices, beliefs and decisions, influence coverage and their in-depth exploration through qualitative research methods can throw valuable insights into programme design. Similarly, understanding the culture and ethnography related to particular geography and population groups become critical to addressing inequities.

[2] SRS: Sample Registration System.
[3] CES: Coverage Evaluation Survey.

Health system-level assessments

While the facility and community level assessments provide an understanding of gaps of availability, accessibility, utilization, timeliness and continuity, an understanding of the enabling environment around health is equally necessary. In this context, the first step should be to map the policies and strategies in place, identify the budget available and its allocations, assess the social norms around essential interventions for RMNCH and map out the various partners and resources available at the district or state levels in order to better understand the bottleneck hampering the health system in the following cross-cutting themes:

1. **Fund flow and utilization at district and subdistrict levels:** Major bottlenecks in the flow of funds from state to the district and further down from district to the subdistrict levels in terms of the amount, timing and clarity on budget items; major hurdles that may prevent the district and subdistrict administration to effectively and fully utilize the planned allocated funds.
2. **Untied funds for facilities and community structures (VHSNCs and RKSs):** Bottlenecks in releasing the funds to the VHSNCs and Rogi Kalyan Samitis (RKSs) on a regular basis.
3. **Infrastructure management:** Bottlenecks in infrastructure management including repairs, maintenance and provisions of additional infrastructure facilities.
4. **Supply chain management:** Major issues in the indentation, procurement, distribution and stock management at the state, district and subdistrict levels.
5. **Human resource management:** Major hurdles in the management of human resources, including recruitment, retention, promotion and transfer.
6. **Emergency transportation:** Major bottlenecks in the provision of emergency transportation across the district/state.
7. **Implementation of entitlements under JSSK and JSY up to the most vulnerable populations:** Bottlenecks in the implementation of incentive schemes for providers and

beneficiaries such as fund flow, approval mechanisms and delays.

8. **Capacity building and roll out trainings:** Major bottlenecks in the roll out of planned training activities such as the SBA, NSSK and F-IMNCI.

9. **Supportive supervision for facilities and FLWs:** Major issues related to the provision of supportive supervision/ mentoring at facilities and for the FLWs.

10. **HMIS and MCTS data quality and use:** The mechanisms adopted by the district and state to ensure quality and use of HMIS and mother and child tracking system (MCTS) data as well as the issues regarding data quality and use.

Tools and Methods for Gap Analyses

The assessment of the RMNCH situation and response includes a number of quantitative and qualitative components, triangulated with secondary sources. This section provides a brief overview of the methodology for each component of primary data collection. Research should be guided by key questions around availability, accessibility, quality and barriers to utilization and coverage of services. The assessments should align with the local ethical and research guidelines with due regards to the privacy and confidentiality of respondents.

In general, the assessments would include the demand side (community) and the supply side (health care provider) perspectives.

Demand side assessment: Surveys can be used to assess the costs, utilization, barriers to use of ANC services, intranatal, PNC services, newborn and child care services. These interviews can be conducted on a sample of population catchment areas. It is important to have an adequate representation of mothers who have children less than one year of age and these surveys should be conducted in the community. Thus, demand side assessments can include sample-based household surveys as well as qualitative exploration with select groups of women and their families.

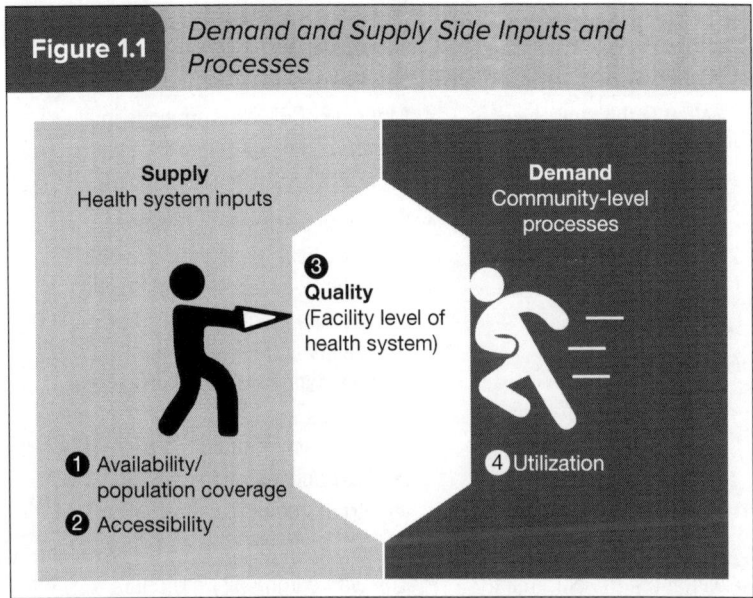

Figure 1.1 *Demand and Supply Side Inputs and Processes*

Supply side assessment: To understand the issues related to provision of care from the supply side, in-depth interviews (IDIs) have to be conducted with the health department officials at the state and the district levels and at various public and private facilities. The IDIs should cover topics under human resources (such as recruitment, training and promotions), drugs, equipment, financial schemes and utilization of services. Facility mapping and quality assessments can also be categorized as supply side assessments (Figure 1.1).

Diverse set of tools and methods will need to be used in the assessments that are listed in Table 1.1.

In addition to the description of the different methodologies employed for primary data collection, one should also review the secondary data sources used—the strengths and limitations of each data source need to be taken into account while assessing differences in findings between sources (Table 1.2).

Table 1.1	Summary of Assessments
Question	**Method**
What is the availability and accessibility of RMNCH services?	• Mapping of RMNCH services in all private and government facilities (SCs, PHCs, CHCs, THs and DHs)

What is the capability of service providers to deliver quality RMNCH services?	• Survey of a sample of facilities and providers (public and private, community-based services) using the following tools:
	  • Facility audit
	  • Knowledge tests including case studies
	  • Case record audits
	  • Direct observations
	  • Structured demonstrations
	  • Exit interviews

What are the community-level facilitators and barriers for utilization of RMNCH services?	• IDIs with community members • Exit interviews • Community surveys
What are the system facilitators and barriers for the provision and utiliza-tion of services?	• Review of policy/programme documents • Review of secondary data • Semi-structured interviews with service providers and block-, district- and state-level health officials • An assessment of all VHSCs in districts
What are the available data sources and how are they used in programme review and planning?	• Discussions with the state monitor-ing and evaluation unit • Analyses of the existing HMIS data

Source: Karnataka Health Promotion Trust (KHPT), 2011, Maternal, Newborn and Child Health in Bagalkot District: A Situational Analysis, the Sukshema Project, Bangalore.

Table 1.2 *Secondary Data Sources: Strengths and Limitations*

Data Source and Sample Size	Information Collected	Strengths	Limitations
NFHS	Demographic, reproductive health and child health information	• Collected periodically, every four years • Provides estimates of different parameters at the national and state levels • Comparable over time • Includes anthropometric data	• Does not provide estimates at the district level • Data collected before implementation of many NHM schemes related to RMNCH (JSY, 108 Ambulance)
DLHS	Demographic and reproductive health information	• Representative of entire household-based population in a district • Captures both those seeking care from private providers and non-care seekers	• Hard to calculate some variables as the sample size becomes too small (e.g., pregnant women who experienced complications and who did not seek care) • Data collected before full implementation of JSY scheme—data not perceived to be current
HMIS data	Administrative records capturing service utilization	• Routine • Comes from the health system itself, important tool for programme/facility management	• Reporting error and bias: over-reporting of service statistics, underreporting of deaths • Does not capture those that seek care from private/informal providers or those who do not seek care

Source: Karnataka Health Promotion Trust (KHPT), 2011, Maternal, Newborn and Child Health in Bagalkot District: A Situational Analysis, the Sukshema Project, Bangalore.

Steps in gap analysis

The responsibility of conducting gap analysis can be shared jointly by the state NHM, the state lead partner (SLP) and district development partners. The district gap analysis team can comprise of representatives from the government (district and state NHM and other departments) and the state development partners. The SLP can provide the required technical support to conduct this exercise. The number of resource persons (RPs) to be involved and the duration of the gap analysis exercise can be jointly decided by the SLP and the state/district authorities. They may take into account the time required for initial team orientation and planning, data collection, preparation of a brief report and a district action plan that clearly identifies the actions to be taken by various stakeholders.

1. **Planning at the state level:** As a first step towards the implementation of district-level RMNCH gap analysis, the state department of health and family welfare and state NHM, along with the development partners, need to discuss and plan for the required human resources, tools and the timelines required for the gap analysis, depending on the number of districts that are to be covered. Officer/s need to be designated at both the state and district levels to undertake the overall responsibilities of coordinating the gap analysis. Consensus need to be reached on the following:

   (a) Adaptation of the suggested gap analysis tools and methods for the state.

   (b) Outputs of the district level gap analysis—reports, data tables and action plan.

   (c) List of gap-analysis team members along with the coordinator for each district. It should be ensured that the team has a member who is well versed in data analysis (HMIS and other survey data) as well as in processing the primary data collected during the gap analysis within the stipulated period.

(d) Dates of gap analysis for each district.

(e) Block-wise list of facilities and services in each selected district that will be covered in gap analysis.

2. **Orientation of the district gap-analysis coordinators:** All the district coordinators need to be well oriented on the protocols and tools to be used in gap analysis. The district coordinators need to be oriented on the district-specific outputs in the form of reports and data tables, which will be deliverables from the district gap-analysis teams. During this orientation, the list of facilities to be included in gap analysis, the district team members and dates of gap analysis have to be reviewed and timelines have to be finalized.

3. **Initial planning for district gap analysis:** The district coordinator has to ensure that the entire district gap-analysis team is oriented on the methods and tools used in gap analysis. Individual members participating in the district gap analysis have to be assigned to specific tasks.

(a) One member who is good in secondary data analysis (HMIS, other survey data) and plotting the locations on maps (geographic information system [GIS]) has to be assigned to work on the available secondary data and to compile. The primary data as it emerges from field visits has to be processed for preparing relevant data tables and graphs.

(b) A team consisting largely of programme officers, oriented on the facility tools, have to visit the identified health facilities to collect the necessary information using relevant tools. The detailed field visit plan has to be prepared and logistics for the field data collection—such as transportation, stay and availability of key staff at the facility for providing information—has to be planned and ensured.

(c) The same team as aforementioned or another team can conduct community-level assessment using the relevant tool.

(d) Another small team can be oriented on conducting key informant interviews. A detailed fieldwork plan in terms of the persons to be interviewed and the date of interview has to be prepared.

4. **Data entry and analysis:** All the facility- and community-level data collected during the gap analysis need to be compiled and the relevant tables have to be generated.

5. **Report writing:** The gap analysis team need to be oriented briefly, for about half a day, on the general outline and data tables to be included in the district gap analysis report. The actual drafting of the report can be completed in a week.

6. **Dissemination of findings with stakeholders:** It is very important that the data is shared with key stakeholders (state and district officials, providers, FLWs and so on). The state workshop should be followed by district workshops to explore specific reasons for gaps, possible solutions that are contextual. These workshops can lead to development of evidence-based project implementation plans. Similarly, consultations with community members for exploration of appropriate solutions to address the gaps can go a long way in using evidence to develop meaningful, field relevant solutions.

7. **Preparing a plan of action:** Based on the gap analysis report, a comprehensive action plan for providing technical assistance and mentoring support has to be drawn up, specifying the targets and assigned responsibilities. At monthly meetings, progress against action plans has to be monitored and health facilities have to be revisited to monitor progress.

Methods of gap analysis

Facility-level methods

The value chain analysis is useful to understand the critical gaps at the facility level (Figure 1.2). The purpose of the value chain tool is to examine and break down the processes and components of critical facility-level service delivery, isolate service-delivery failures and pinpoint specific gaps that contribute to mortality. The framework begins with mortality, undergoes a

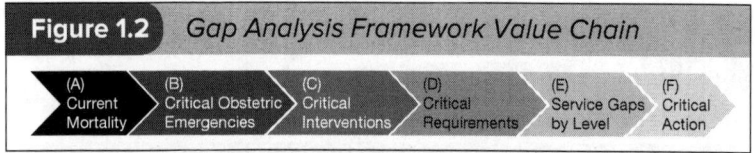

Figure 1.2 *Gap Analysis Framework Value Chain*

(A) Current Mortality | (B) Critical Obstetric Emergencies | (C) Critical Interventions | (D) Critical Requirements | (E) Service Gaps by Level | (F) Critical Action

process of reverse engineering and determines the specific facility data that need to be collected and analysed. The tool begins with maternal and neonatal mortality, and then suggests investigating the critical health complications that cause mortality (critical change areas such as haemorrhage, sepsis and asphyxia); next, it suggests the study of the necessary preventative and treatment interventions and finally, from here, the framework arrives at the critical requirements essential for delivering those treatments (infrastructure, staff, training, equipment, drugs, supplies and so on).

The critical requirements of this value-chain analysis are then compared to facility-level mapping data, which calls attention to service gaps that have damaging—and potentially fatal—effects on maternal and newborn health (MNH). These are the specific service gaps that we will focus. It is important to rectify specific gaps in essential drugs; however, it is important that one should always be aware of how specific drugs and other inputs influence the larger goal of integrated BEmONC and CEmONC interventions (Figure 1.3).

Facilities could be identified through lists provided by the state and district officials. As these lists may not be complete, snow-balling could be conducted to identify unlisted public and private facilities. Private facilities comprise all those private hospitals, nursing homes or clinics that provide any RMNCH services, either in-patient or out-patient. Clinics that only provided diagnostic facilities need not be included.

The mapping tools (specific to facility types) could be developed by a team of experts from the National Rural Health Mission (NRHM) and development partners in accordance

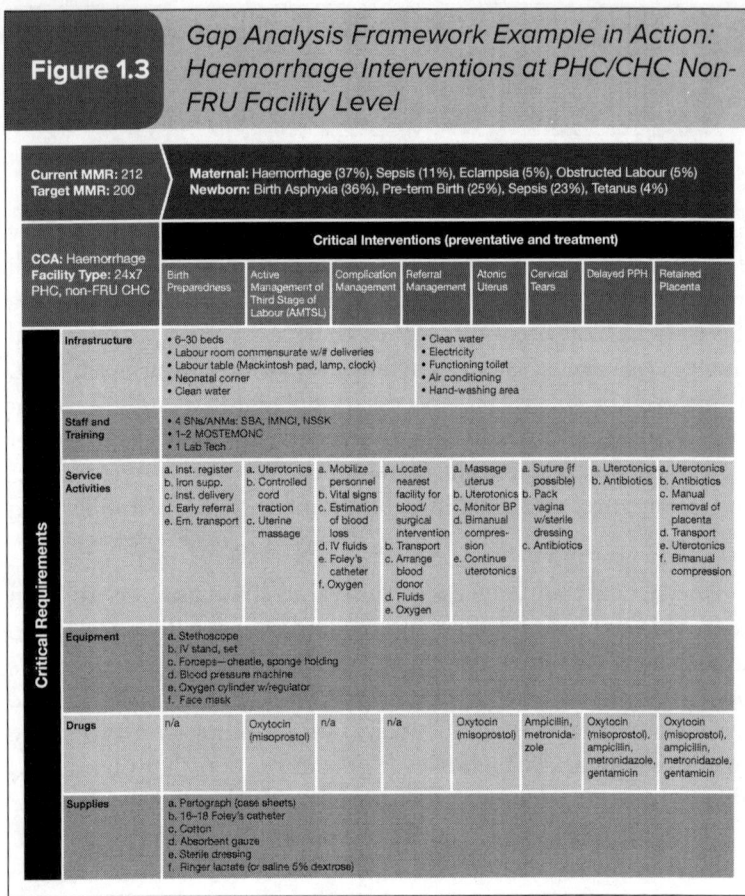

Figure 1.3 Gap Analysis Framework Example in Action: Haemorrhage Interventions at PHC/CHC Non-FRU Facility Level

Current MMR: 212 Target MMR: 200	**Maternal:** Haemorrhage (37%), Sepsis (11%), Eclampsia (5%), Obstructed Labour (5%) **Newborn:** Birth Asphyxia (36%), Pre-term Birth (25%), Sepsis (23%), Tetanus (4%)								
CCA: Haemorrhage **Facility Type:** 24x7 PHC, non-FRU CHC	**Critical Interventions (preventative and treatment)**								
	Birth Preparedness	Active Management of Third Stage of Labour (AMTSL)	Complication Management	Referral Management	Atonic Uterus	Cervical Tears	Delayed PPH	Retained Placenta
Infrastructure	• 6–30 beds • Labour room commensurate w/# deliveries • Labour table (Mackintosh pad, lamp, clock) • Neonatal corner • Clean water			• Clean water • Electricity • Functioning toilet • Air conditioning • Hand-washing area				
Staff and Training	• 4 SNs/ANMs: SBA, IMNCI, NSSK • 1–2 MOSTEMONC • 1 Lab Tech							
Service Activities	a. Inst. register b. Iron supp. c. Inst. delivery d. Early referral e. Em. transport	a. Uterotonics b. Controlled cord traction c. Uterine massage	a. Mobilize personnel b. Vital signs c. Estimation of blood loss d. IV fluids e. Foley's catheter f. Oxygen	a. Locate nearest facility for blood/ surgical intervention b. Transport c. Arrange blood donor d. Fluids e. Oxygen	a. Massage uterus b. Uterotonics c. Monitor BP d. Bimanual compres- sion e. Continue uterotonics	a. Suture (if possible) b. Pack vagina w/sterile dressing c. Antibiotics	a. Uterotonics b. Antibiotics	a. Uterotonics b. Antibiotics c. Manual removal of placenta d. Transport e. Uterotonics f. Bimanual compression
Equipment	a. Stethoscope b. IV stand, set c. Forceps – cheatle, sponge holding d. Blood pressure machine e. Oxygen cylinder w/regulator f. Face mask							
Drugs	n/a	Oxytocin (misoprostol)	n/a	n/a	Oxytocin (misoprostol)	Ampicillin, metronida- zole	Oxytocin (misoprostol), ampicillin, metronidazole, gentamicin	Oxytocin (misoprostol), ampicillin, metronidazole, gentamicin
Supplies	a. Partograph (case sheets) b. 16–18 Foley's catheter d. Cotton d. Absorbent gauze e. Sterile dressing f. Ringer lactate (or saline 5% dextrose)							

(left margin label: Critical Requirements)

with appropriate service guidelines and should be pretested. The tools could be designed to capture details of population/villages covered, physical infrastructure, staff, drugs, equipment and supplies, services (antenatal care, delivery, postpartum, postnatal, abortion, newborn and child), certain service statistics and use of facility-untied funds.

All field investigators need to be trained and provided with data collection manuals. In addition, the data collection can be monitored for quality by a central team of public health experts (with experience in monitoring and evaluation) through field visits and spot checks. For each RMNCH care component at each level, the primary respondent will be asked if they are routinely offering services, according to the standards listed in the NRHM guidelines. Both spontaneous and probed responses can be collected. Spontaneous responses will provide an insight into the knowledge of guidelines and provider preparedness. Taking into account different response biases (recall, social desirability and so on), neither spontaneous nor probed responses necessarily indicate actual services provided. Service statistics too may be inconsistently maintained, and therefore, the quality and completeness of the data cannot be assured.

The following mapping tools can be used at each level of care:

Subcentre: Facility-related information along with the (a) villages and populations covered, and for each village covered by the SC, the number of ASHAs and AWWs sanctioned and in position, training status of these FLWs, functioning of VHSNCs in each village, frequency of conducting VHND and immunization days; (b) infrastructure; (c) equipment; (d) drugs and supplies; (e) services including referral services; (f) service utilization data; (g) untied funds and (h) community outreach services.

Non-FRU facility: To be used for the additional PHCs, block PHCs or community health centres (CHCs) that are not designated as FRUs. The tool has to cover staffing, infrastructure, equipment, drugs and supplies, services including referral services, service statistics, information, education and communication (IEC) display and untied funds.

FRU facility: To be used for block PHCs and CHCs that are designated as FRUs. The tool should cover staffing, infrastructure, equipment, drugs and supplies, services including referral services, service statistics, IEC display and untied funds.

District hospital: To be used for the district hospital (DH). The tool should cover staffing, infrastructure, equipment, drugs and supplies, services including referral services, service statistics, IEC display and untied funds.

Additional tools that facilitate the assessment of various aspects of facility-based care as currently envisaged in delivery points, labour room, newborn care corner, nutrition rehabilitation centre and complication management could be used. These are provided along with specific national operational guidelines issued by MoHFW. The recently released MNCH toolkit can be appropriately used to assess the provision of maternal and newborn-health facilities and services (Table 1.3).

For assessing provider competency and to assess the quality of services provided, a variety of tools and methods will need to be employed (Table 1.4). They include a facility checklist, case record audits, exit interviews, knowledge questionnaires including case vignettes, direct observations and demonstrations of skills. Some of the tools are facility specific and some are provider specific. Tools should be aligned with current government guidelines for standards of care.

Community-level methods

To understand community-based facilitators and barriers to service utilization, IDIs can be conducted with women and families selected from facility records. The objectives of the qualitative assessments are:

1. To determine participants' understandings of a healthy pregnancy, including delivery and ill health of the neonate
2. To determine the actions or behaviours undertaken by participants to facilitate a healthy pregnancy and delivery and to promote good health in the neonate
3. To determine the available and preferred health care alternatives for pregnancy and delivery and care of the neonate
4. To determine the decision-making processes involved in pregnancy and the delivery and care of the neonate

Table 1.3   *Facility Mapping Data: Strengths and Limitations*

Data Source and Sample Size	Information Collected	Strengths	Limitations
Mapping data: Three different instruments	An audit of facilities covering: • Villages covered, other health care facilities and providers in the area (for SCs only) • Physical infrastructure • Staff in position • Equipment availability and functionality • Drugs and supplies • Select output parameters from facility health records • Untied funds and RKSs • Monitoring activities • Service provision	• Comprehensive; covers most facilities in districts • First data set to provide such information • Provides a baseline for evaluation of interventions	• Population data not available for non-census villages covered by facilities • As the health system is dynamic, data is very time sensitive. Many changes can be made after mapping is completed

Source: Karnataka Health Promotion Trust (KHPT), 2011, Maternal, Newborn and Child Health in Bagalkot District: A Situational Analysis, the Sukshema Project, Bangalore.

Table 1.4 *Provider Competency Data: Strengths and Limitations*

Data Source and Sample Size	Information Collected	Strengths	Limitations
Case studies and knowledge questionnaires	Provider knowledge about various issues of mother, newborn and child care and complications; in assessing the patient and recommending management of the health condition in the given case scenarios	• Captures both knowledge and problem-solving skills. • Provides a baseline for evaluation of interventions	• Findings may not be representative at the district level because of the smaller sample size • Does not capture ability to apply knowledge/skills in authentic setting
	Assesses skills and practice of ANC, PNC and neonatal health	• Authentic context • Provides a baseline for evaluation of interventions	• Hawthorne effect: Providers might be more conscientious than normal • Sample size means findings are not representative at the district level; findings are presented for all the programme districts
Structured demonstrations	Assesses skills and practice while performing a task to provide health care for neonatal and child health	• Does not affect patient confidentiality/privacy • Conducted when direct observation is not possible	• Inauthentic context
Exit interviews	Assess client satisfaction, experience of ANC and PNC, delivery, also covers costs of services	• No recall bias	• Convenience sample, not representative

Method	Purpose	Considerations
Facility checklist	To assess infrastructure, systems for infection prevention/waste management, signal functions performed in emergency obstetric care/child care, protocols, referrals, waste management, abortion care, cause of maternal and infant deaths	• Provides snapshot in time of facility operations
Clinical audit	Assessments of case sheets/registers recording client history and case management around specific conditions in the area of maternal, neonatal and infant health	• Reveals facility's record-keeping practice • Should demonstrate case-management skills and practice • Data quality depends on clinical record-keeping practice of facility
Direct observations	Provider practices in with relation to antenatal, intranatal and postnatal services	• Reveals provider practices in real-life situations • The presence of the observer may influence the practice • Complications being rare events may be hard to cover during assessments

Source: Karnataka Health Promotion Trust (KHPT), 2011, Maternal, Newborn and Child Health in Bagalkot District: A Situational Analysis, the Sukshema Project, Bangalore.

The sample has to be drawn to include women at various stages in the life cycle—pregnant women and women with young children. The sample can be recruited through ANMs and AWWs; part of the role of the ANMs is to maintain a register of all pregnant women in their community. All interviewers can be trained in qualitative interviewing, and data could be collected in pairs. Prior to each interview, informed consent has to be collected.

To further assess the client perspective, a community-based survey has to be conducted. For the community-based component, respondents can be selected through a multistage sampling technique; SCs can be randomly sampled, and then villages within the catchment area can be selected to ensure a sample that includes both care seekers and non-care seekers (Table 1.5).

VHSCs are an important intervention under NRHM to facilitate community participation in governance of health facilities. The programme implementers could undertake an assessment of VHSC functioning. Their field investigators can undergo a two-day training and then collect data.

The objectives of the assessment are:

- Understand the structure and activities of the VHSCs
- Collecting baseline information for community monitoring
- Classifying the VHSCs according to the level of support required

To achieve these objectives, a variety of methodologies can be employed, including structured interviews with VHSC functionaries (ex-officio members which include Panchayat president, ANM, ASHA and Anganwadi teacher) and VHSC members who are non-functionaries. In addition, focus group discussions can be held with the marginalized beneficiaries such as SC/ST women (Table 1.6).

Table 1.5 *Community Assessment Data Sources: Strengths and Limitations*

Data Source and Sample Size	Information Collected	Strengths	Limitations
IDIs with women of reproductive age (18–49) (sample from facility records), pregnant women, new mothers, husbands, grandmothers.	Cultural facilitators and barriers to accessing care	• Non-structured format allows interviewer to probe for depth on specific issues • Allows participants to respond in their own words, in a culturally salient way	• Sample bias: Only women who have contact with health system (ANMs/AWWs) included in sample (sampled from register of pregnant women)
Exit interviews—questionnaire	Cost of maternal and newborn services, care received, provider attitudes	• Provides a perspective on quality of care with no recall bias • Quantitative survey data is comparable across districts • Captures formal care-seeking population	• Convenience sample

(Continued)

Table 1.5 *Continued*

Data Source and Sample Size	Information Collected	Strengths	Limitations
Beneficiary interviews in community. Sample drawn from facility records of women who have given birth in the last 12 months and with help of ASHAs. • For mothers with children under 3 months: Questions cover postnatal and new-born care • For mothers with children over 3 months and less than 12 months: Questions cover immunizations	• Where services are received • Cost of maternal and newborn services • Attitude of providers • Episodes of child-hood illness/care seeking • PNC care • Barriers to accessing care • Details on govern-ment schemes	• Specificity of time period reduces recall bias	• Excludes women who have no contact with ASHAs • Small sample-size limits generalizability

Source: Karnataka Health Promotion Trust (KHPT), 2011, Maternal, Newborn and Child Health in Bagalkot District: A Situational Analysis, the Sukshema Project, Bangalore.

Table 1.6 *VHSC Assessment Data Sources: Strengths and Limitations*

Data Source and Sampling Size	Information Collected	Strengths	Limitations
Structured interviews	To compare activities and practice of VHSC with the guidelines and involvement/role of non-functionary members	• Structured format means data is comparable across districts • Provides a baseline for evaluation of interventions	• Low level of awareness means a high level of non-response
Focus group discussions with beneficiaries	Health-related needs of high-need groups	• Non-structured format allows interviewer to probe for depth on specific issues • Allows participants to respond in their own words, in a culturally salient way • Discussion format allows participants to flesh out their responses with peers • Provides a baseline for evaluation of interventions	• May not capture personal or private information/minority viewpoints/experiences

Source: Karnataka Health Promotion Trust (KHPT), 2011, Maternal, Newborn and Child Health in Bagalkot District: A Situational Analysis, the Sukshema Project, Bangalore.

Health system-level methods

The health system-level gaps or bottlenecks need to be assessed through mixed methods:

1. Review of policy/scheme-related documents, official circulars and the like
2. Secondary data
3. Interviews with the concerned key officials at the state and district levels

The goal of the health systems assessment is to understand the system-level facilitators and barriers to the delivery of RMNCH services from the supply side (Table 1.7). Semi-structured interviews need to be conducted with health department officials at state and district levels and providers at various facilities across DHs, taluk hospitals (THs), CHCs, PHCs, SCs and private facilities. The interviews have to cover human resource systems, governance, health service delivery, HMIS, finance and infrastructure relating to MNCH service delivery. Interviewer training (two days) and data collection should be given importance. Before each in-depth or exit interview, verbal consent needs to be obtained.

Gap Analyses and Technical Interventions for RMNCH+A

Gap analysis, done as described in this chapter, will help in the selection of a critical technical intervention package that is relevant to the local context and is based on strong evidence. This technical intervention package forms the basis for the improvements in RMNCH that the states/districts wish to attain and represents the 'what' of the implementation. It consists of two types of interventions:

1. **Primary:** Interventions that have been prioritized to be included in the implementation plans due to (a) strong evidence and (b) need for the intervention in high-priority districts driven by current levels of utilization and coverage.

Table 1.7 *Health Systems Assessment Data Sources: Strengths and Limitations*

Data Source and Sample Size	Information Collected	Strengths	Limitations
IDIs with providers and officials	Provider's perspective on system-level issues	• Allows participants to respond in their own words, in a culturally salient way • Semi-structured format allows interviewer to probe for depth on specific issues • Semi-structured format captures provider's own perspectives and priorities • Large sample size increases transferability (application of results for other sites/contexts) • Exploratory, reveals areas for further investigation	• Exploratory rather than conclusive
Literature review of • Policy and administrative documents • Journal articles		• Policies and guidelines tell us how situation 'should be': Allows a framework against which the situation can be assessed • Budget and spending analysis can reveal political will that accompanies policies	• Policies and guidelines may not always reflect implementation

Source: Karnataka Health Promotion Trust (KHPT), 2011, Maternal, Newborn and Child Health in Bagalkot District: A Situational Analysis, the Sukshema Project, Bangalore.

2. **Innovations:** Interventions that are either new or need to be adapted to the local context. These need to be piloted to assess effectiveness and readiness for scalability.

In order to ensure that the package of interventions selected is relevant to the local context, the following process could be utilized:

1. A list of interventions for technical areas could be identified. This can be done using a variety of local, national and international sources, including NRHM documents, Indian Public Health Standard documents, UN agency documents such as WHO and UNICEF.

2. The current evidence on all interventions has to be reviewed. A variety of sources could also be used for review of the evidence, including peer-reviewed published journal articles, programme documents, technical reports and strategies from international agencies such as Bill & Melinda Gates Foundation (BMGF), jhpiego (Johns Hopkins Program for International Education in Gynecology and Obstetrics), Engender Health, USAID and UN agencies such as the WHO and UNICEF.

3. The local evidence from baseline assessments from the programme and secondary data sources have to be reviewed to identify coverage gaps. Data from secondary sources such as the DLHS, NFHS and Reproductive Health Survey (RHS), as well as data from the programme's own baseline assessments on availability and quality of MNCH services, have to be used to determine the need for prioritization of interventions in the programme districts.

4. In order to both avoid duplication and synergize efforts, the role of other agencies/actors in the field of MNCH need to be considered in the districts where the programme is implemented.

5. A matrix/framework for criteria for inclusion in the critical package has to be developed and presented to all key stakeholders. This matrix can summarize the aforementioned Steps 1–4, and form the basis for discussion with

all partners as to which interventions need to be prioritized for inclusion in the critical technical intervention package.

Following this process, interventions can be prioritized for inclusion, if they meet all of the following criteria:

- Strong evidence of effectiveness of the intervention at improving MNCH outcomes (morbidity and mortality)
- Need (poor coverage) for the intervention
- Intervention a priority for NRHM and Government of Karnataka (GoK)
- Minimal duplication of the intervention with other programmes
- Implementation of the intervention feasible and scalable in the local context

These selected interventions then can be reviewed, discussed and finalized with the partners and the state governments, NRHM and funding agencies. Table 1.8 provides an illustration of the critical package of interventions developed in the context of Karnataka as a part of the technical assistance grant between 2009 and 2016.

The non-prioritized interventions refer to those that are not considered due to recognition of larger priorities, gaps in funding and so on. The proposed interventions through the continuum of care indicating the location of intervention (facility, community or both) are indicated in Figure 1.4.

While the package should include the continuum of care from pre-pregnancy to the postnatal period and 12 months of age for the infant, extra priority has to be given to interventions at the time of delivery and the 48 hours to one week after birth, as this represents a critical time period where more than half of maternal and neonatal deaths occur. With over 80% of pregnant women now delivering in facilities in India owing to new schemes and programmes by NRHM, there is a need to prioritize interventions that specifically target improved MNCH care at the facility level.

Table 1.8 *Technical Intervention Package for MNCH*

	Primary Interventions	Innovations	Not Prioritized

Maternal care interventions	• Quality delivery of ANC services
	  — Counselling on birth plan and emergency preparedness
	  — Screening for infections and hypertensive disease
	• Quality management of normal/routine deliveries
	  — Clean delivery/infection prevention
	  — Use of partograph
	  — active management of the third stage of labour (AMTSL)
	  — Rapid assessment, stabilization and referral of complications
	• Build and enhance basic emergency obstetric care (BEmOC) competencies at PHC level
	• Postpartum care
	  — Assessment, stabilization and referral
	  — Counselling for family planning, exclusive breastfeeding and nutrition
		• Use of corticosteroids for preterm labour/birth
		• Community-based rapid diagnostic tests for infections
		• Integrated maternal and neonatal care assessment and protocol tools—'Healthy Beginnings'
			• Community-based use of misoprostol
			• Community-based routine delivery
			• CEmOC capabilities

| Newborn and infant care interventions | • Basic newborn care
  – Warmth/KMC
  – Clean cord care
  – Breastfeeding within one hour of birth
• Basic neonatal resuscitation
  – Bag and mask
  – Assessment, initial management and referral of complications
• Community-based assessment, identification and referral of illness
• Management of sepsis and low birth weight (LBW) (including preterm birth)
• Increased coverage of full vaccination schedule in infants
• Nutrition
  – Exclusive breastfeeding
  – Timely complementary feeding
  – Treatment of diarrhoea with zinc | • Chlorhexidine application for cord care
• Integrated maternal and neonatal care assessment and protocol—'Healthy Beginnings' | • Community-based management of neonatal infections
• Broader IMNCI at facility level
• Nutritional powders to improve nutrition and prevent illness |

Source: Karnataka Health Promotion Trust (KHPT), 2011, Maternal, Newborn and Child Health in Bagalkot District: A Situational Analysis, the Sukshema Project, Bangalore.

Figure 1.4   Interventions Across Continuum of Care

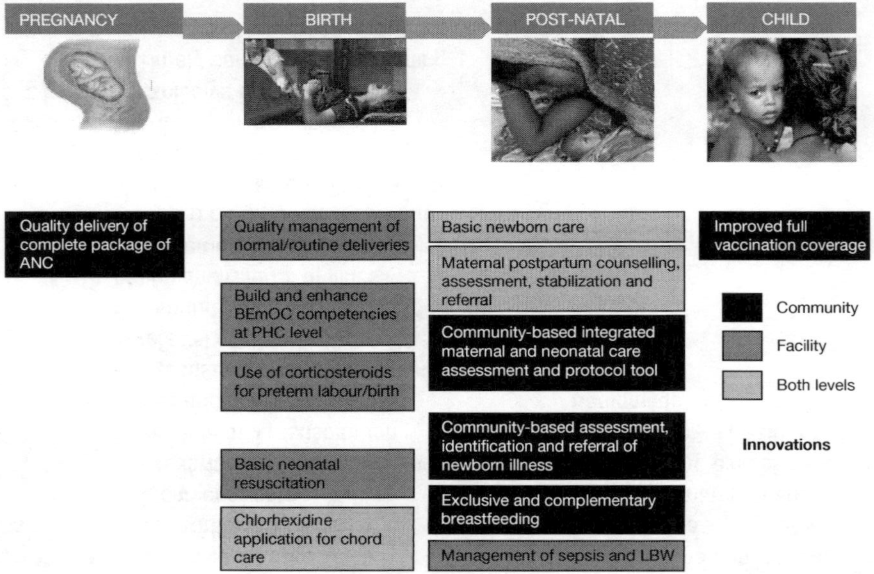

PREGNANCY   BIRTH   POST-NATAL   CHILD

Quality delivery of complete package of ANC

Quality management of normal/routine deliveries

Build and enhance BEmOC competencies at PHC level

Use of corticosteroids for preterm labour/birth

Basic neonatal resuscitation

Chlorhexidine application for chord care

Basic newborn care

Maternal postpartum counselling, assessment, stabilization and referral

Community-based integrated maternal and neonatal care assessment and protocol tool

Community-based assessment, identification and referral of newborn illness

Exclusive and complementary breastfeeding

Management of sepsis and LBW

Improved full vaccination coverage

■ Community
■ Facility
■ Both levels

Innovations

Solution levers

The solution levers represent the 'how' of our package, that is, these are the activities that need to be undertaken for effective implementation of the technical package. These solution levers address critical root causes/barriers and have impacts across the objectives and technical foci of several programmes.

Two types of solution levers are:

1. **Primary:** Prioritized solution levers that have been shown effective in India or elsewhere globally and integrate readily with existing platforms; these typically can be taken to scale quickly.
2. **Innovations:** Solution levers that have less evidence to support their effectiveness, that are applied in a significantly different way or that involve a fundamentally different operating model and may need targeted creation of infrastructure or new capabilities. Pilot testing for feasibility of implementation and/or effectiveness would be needed before scale-up.

The rationale for the solution categories identified is provided in Table 1.9.

Within each category, specific solution levers have been identified as key. The shaded areas represent innovations (Table 1.10).

Figure 1.5 describes the 'critical path' and deliverables of each solution category and how they relate to outcomes and impact.

Table 1.11 summarizes the implementation framework, including the indicators of success and critical activity milestones under each of the objectives and solution levers.

Table 1.9 Critical Gaps/Barriers and Solution Categories

Levels of Change	Objectives of Change	Critical Gaps/Barriers	Solution Categories
Health systems	Enable expanded **availability** and **accessibility** of critical MNCH interventions for rural populations	• Inadequate distribution of facilities and staff across populations and geographies • Inadequate availability of supplies and equipment • Inadequate access for the rural poor to specialist services for delivery and newborn care	1. Influencing policy and planning
Facility	Enable improvement in the **quality** of MNCH services for rural populations	• Weak clinical, managerial and administrative competencies inhibit the ability to deliver critical health interventions and services	2. Improving quality of care at birth and immediate postpartum care at facilities
Community	Enable expanded **utilization** and population **coverage** of critical MNCH services for rural populations	• Limited awareness of available services and incentives for MNH • Cultural practices and beliefs that determine health-seeking behaviour • Poor community engagement in exercising rights to quality services • Poor coverage of target populations by FLWs for MNCH services—unreached target populations and reached by incomplete package of services	3. Improving management and delivery of outreach services 4. Strengthening accountability
Cross-cutting	Improve **data quality and use**	• Poor data quality and analytical skills weaken programme management delivery and improvement	5. Strengthening data management and use

Source: Karnataka Health Promotion Trust (KHPT), 2011, Maternal, Newborn and Child Health in Bagalkot District: A Situational Analysis, the Sukshema Project, Bangalore.

Table 1.10 *Specific Solution Levers*

1. Influencing policy and planning	2. Improving quality of care at birth and immediate postpartum care at facilities	3. Improving management and delivery of outreach services and shaping demand	4. Strengthening accountability	5. Strengthening data management and use
1. Facilitation of policy changes that respond to critical issues related to infrastructure, staff, supplies and financial incentives 2. Improvement of public–private partnerships (PPPs)	3. On-site mentoring for improved clinical care and service delivery	4. Enumeration and tracking tools (ETTs) and methods for ASHAs to improve coverage 5. Integrated maternal and newborn management tool for ASHAs to improve identification and actions for postnatal danger signs 6. Family-focused communication tools and materials for ASHAs to use with families to influence awareness and practices	7. Community monitoring tools for VHSCs and Aarogya Raksha Samitis (ARSs) to strengthen accountability	8. Development and implementation of data quality controls and audits 9. Development and implementation of protocols for data analysis and use for programme review, planning and problem-solving at district and taluk levels

Source: Karnataka Health Promotion Trust (KHPT), 2011, Maternal, Newborn and Child Health in Bagalkot District: A Situational Analysis, the Sukshema Project, Bangalore.

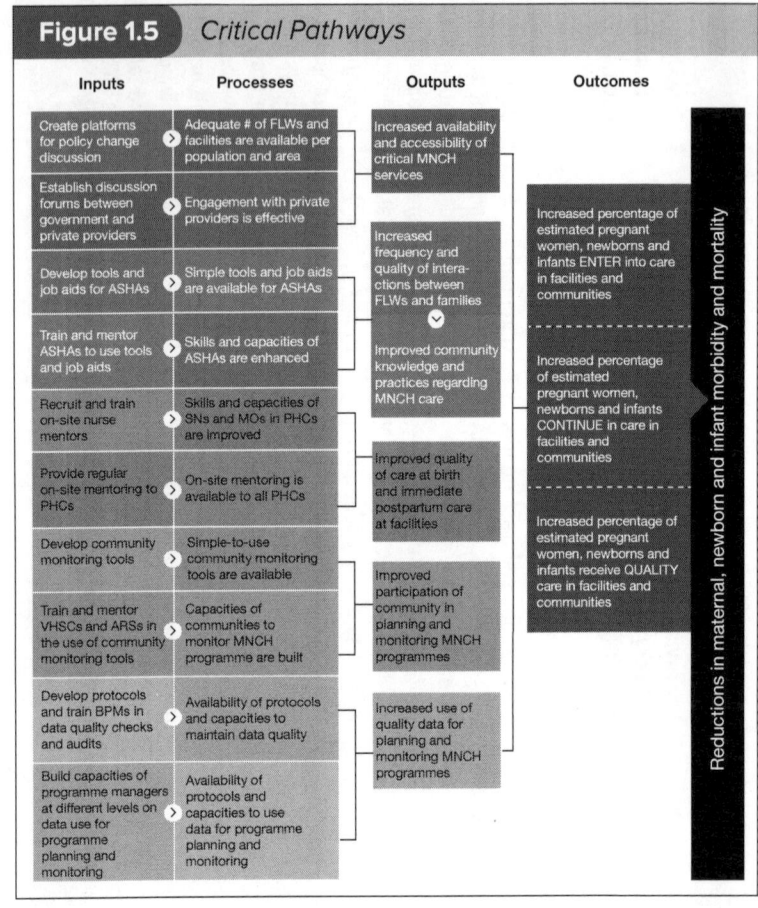

Figure 1.5 Critical Pathways

Table 1.11 *Implementation Framework: Indicators of Success and Critical Activities*

Goal	Indicators of Success	Monitoring and Evaluation	Assumptions
To support the government to improve maternal, neonatal and child health outcomes in rural populations through the development and adoption of effective operational and health system approaches within the NRHM.	**Process Indicators** 1. Development, piloting and implementation at scale of a strategy to improve quality of delivery and postpartum care services in 24x7 PHCs in the districts 2. Development, field testing and implementation at scale of appropriate tools, job-aids and mechanisms to improve the frequency and quality of interactions between FLWs and target families in the districts 3. Development, field testing and implementation at scale of a community monitoring tools and processes involving VHSCs and ARSs to strengthen accountability in the districts	1. Endorsement by the state NRHM and state Department of Health & Family Welfare of the programme strategies and implementation design 2. Systematic documentation by the programme and review of implementation process and progress in the focus districts by the government and an expert panel. 3. Approved design and documentation of a monitoring and evaluation plan, including review of published reports.	Constructive partnership with NRHM team can be established. Leadership of NRHM supports strategic focusing and innovation. NRHM leadership and functionaries at the district level will be engaged and supportive of programme initiatives. The national NRHM will seek evidence-based approaches and operational models for endorsement and incorporation into the NRHM design.

(Continued)

Table 1.11 Continued

Indicators of Success	Monitoring and Evaluation	Assumptions
4. Facilitate policy changes through consultative workshops on infrastructure, staff, drugs and supplies, incentives and PPPs	4. Evidence of endorsement of programme-derived strategies, tools and job-aids for scaling up through the NRHM by the GoI.	
5. Concurrent evaluation and documentation of results of the implementation in districts.		
6. The strategies, tools and job-aids for improving MNCH endorsed for scaling up by the NRHM at the state and national levels.		
Outcome indicators in the implementation districts	Measurement of baseline and endline indicators using routine HMIS/MCTS, existing health surveys and special surveys (where required) to document changes in service delivery endpoints.	
1. At least 80% of pregnant women receive designated antenatal services included in agreed package of interventions.		
2. At least 85% of all deliveries occur in institutions.		

3. At least 80% of all deliveries (home and institutional) include designated services included in agreed package of interventions at birth.

4. At least 80% of mothers and newborns receive designated services included in agreed package of interventions during the neonatal period.

5. 80% of newborns and mothers are visited by a health care worker at Day 2 and Day 7 after delivery.

6. Percentage of fully immunized children increases by 30% over current levels.

7. Proportion of women with obstetric emergencies treated in facilities providing designated intervention package will reach 100%.

8. Obstetric case fatality rate in facilities providing designated package of interventions is less than 1%.

Built-in evaluation system to measure maternal and neonatal mortality at baseline, mid-point and end-of-programme.

(Continued)

Table 1.11 Continued

	Indicators of Success	Monitoring and Evaluation	Assumptions
Objective 1. Enable expanded availability and accessibility of critical MNCH services for poor populations, especially in rural areas. **Solution category** • Influencing policy and planning • Strengthening data management and use	1. Increased availability and accessibility of critical MNCH services through optimization of existing public and private sector provider mechanisms such that: • There is at least 1 facility providing SBA services for every 30,000 population. • There is at least 1 BEmOC facility for every 100,000 population. • There is at least one CEmOC facility for every 500,000 population. • Each taluk in focus districts has at least one facility providing a package of critical MNCH interventions. 2. Incentive systems for providers and beneficiaries are modified to improve PNC coverage.	Programme end-line mapping of public and private health facilities to assess availability and accessibility of critical MNCH services per population and area.	The NRHM at the national and state levels participates in policy discussion forums and provides sufficient funds for redistribution of functional facilities and modifications of schemes based on evidence.

3. Thayi Bhagya Scheme is modified for an effective enrolment of high-volume private providers for providing specialist care for the rural poor.

4. Improved utilization of programme monitoring data by NRHM functionaries at the state, district and local levels to increase availability of MNCH services.

Activities:

1.1 Organize a state-level policy workshop on equitable distribution of functional SCs, PHCs, BEmOC and CEmOC centres according to population and area coverage.

1.2 Organize a state-level policy workshop on staff, drugs and supplies.

1.3 Organize a state-level policy workshop on improving PNC through demand and supply side incentives.

1.4 Train district programme managers (DPMs) and block programme managers (BPMs) in data quality audits.

1.5 Train DPMs and BPMs in data analysis, interpretation and use for programme planning and review.

(Continued)

Table 1.11 *Continued*

Objective	Indicators of Success	Monitoring and Evaluation	Assumptions
2. Enable improvement in the quality of critical MNCH services for poor populations, especially in rural areas. **Solution category** • Improving quality of care at birth and immediate postpartum period in facilities	1. Enhanced capabilities and performance of staff nurses (SNs) and medical officers (MOs) in 24x7 PHCs in delivering quality services at birth and immediate postpartum period. 2. 80% of SNs and MOs meet minimum performance requirements in delivering critical MNCH intervention during delivery and immediate postpartum period in 24x7 PHCs. 3. Improved referral mechanisms, documentation and review processes in facilities.	Baseline and endline assessments of quality of services provided by 24x7 PHCs. Routine monitoring of outputs of SNs nurses and MOs in 24x7 PHCs in key domains related to the delivery of critical services during delivery and immediate postpartum period.	The NRHM will facilitate the programme to develop, pilot and implement at scale the strategies to improve quality of services in 24x7 PHCs in the implementation districts. Sufficient resources will be available through the NRHM and the health system to ensure that key staff, equipment, medicine and other materials are available to deliver critical interventions.

Activities:

2.1 Pilot the on-site mentoring strategy for improved quality of services during delivery and postpartum period in 24x7 PHCs in implementation districts.

2.2 Roll out the on-site mentoring strategy in all 24x7 PHCs in all implementation districts.

2.3 Organize state- and district-level workshops to share the implementation experiences and advocate for the inclusion of PHC-level quality improvement strategies in the district and state PIPs.

	Indicators of Success	Monitoring and Evaluation	Assumptions
Objective 3. Enable expanded utilization and coverage of critical MNCH services for poor populations, especially in rural areas. **Solution category** • Improving management and delivery of outreach services and shaping demand • Strengthening accountability	1. Increased levels of knowledge among women in reproductive age groups and their families regarding effective preventive and curative interventions for reducing maternal and newborn morbidity and mortality. • Increased demand for quality care, including package of critical MNCH interventions. 2. Improved frequency and quality of interactions between beneficiaries and FLWs to improve entry and continuity of beneficiaries in the continuum of MNCH care. • Increased proportion of pregnant women, newborns and infants 'enter' into MNCH care continuum. • Increased proportion of pregnant women, newborns and infants 'continue' in MNCH care continuum	Baseline and follow-up knowledge, attitude practices (KAP) surveys of rural women and families in focus districts. Monitoring system data, programme audits and participatory assessments.	NRHM will facilitate the implementation to develop, field test and implement at scale the tools and job aids for FLWs and community structures

(Continued)

Table 1.11 *Continued*

Indicators of Success	Monitoring and Evaluation	Assumptions
3. Improved participation of community-level structures in planning and monitoring of utilization and coverage of MNCH services.		

Activities:

3.1 Develop and field test simple-to-use tools and job aids for FLWs to increase utilization and coverage of critical MNCH services through enumeration and tracking, improved PNC and improved family-focused communication in implementation districts.

3.2 Train and support the FLWs in implementation districts in the use of these tools and job aids.

3.3 Develop and field test simple-to-use community monitoring tools for VHSCs and ARSs.

3.4 Train and support VHSCs and ARSs in implementation districts in the use of these tools and job aids.

3.5 Organize district- and state-level workshops to share the implementation experiences and advocate for the inclusion of tools and job aids for FLWs and community structures to increase utilization and coverage as well as accountability in the PIPs of implementation districts.

Source: Karnataka Health Promotion Trust (KHPT), 2011, Maternal, Newborn and Child Health in Bagalkot District: A Situational Analysis, the Sukshema Project, Bangalore.

Case Study 1A: An Overview of Karnataka Health System

This case study provides an overview of the health system in Karnataka, with a special focus on the assessments done in relation to the health systems. It shows how gap analysis and assessments at various levels of health system help in creating a very rich picture of what needs to be done to strengthen the health system and what are some of the cost-effective solutions to existing problems that plague the system. It is hoped that gap analysis in other settings and contexts would lead to such a detailed picture that help prioritize interventions.

With the introduction of NRHM, there has been a big push towards increasing the availability of MNCH services through the improvement of PHCs to 24×7 PHCs and CHCs to FRUs by providing additional infrastructure. The NRHM has also been successful in providing alternative solutions to the low level of human resources through contracting. This case study highlights the many aspects of the NRHM in strengthening the health system as well as identifying remaining gaps. It provides an overview of the policy environment, the service delivery framework, community support systems and linkages, referral systems, human resource systems, procurement, HMIS, financial schemes and budgeting and spending. The primary sources of data for this case study are drawn from various health systems assessment, quality assessment and facility mappings, including self-reporting and audits of facility records that were done as part of the Sukshema Project, a project that was implemented in Karnataka with funding from the BMGF. Due to the dynamic nature of the health system, changes may have been made since this assessment was completed (July–August 2010) and the figures may not reflect the current reality but still provide a snapshot of NRHM progress.

Policy and programmatic environment

The health delivery system at the district level is governed by state and national programmes. Health policy in India is formulated at the central level by the MoHFW and implemented at the state level by the Department of Health & Family Welfare. A National Health Policy was written in 2002, which allowed for a state policy to be developed, adapting the key elements to the needs of the state.[4] In Karnataka, the Integrated Health Policy was written in 2004, and as with the national policy, some of the main pillars include equity, quality of care and client satisfaction, PPPs and continuing medical education.[5] Planning is done at state and district levels according to these policies and other guidelines.

The state also has legal stewardship over the private sector, although this is not necessarily practised. A 2007 bill ordered that all private facilities should be registered with the district authorities for the purposes of oversight, but not all private facilities have registered.[6,7] Private providers also engage with the state in PPPs, such as the Suvarna Arogya Suraksha Trust, Thayi Bhagya Scheme, the 108 ambulance services, contracting in of specialist providers and contracting out of PHC management.

While there are both national and state policies and guidelines, health is constitutionally a state concern and health expenditure is met largely by the state budget.[8] In the field of public health policy, Karnataka is a leader. Prior to the central government's introduction of PHCs throughout India, the state of Karnataka had already established a number of primary health units for providing comprehensive health, including curative, preventive

[4] GoI, National Health Policy, 2002. Available at http://stg2.kar.nic.in/healthnew/PDF/NATIONAL%20HEALTH%20POLICY%202002.pdf (accessed on 2 November 2017).

[5] GoK, The Karnataka State Integrated Health Policy, 2004. Available at http://stg2.kar.nic.in/healthnew/PDF/STATE%20HEALTH%20POLICY.pdf (accessed on 2 November 2017).

[6] GoK, Karnataka Act No. 21 of 2007: The Karnataka Private Medical Establishments Act, 2007.

[7] A. Yasmeen, 'Many Hospitals Yet to Register Under KPME Act', *The Hindu*, Saturday, 16 October 2010.

[8] GoK, The Karnataka State Integrated Health Policy, 2004. Available at http://stg2.kar.nic.in/healthnew/PDF/STATE%20HEALTH%20POLICY.pdf (accessed on 2 November 2017).

and rehabilitative care.[9] Karnataka has also provided national leadership in terms of tackling corruption within the health sector.[10] The state also has premier scientific, technical and research institutions that can provide the evidence required to improve health systems. Karnataka also has a strong tradition of excellence in tertiary education. Rajiv Gandhi University and its affiliated colleges help provide the state and nation with the human resources they need to provide health for all.

Key health programmes in Karnataka

As well as national and state policies, maternal and child health (MCH) has been guided by a number of key programmes, a series of which are outlined in Table 1a.1. The current ones are the NRHM and the Karnataka Health Systems Development Reform Project (KHSDRP), both of which work hand in hand to improve systems and infrastructure. The RCH Programme also has key relevance to MNCH issues, but it ended in 2010. RCH officers still exist at the district level.

NRHM

The NRHM (2005–2012) was launched to provide accessible, affordable and accountable quality health services to the rural population, including the poorest and those in the most remote areas. States with the poorest health indicators are classified as special focus states and provided with more intensive support. Karnataka is classified as high performing. The thrust of the mission is on establishing a fully functional, community owned, decentralized health delivery system with inter-sectoral convergence at all levels, to ensure simultaneous action on a wide variety of determinants of health such as water, sanitation, education,

[9] NRHM, Department of Health and Family Welfare Services, 2009, GoK. Programme Implementation Plan, 2010–2011, Bangalore.
[10] H. Sudarshan and N.S. Prashanth, 'Good Governance in Health Care: The Karnataka Experience', *The Lancet*, published online, 12 January 2011. doi: 10.1016/S0140-6736(10)62041-7

Table 1a.1	Timeline of Key National and State Health Programmes Relating to MNCH in Karnataka	
Years	**Programme**	**Implemented by**
1992–1993 and 1998–1999	CSSM (Child Survival and Safe Motherhood)	GoI, UNICEF
1997–1998 and 2004–2005	RCH 1	GoI
2005–2010	RCH 2	GoI, World Bank
2006–2012	KHSDRP	GoK, World Bank
2005–2012	NRHM	GoI

Source: Karnataka Health Promotion Trust (KHPT), 2011, Maternal, Newborn and Child Health in Bagalkot District: A Situational Analysis, the Sukshema Project, Bangalore.

nutrition, social and gender equality. In such an integrated framework there is a move away from health as a vertical programme, with an understanding of the many contextual factors affecting health of populations.[11]

Some of the NRHM's most important interventions include the 108 ambulance service, ASHAs and PHCs that are open all hours.

The Karnataka Health Systems Development Reform Project

The KHSDRP is a project supported by the World Bank to improve health service delivery across all 30 districts in Karnataka. It commenced in 2006 and after its commencement began working hand in hand with the NRHM. The project aims to increase utilization of essential health services (curative, preventive and public health), particularly in underserved areas and among vulnerable groups, to accelerate achievement of the health-related MDGs. The activities include the following:

[11] GoI, NRHM, 2005. NRHM Mission Document, 2005–2012.

- Implement an organizational development plan, to cultivate an environment geared towards results-based management and PPPs.
- Expand coverage of existing government programmes in primary care and public health through increased spending and better performance.
- Introduce innovations in service delivery and health financing along four different dimensions of service: infrastructure development and maintenance, delivery of priority curative services, planning and delivery of public health services and accessibility to safe delivery and hospital inpatient services.
- Support all project management, monitoring and evaluation activities.
- Support innovations in PPPs (including mobile clinics, citizen help desks, contracting in of specialists from the private sector and contracting out of PHCs).
- Develop a new HMIS.
- Improve procurement, distribution and quality control systems.
- Support the Suvarna Arogya Suraksha Trust, a health insurance scheme for BPL families in the five districts of Gulbarga division.

Administration

There is a multilayered apparatus at the state level to translate policy into practice, from the MoHFW in Bengaluru to district surgeons in each DH. The MoHFW converts the 2004 State Integrated Health Policy into actionable plans. The principal secretary of health provides the administrative support to formulate, monitor and implement these plans. The Department of Health & Family Welfare's commissioner coordinates and monitors the working of various programmes and project wings of the department. The director of health and family welfare services heads the department and is assisted by additional directors for each programme component.

At the district level, there are a number of officers implementing and reporting state and national programmes including district health and family welfare officer (or district health officer; DHO), the district leprosy officer, the district reproductive health officer (DRHO), the district malaria officer, district TB officer, district family welfare officer (DFWO), District AIDS Preventions Control Units (DAPCUs) and district surveillance officer. With the merger of the NRHM and KHSDRP, the district programme management officers assist the DHOs in other tasks relating to these programmes. The district programme management unit and the block programme management unit add managerial inputs into programme implementation. Clinically, district surgeons at DHs oversee curative and preventative services. In addition, there are 176 taluk health officers who implement programmes at the taluk level.[12]

Information management

Clinical record-keeping

Up-to-date, accurate and comprehensive patient records facilitate case management and accurate clinical decision-making and referral. The data collection process for the quality assessment revealed that clinical records are not well maintained. For example, out of 593 attempted case record audits for eclampsia, only 146 were completed (25%); for abortion audits, 215 were completed (35%) due to incomplete record-keeping (Figure 1a.1).

Health management information system (HMIS)

The broad range of interventions under the NRHM has increased the demand for disaggregated data on population and health for use in both microlevel planning and programme implementation. The HMIS would ideally provide a continuous flow of good quality information on inputs, outputs and outcome indicators

---

[12] GoK, 2011. DHFW, NRHM, Programme Implementation Plan for 2010–2011, Bangalore.

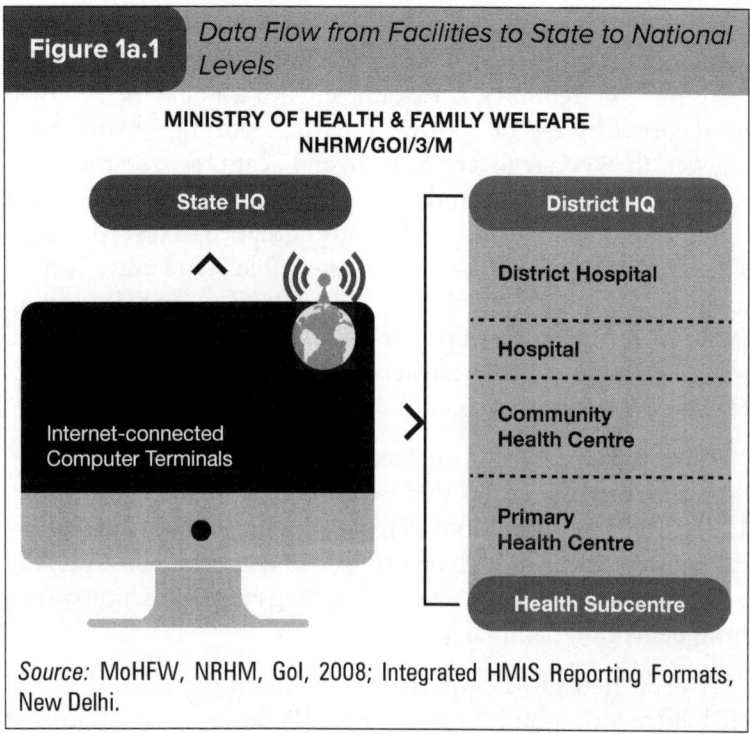

Figure 1a.1 *Data Flow from Facilities to State to National Levels*

MINISTRY OF HEALTH & FAMILY WELFARE
NHRM/GOI/3/M

State HQ

District HQ

District Hospital

Hospital

Community Health Centre

Primary Health Centre

Health Subcentre

Internet-connected Computer Terminals

Source: MoHFW, NRHM, GoI, 2008; Integrated HMIS Reporting Formats, New Delhi.

facilitating monitoring of the objectives of NRHM, ensuring information is available for decision-making regarding scale-up and replication.

Previously, reporting was done by taluk, however, this system frequently double-counted individuals as they visited more than one facility during, for example, a pregnancy. To improve data quality, reporting formats were established by the MoHFW, GoI, in 2008 to facilitate standardized entry at the facility and the district level. These were only rolled out for use in Karnataka in September 2010, when facility-based reporting began with these formats, whereby each facility sends monthly reports to the taluk health office for data entry, upload and aggregation. Computers have also been introduced at the PHCs to enable data entry at this level as well.

Reporting responsibility at the SC level includes not just the facility, but also the catchment area. In the case of a care delivered in the community, for example, with a home birth, it will be reported by the SC (lowest level of reporting) in the ANC register, the PNC register, the birth and death register, the referral register and the like, and then sent to the PHC or taluk health office for data entry (not all PHCs are equipped to do reporting). The reporting facility has an Internet-enabled data-entry facility to enter and upload the data to the MoHFW server. Reporting facilities can also download data for analysis and data users (policy decision-makers) can access the monthly report data from HMIS portal for analysis.

While this system has benefited from recent rationalization, the large number of registers that need to be maintained (currently, 13 for MCH, reduced from 17), with overlap between the different registers, means a high reporting load for providers, especially at the SC level. The high level of reporting may distract providers from delivering essential services.

A dedicated HMIS web portal has been established at the URL http://nrhm-hmis.nic.in. The HMIS facilitates standardized compilation and calculation of the various indicators at different levels of the health care delivery system and allows programme managers to track monitoring indicators for management decision-making.

Commenced in January 2011, the MCTS is a scheme whereby ANMs use mobile phones to 'text' details from the Thayi card to a central database. This scheme is in its nascent stages but is expected to increase the quality of data available for improved planning at the district level.

The next sections provide more in-depth view of the NRHM by taking northern districts of Karnataka as a case in point.

Community support systems and linkages

Positive outcomes for maternal, newborn and child health do not just rely on service delivery but also require active community participation and support. Community mobilization for MNH is the process whereby community members gain the knowledge, optimism and level of organization to achieve quality health care service. This might include providing peer health education, organizing transport linkages for pregnant women to reach facilities or encouraging families to delay the age of marriage of their daughters. Marginalized and vulnerable sections of the community require more intensive efforts in the process of mobilization and service delivery. The key mechanisms to ensure the continuum of care in the community include ASHAs, VHSCs, Anganwadi centres and AWWs. ANMs also provide care at the SC or community level; however, they are part of the health care system and so are described in the service delivery framework section.

Accredited social health activist (ASHA): ASHAs are a part-time, community-based volunteer workforce at the village level created under the NRHM. Their primary role is in building the community's awareness of their health care entitlements, in providing health education, in facilitating the community's access to essential health services and in delivering preventive and first contact curative care. The key roles to be performed by ASHAs include; track and mobilize women to attend monthly clinics, prepare birth preparedness plans, conduct home visits, support institutional delivery, make postnatal and newborn home visits, counsel on family planning and support the ANM in updating the MCH card. Under the JSY scheme, ASHAs are provided cash incentives to support mothers to deliver in facilities for their first two births.

ASHAs are meant to serve an average population size of 1,000. For instance, about 1,064 ASHAs have been recruited in Bagalkot district and each ASHA covers an average population size of 1,088. Again, aggregate coverage figures are good, but about 21% villages in the district do not have an ASHA. IDIs with ASHAs found that the workload varies—for some it is a full-time job and some have a lighter load and see few maternity cases. Furthermore, ASHAs called for more skills-based trainings to ensure knowledge can be translated into practice.

Village health and sanitation committees (VHSCs): The VHSCs are village-level bodies comprised of key stakeholders in a village and serve as a forum for village planning and monitoring. VHSCs were developed under the NRHM to ensure that:

- No section of the village community is excluded from services.
- An understanding is engendered in the community about health services and health-related rights.
- A village health plan is drawn to suit local realities and necessities, including transport for MNCH emergencies.
- Monitoring and oversight is provided to all village health activities, and guidance is provided for improvements.
- Untied funds are appropriately used in the village for improving maternal and neonatal health in the village.

The VHSC comprises 15 members including a minimum of 8 women members, and among the women members 3 of them should belong to SC/ST and 2 self-help group (SHG) members. Among the remaining 7 (male) members, a minimum of 2 should be belonging to SC/ST. The junior woman health assistant (ANM), junior male health worker (MHW), primary school teacher (preferably women), all AWWs and ASHAs of that particular village will be the ex-officio members. The Gram Panchayat member of the village is the VHSC president and one of the ASHAs from the locality its secretary.[13]

While the VHSC has a role in MNCH, assessments of VHSC activity, however, reveal that efforts are mostly around sanitation such as cleaning tanks, drains and getting rid of vermin. Since VHSCs are given untied funds, most respondents did not know how these were spent. These figures suggest that some VHSC efforts could be redirected towards maternal, newborn and child health.

[13] Karnataka Health Promotion Trust, 2010. VHSCs, Bangalore.

Anganwadi centres: Anganwadi centres were established under the Integrated Child Development Services (ICDS) Scheme as child care centres, providing nutrition support to young children and pregnant women through midday meals, preschool education, supplementation for children from six months to six years, iron supplementation for pregnant women, awareness raising meetings and growth monitoring. The ICDS is a centrally run programme implemented by the Ministry of Women & Child Development (MWCD) (not the Department of Health & Family Welfare, which oversees much of MCH service provision). All pregnant women and children are registered at the Anganwadi centres. Vaccinations are also provided by ANMs at Anganwadi centre sites.[14]

Anganwadi workers (AWWs): AWWs are concerned with infant and child health through nutritional supplementation, growth monitoring, vaccinations and child care provided at the Anganwadi centres. They are employed under the ICDS Scheme, under the MWCD.

According to the ICDS protocols, there should be 1 AWW per 400–800 population in rural areas.[15] In Bagalkot, for instance, there are in total 1,666 AWWs in the entire district, with more than 1 AWW (1.44) for every 1,000 people. The aggregate coverage figures are good; however, about 4% villages in Bagalkot district do not have any AWW. The proportion of villages with no AWW is relatively high in Bilgi (8%) and Bagalkot (5%) taluks.

According to an interview with the joint director of ICDS, since the introduction of ASHAs, a new set of guidelines for AWWs has been introduced to clarify roles between ASHAs, AWWs and ANMs. For example, AWWs used to distribute Vitamin A, tetanus toxoid (TT) vaccines and IFA tablets, however, now this is done by ANMs. In terms of antenatal care, both ANMs and

---

[14] ICDS Guidelines. Available at http://wcd.nic.in/icds.htm (accessed on 2 November 2017).
[15] Ibid.

Table 1a.2	Availability of Personnel at Village Level for MNCH Services	
Staff	Number	Number per SC Catchment Area
ANM	203	0.84
MHW	107	0.44
AWW	1,666	6.91
ASHA	1,064	4.41

Source: Mapping data.

AWWs register pregnant women, make home visits, check swelling in hands and legs, counsel on nutrition and make referrals. Hence, there is still duplication and confusion about roles. This is augmented by the many departments who give work to the AWWs, the health department, Sarva Shiksha Abhiyan, food and civil supplies, rural development and the Panchayat Raj department (Table 1a.2).

Referral systems and transport connections

The *Operational Guidelines on Maternal and Newborn Health* prescribes that all facilities accredited for safe deliveries should have an assured referral transport linkage and an assured referral facility linkage. An assured referral facility linkage is a CEmONC centre that agrees to provide emergency services on a cashless basis to any patient referred from a lower facility. It could be a public hospital or an accredited private hospital. The ideal situation is where every mother delivers in an institution with access to a referral centre within one hour, in case of complications requiring surgery and blood transfusion. The facility referred to should be contacted by phone about the referral with a brief history of the patient, so that on arrival the women is received and treatment started immediately. In addition, road access is required connecting homes to facilities and facilities with one another.

Referral systems

Mapping data and quality assessment data have found that the process of referrals and communication between different facility levels is ad hoc and unstructured with little follow up. In the northern districts of Karnataka, the quality assessment found that only 9% of SC facilities (the most proximate level of the health system) had referral services chart with contact details available, 15% had separate referral-out register maintained and 11% had referral slip/card available. As the SC is the most proximate point of contact between communities and the health system, this needs to be improved so that SCs can operate as a conduit to appropriate levels of care as needed. At 130 PHCs assessed, 27% had referral charts displayed, 56% had out-referral registers and just 29% had referral slips.

Higher-level facilities have higher levels of referral mechanisms in place with 42% of THs displaying referral charts and 60% having referral slips; however, it is still inadequate to ensure facility linkages for comprehensive care. In the self-reportage of service provision in the facility mapping, referrals were rarely provided, ranging from 42% for ANC and intranatal care at PHCs and 40% for safe abortion at PHCs (Table 1a.3).

Referral audits

Since delays in referring and transfer of cases increases risks of maternal and newborn mortality, it is essential that referrals are documented properly to monitor their timeliness and effectiveness. The referring facility should use forms provided to note the particulars of the case to be transferred, the time of admission, time of referral, the details such as diagnosis, indication for referral and the treatment given at the facility. The referring facility should inform the referred facility about the patient and note in their referral register who is accompanying and what mode of transport is arranged. All these steps would ensure that the mother or child being referred out reaches the destination facility on time and is received and followed up promptly. Each case

Table 1a.3	Percentage of Facilities with Established Referral Systems in Project Districts					
Referral System Component	DH (7)	TH (33)	CHC (33)	PHC (130)	SC (370)	Private (78)
Referral service chart displayed	28.6	42.4	30.3	26.9	8.7	33.3
Referral out register maintained	71.4	81.8	69.7	56.2	15.1	15.4
Referral slip/card available	42.9	60.6	33.3	28.5	11.1	33.3

Source: Service Provider Assessment.

referred out should be followed up and the outcome documented in the referring facility.

Audits of referral records were carried out at PHCs, higher-level facilities and private facilities. Among the 621 records of referral audited, 55% had the time of admission and 51% had the time of referral. 16% recorded the treatment given at the facility (Figure 1a.2).

Only 8% of the 621 audits completed had a note of the person accompanying from the referring facility, and 21% of the records had documented the mode of transport. Among them, the 'Number 108' ambulance service was listed in 22%; however, there was no documentation in 45%. The highest number of referrals was made to the DH (42%), 54% from THs, 51% from CHCs, 34% from private hospitals and 34% from PHCs. A significant 38% of cases had a different destination facility listed, such as THs and CHCs. Clinical outcome of the client at the referred facility was documented through follow up in only 9% of referral records.

Transport connections to subcentres

A significant barrier in accessing health care is transport to the facility. Mapping data demonstrated in the district, 27% of

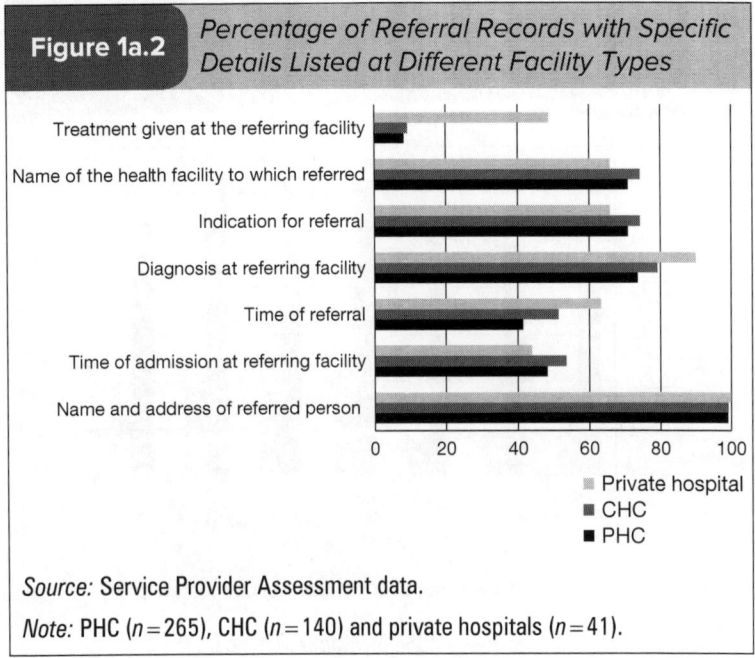

Figure 1a.2 *Percentage of Referral Records with Specific Details Listed at Different Facility Types*

Source: Service Provider Assessment data.

Note: PHC (*n* = 265), CHC (*n* = 140) and private hospitals (*n* = 41).

the villages are not connected to an SC by pucca road, ranging from 20% of villages in Badami to 32% in Mudhol taluk. Furthermore, 10% of the villages have no public or private transport facility, ranging from 4% in Bilgi to 14% in Bagalkot taluk. Unsurprisingly, the larger the village population size, the greater the chance they are linked to the SC with a pucca road and have transport facilities available. This provides a challenge for ANMs to pursue their domiciliary fieldwork in smaller villages as well as for women living in remote rural areas to access facilities (Figure 1a.3).

108 Ambulance Service

DLHS 2007–2008 data reveal that the poor often rely on ambulance services to reach facilities for deliveries. IDIs with ASHAs reveal that the 108 ambulance service is crucial and is often the only mode of transport available for mothers. Commenced in 2008–2009, the 108 ambulance scheme is a PPP between the Department of Health & Family Welfare, GoK and Emergency

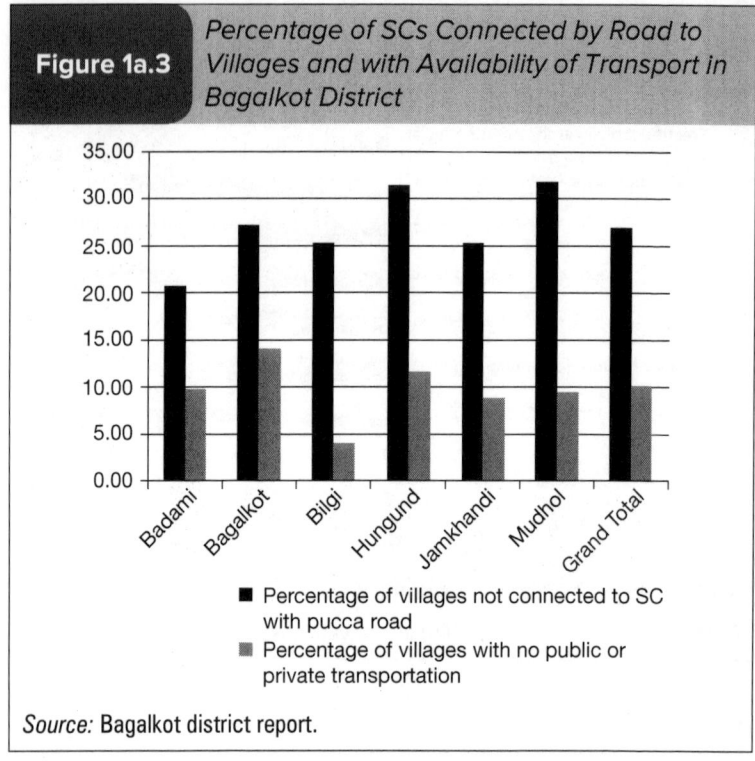

Figure 1a.3 *Percentage of SCs Connected by Road to Villages and with Availability of Transport in Bagalkot District*

■ Percentage of villages not connected to SC with pucca road
■ Percentage of villages with no public or private transportation

Source: Bagalkot district report.

Management and Research Institute (EMRI, AP).[16] Under the scheme, the GoK provides funds for these services under its state budget, the NRHM and other relevant schemes, running it on a no-loss, no-profit basis. EMRI provides comprehensive emergency response services (medical, police, fire) using a single toll free number on a 24×7 basis. Response is supposed to be provided within 30 minutes in rural areas and 20 minutes in urban areas, with an average per trip distance of 25 kilometres. There are 517 ambulances deployed throughout the state, with roughly one for each lakh population, providing either advanced or basic life support. This is a little below the WHO recommendation of

[16] Department of Health & Family Welfare, GoK; Emergency Management and Research Institute, 2008. Memorandum of Understanding for Providing Emergency Response Services in Karnataka.

one ambulance per 60,000 people, but there are plans to scale up once community demand increases. The 108 scheme also involves accreditation of destination health facilities to ensure that they can provide the care required.

Private sector partners in Bagalkot district

As utilization data demonstrates private providers are an important source of the health care for all population groups. The *Operational Guidelines on Maternal and Newborn Health* suggest that whenever suitable private providers of care for MNH exist, effort should be made to engage with them based on transparent and clear standards of care, timely payments and appropriate supervision.

With little regulation, the private health care sector varies in quality of service provision and technical proficiency, from informal providers to specialist doctors. IDIs with private providers in project districts found that few participate in the Thayi Bhagya Scheme and deaths are reported for the HMIS, and so these facilities are partially networked into the public system.

Human resource systems and training

According to the *Operational Guidelines on Maternal and Newborn Health*, the district needs to have one senior programme manager (reporting directly to the DHO) and one contractual programme manager to ensure training, hiring and supportive supervision is run according to plan. This is not the case in the project districts. In Karnataka under the NRHM, at the state level there is a district programme manager and an accounts manager who oversee human resources.

The key issues in human resources for service delivery in MNH are:

- Getting an adequate number of skilled providers in place, including leveraging partnerships with private providers

- Ensuring that the skills of providers are adequate to deliver quality services
- Ensuring that there is a positive workforce environment and supportive supervision
- Ensuring that there is human resource planning for managers and supervisors

Hiring

To ensure an appropriate number of skilled providers are in place, the government has two pathways through which to employ people in the government health system—the regular system for permanent posts and contractual appointments under NRHM. For human resources to be hired through the regular system, the DHO assesses vacant positions and provides the details to the directorate. Regular appointments are done through the Karnataka Public Service Commission and it takes 1 to 1.5 years. Contractual recruitment has occurred through a number of different avenues: direct special recruitment by the state government and recruitment under the NRHM by the district health society (DHS) through district recruitment committees (DRCs) for MOs or ARS for paramedical staff.

With the Department of Health & Family Welfare, there are about 70,000 employees in the state with one chief administration officer providing oversight. Unfortunately, the DHOs are frequently unable to assess the vacancy positions in a timely manner, and do not have details about vacancies in different districts. District officers have a limited role in planning HR for the district. Many vacancies exist, and hiring specialists for rural posts in particular remains challenging.

The NRHM has been successful in rapidly increasing the availability of human resources for health in rural areas through recruiting additional staff on a contractual basis. However, there are large differences between the pay and status of regular staff and contractual staff for similar work, and contractual staff have little administrative, financial and management decision-making power. IDIs with providers found that across all cadres, there is discomfort with the discrepancy in pay, status and conditions between regular and contractual staff, and that typically, contract workers are stronger performers than regular staff. From interviews with district programme MOs and RCH officers, the suggestion to regularize positions after a fixed period was raised.

Another incentive to facilitate the appointment of staff in rural areas is the Remote Area Allowance (RAA), and the Tribal Areas Allowance and mobility support.[17] RAA is given to all staff at the PHC level. However, the implementation of this scheme varies across districts. For the most part, incentives are given based on remote postings, but not on actual residence in the locality. This means frequently providers are not residing in the area of their posting, undermining their ability to be on hand in an emergency. There are no performance-based incentives. From IDIs with district programme MOs and RCH officers, the suggestion emerged to provide good quality housing to attract and retain staff in remote facilities.

In addition to hiring, specialist staff have been deployed through in-sourcing at the FRU level since 2009, in attempt to fill gaps at higher levels of care.[18] Recently (in 2011), the High Court of Karnataka ordered a redistribution of specialist medical staff to government facilities in rural areas to increase equity in service provision.[19]

Training

To ensure that the skills of providers are adequate to deliver quality services, the government has a system in place to provide

[17] GoK, DHFW, NRHM, Programme Implementation Plan for 2010–2011, Bangalore, 92.

[18] GoK, DHFW, NRHM, Programme Implementation Plan for 2010–2011, Bangalore.

[19] Staff Reporter, *The Hindu*, 2 May 2011. Available at http://www.hindu.com/2011/05/02/stories/2011050261810500.htm (accessed on 2 November 2017).

regular training programmes. The coverage of trainings, including induction trainings, is uneven. Only 18% of ANMs in the SCs are trained in integrated skills development programme (ISDP) compared to 69% in immunization and 79% in integrated management of neonatal and childhood illnesses (IMNCI) training. Among the SNs, most of the PHC/CHC staff has received trainings in IMNCI, SBA while the coverage for all other trainings such as ISDP, immunization and BEmOC training is inadequate at all levels of facilities. Coverage of trainings for medical officers is inadequate at all levels of facilities except ISD trainings at district level and IMNCI trainings at PHC and CHC levels.

All training provided by the health system is in-service training rolled out by the State Institute of Health & Family Welfare (SIHFW). All trainings are delivered according to NRHM/ GoI guidelines and modules are adapted for use in Karnataka. Training of the trainer (TOT) sessions are held centrally and then delivered through district training centres (DTCs) and medical colleges across the state. In addition, direct trainings are provided by various government agencies and departments, for example the Karnataka State AIDS Prevention Society (KSAPS) provides training relating to HIV prevention and care. Initially training needs assessments were performed under the first RCH programme (1996–2004-RCH1), but this has been discontinued in the second phase of the programme. Priority for training is currently given to inadequate performing districts.

Administration and management training is scheduled once in two years for the health department's administration cadre, with content developed by the Administrative Training Institute in Mysore.

According to data from interviews, trainings are typically evaluated at two intervals, one immediately after the training and one three months after the training to assess skills and knowledge. However, the evaluations often do not capture the relevance and applicability of the trainings to job roles.

Further, interviews also reveal there are delays in the preparation of training modules and inadequate availability of materials. For example, the module for the 2009 SBA training was not available by December of 2009. Sometimes, a lower cadre of staff gets trained while the higher cadres do not; undermining the lower cadres' ability to apply the new skills they have learned. Additionally, a lack of scheduling results in trainings occurring haphazardly, sometimes over burdening a particular cadre and repeating material. SIHFW is sometimes not able to spend its entire training budget.

Certain cadres are not provided training, such as contract staff and AYUSH doctors. For example, the SIHFW has commenced a 15-day induction training for MOs recruited to permanent positions, but MOs on contract (as opposed to permanent staff) receive no such training. It means key providers are not able to provide the essential package of care (Table 1a.4).

Supportive supervision, mentoring and monitoring

Along with training, periodic on-the-job mentoring visits provided by a team of supervisors is also central to improved performance. Supportive supervision is key to translating trainings into improved practice, to ensure that knowledge and skills are applied appropriately in the job setting. Ideally, during a supportive supervision visit, the supervisor assists the service provider in her tasks, follows up to see that gaps in supplies are bridged, provides training and encouragement as needed. According to successful models of supervision, a supervisor follows a checklist to ensure that every skill is rehearsed, every protocol is understood and followed, all the inputs are in place and all processes and outputs recorded appropriately.[20,21] The assessments found that there was no mechanism in place for supportive supervision, and protocols are not available.

---

[20] A. Rowe, D. de Savigny, C. Lanata, and C. Victora, 'How Can We Achieve and Maintain High-quality Performance of Health Workers in Low-resource Settings?' *The Lancet*. 2005. doi: 10.1016/S0140-6736(05) 67028-6

[21] NRHM, MoHFW, GoI, 'Quality Assurance for District Reproductive and Child Health Services in Public Health System' (New Delhi: MoHFW, GoI, 2008).

Table 1a.4	Percentage of Staff Trained in Various Skill Areas				
Cadre and Skill Area	**Facility Type**				
ANM	SC				
Integrated skill development training	18				
Immunization training	69				
IMNCI training	79				
SN	**DH**	**TH**	**CHC**	**PHC**	**PVT**
Integrated skill development training	28.4	13.6	11.9	3.8	1.1
Immunization training	52.3	40.3	37.3	22.5	16.7
BEmOC	28.4	10.7	3.7	6.7	8.2
IMNCI training	36.6	27.9	48.5	60.9	8.9
SBA training	38.3	27.6	51.5	63.2	16.7
Medical officer	**DH**	**TH**	**CHC**	**PHC**	**PVT**
Integrated skill development training	79.7	17.2	26.6	17.6	3.3
Immunization training	6.4	15	50	35.7	19.9
Non-scalpel vasectomy	1.2	11.3	20.3	7.2	10.6
Medical termination of pregnancy	2	14	23.4	10.9	25.8
Minilap	2.3	17.2	36	14.5	23
BEmOC	2	14.5	25	11.9	24.5
IMNCI	4	22.7	78	52.8	19.8

Source: Service Provider Assessment.

Career advancement

There is a lack of merit-based career advancement in the health system among all cadres. Very few promotional opportunities are available to ANMs to become lady health visitors (LHVs) or SNs, and progress is slow. SNs also experience slow professional development. The SNs start their career at the PHC level and progress to senior staff at the PHC and then Grade II at the TH.

On the other hand, MOs have automatic time-bound promotions every 6 or 13 years, moving from PHC to CHC level. Interviews found that many MOs who move to the district level are given a high level of administrative responsibilities, for which they are given no training and are ill prepared. Interviews with MOs found that the suggested solution to this burden was a parallel cadre to deal with management and administration or training in administration.

Procurement and logistics

Many facilities are short on equipment, drugs and supplies. While these shortfalls do not entirely account for the partiality of service provision, they do undermine the ability of providers to offer comprehensive and quality care. This has been given policy attention; the 2004 state Integrated Health Policy outlines the need for rational and efficient drug purchase and use. Further, the *Operational Guidelines on Maternal and Newborn Health* provides clear ground rules which are as follows:

- Drugs and supplies needed for the provision of care through the continuum of care should be available as per the approved drugs and supplies list, without interruption, in each and every facility.
- Every district should have a district warehouse with a minimum stock of three months of all the drugs and supplied required, with an inventory management system.
- Every facility should indent when their stocks fall below an estimated three months requirement. Transport of supplies to the periphery should be assured to the district SCs

and all facilities without a vehicle to transport the stocks immediately.

- Procurement systems must ensure that drugs, supplies and equipment at the district level are replenished when stocks fall below a three-month threshold.

Drug supply and logistics

Each facility has a budget limit for the purchase of drugs which is as follows:

- PHCs have 1 lakh
- CHCs have 5–10 lakh
- THs have 20–25 lakh

Facilities submit an annual indent to the district drug warehouse (DDW). A consolidated list is then submitted to the Karnataka Drug Warehousing and Logistics Society (KDWLS). The KDWLS floats the tender and these are scrutinized by a technical committee. Once the tender is selected, drugs are supplied straight to the DDW within 60 days. Quality control includes certificates from suppliers and sending random samples to labs for analysis.

According to IDIs, those preparing the indents for the drugs do not have much training in forecasting and are not able to prepare a realistic indent. Additionally, national programmes also supply drugs in addition to the indent, causing excess drug stock. Due to the limited budget, not all drugs are ordered at replacement levels. According to IDIs, when there is a shortage, untied funds are often used to maintain stock.

Equipment

KDWLS supplies all equipment including furniture and office equipment based on an approved list. The process typically takes 8 months to one year. The maintenance unit of KDWLS takes care of repairs, replacements and warranties. There is no routine equipment audit across all facilities. Since NRHM, facilities no longer procure equipment through KDWLS and so funds are now unspent.

Government schemes and incentives

There are two conditional cash transfer programmes in the state to promote MCH care seeking among disadvantaged groups, primarily BPL card holders. All schemes provide support for the first two births only. These schemes have uneven uptake due to low awareness, irregular funding and uneven implementation.

JSY and Prasuthi Araike: JSY is a central scheme under the NRHM introduced in 2005 that provides cash transfers to pregnant woman from poor and marginalized families, to cover the transport, diet and medical care costs of delivering in an institution (amounts provided listed in Table 1a.5). The scheme also involves the ASHA drawing up a 'microbirth plan' with each beneficiary to ensure that they are ready to go to the most convenient facility at the time of delivery. Eligibility for the scheme is with a BPL card or if they are from an SC or ST community. However, if the mother has no BPL card but her annual income is under 17,000, she can obtain an income certificate with the assistance of ASHAs and AWWs. In rural areas, most of the people seeking care at public facilities are eligible for such a certificate.

Table 1a.5	Incentive Schedule for Mothers and ASHAs Under the JSY Scheme			
Place of Delivery	**Rural**		**Urban**	
	Mothers	**ASHAs**	**Mothers**	**ASHAs**
Institutional deliveries	700	200	600	200
C-sections	1,500	200	1,500	200
Home deliveries	500	Nil	500	Nil

Source: Operational Guidelines on Maternal and Newborn Health, 2010.

The scheme also provides incentives for ASHAs to promote institutional deliveries and guide and support the pregnant woman to seek appropriate care. The scheme also provides a smaller sum for women who opt to deliver at home using skilled birth attendance (Table 1a.5).

As well as supporting deliveries in public hospitals, there is an additional state-funded scheme, Prasuthi Araike, which provides benefits (₹2,000) for deliveries by BPL mothers in accredited public or private institutions. IDIs with providers and mothers suggest that this scheme is not working well across the project districts, mainly due to unavailability of state funding to support this scheme.

The service provider assessment found that 78% of SC facilities in the project districts had information about the JSY scheme on display. Despite this, community survey data demonstrate that only 47% of women know about the JSY scheme. Low levels of awareness translate to a low level of uptake; a number of data sources suggest low coverage of JSY. DLHS 2007–2008 data finds that only 7% of rural women in Bagalkot benefit from JSY or state specific schemes. More recent data shows higher numbers of recipients. Among respondents of exit interviews with recently delivered women, only 14% of women reported receiving the JSY stipend at discharge. Community survey data found that 34% of eligible women received the incentive, of which 28% received it at discharge and the remainder were asked to collect it later. Service statistics collected during facility mapping on the other hand, record 55% of women benefitting from the JSY/Thayi Bhagya Scheme (recipients of both schemes are included in the same indicator). This data on low uptake of the JSY scheme suggests that the key to the schemes success may lie in the incentive paid to the ASHA, rather than to the mother.

Madilu Kit (MK) Scheme: This scheme provides below poverty line (BPL) mothers with a kit of 19 key items relating to maternal and infant health and hygiene. Supply of the kits has been irregular, and a backlog has been created from an irregular and inadequate supply. At the time of assessment, the current supply was being used to cover new mothers, and the remaining stock provided to mothers who have given birth over the last three months but did not receive the kit. Awareness of the scheme is also low; only 51% of mothers in the community survey knew about it (more than the rate of women who know about the JSY scheme, standing at 47%). Facility service statistics record only 25% of recently delivered women receiving the kit. The quality assessment found that only 54% of SC facilities had information about the scheme on display.

Thayi Bhagya Scheme: Based on the well-known Chiranjivi model from Gujarat, this scheme provides free services to BPL pregnant women delivering in registered private hospitals. The hospitals are paid ₹300,000 for each 100 deliveries, with 10% paid in advance. According to interviews, at the time of the assessments the scheme has not been popular across the project districts, with the exception of Bagalkot district (where facility statistics record 41% of women who recently delivered as beneficiaries).[22] Some private providers reported that they find the compensation inadequate to cover the cost of deliveries. This is primarily because of the high rates of C-section referrals to these hospitals, increasing the cost of care (Figure 1a.4).

One reason why the Thayi Bhagya Scheme may have low uptake is low awareness among providers in the government system regarding which private providers they can refer to, that is, which private providers will be participating in the scheme. As part of efforts to improve referral systems, the private facilities that are part of the scheme should be made known to government providers (Table 1a.6).

Understandings of the schemes

The qualitative assessment found that incentives were a factor in the decision to deliver in a government facility. Respondents reported that in order to qualify Thayi card (mother's card) must

---

[22] The Thayi Bhagya Scheme has been rolled out in other districts since the assessments.

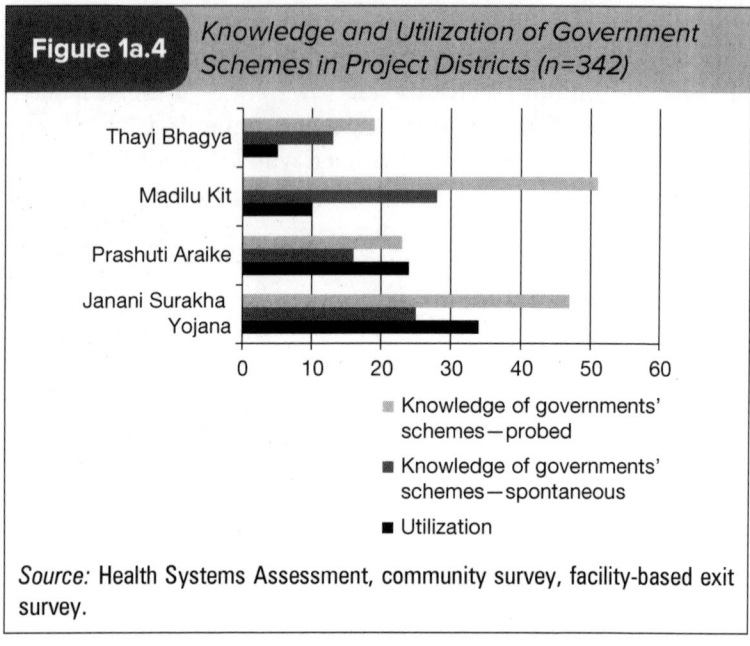

Figure 1a.4 Knowledge and Utilization of Government Schemes in Project Districts (n=342)

Source: Health Systems Assessment, community survey, facility-based exit survey.

be created during pregnancy and delivery must be conducted in the government hospital; also, home deliveries were ineligible to receive benefits. Most were informed of the scheme from the ASHA, AWW or other villagers. Benefits discussed by respondents included coverage of delivery cost and a kit of useful items for the mother and child. In accordance with the community survey, of the respondents who had registered and created a mother's card, only a fraction had actually received any of the expected incentives.

Implications

A variety of data sources were utilized to provide an overview of the health system. From the compilation of the findings, a number of clear implications emerge, outlining clear areas for action or intervention. These are outlined further.

Table 1a.6 *Knowledge and Benefit from Government Schemes*

| | Knowledge of Schemes % | | | | Benefit from Schemes % | |
| | Community interview (n = 320) | | Exit interview (n = 305) | | Community interview (n = 301) | Exit interview (n = 291) |
	Spontaneous	Probed	Spontaneous	Probed		
JSY	25	47	28	41	34	14
MK	16	23	20	23	24	15
PA	28	51	30	44	10	1
TB	13	19	12	14	5	1

Source: Health System Assessments, community interviews and exit interviews.

Information Management

Clinical record-keeping needs to be improved, to facilitate better clinical decision-making. Standard case sheets for key maternal and neonatal health issues should be provided to all facilities and providers required to maintain them as this helps ensure providers follow standard practice (according to protocols). Introducing audits every six months to see quality improvement will allow staff to take ownership, feel that they are participating in change and actually see the improvement. Audits also allow the programme planners to monitor the practice and adherence to standard protocols.

Referral Systems and Transport Connections

A structured referral system: The referral system at present is not structured in a way to direct the flow of patients from lower facilities to FRUs and higher facilities thereafter. This results in, for example, a high burden of normal deliveries at higher facilities such as TH and DH, and thus specialist care is compromised. Formal referral systems should be established starting with the supply of standard referral registers, referral slips to the facilities and sensitization to the staff towards maintaining a good system for referral linkages. Training is needed for providers at all levels to refer promptly, communicate with the referred facility and follow up on the outcome. Such a system would streamline the flow of patients correctly in order to distribute the patient load among the facilities to ensure better service delivery.

Greater coordination with private providers: The high rates of care seeking in the private sector suggest that the private sector has better population reach, making PPPs an attractive option to address gaps in the public sector. The National Health Policy of 2002 and the State Integrated Health Policy of 2004 both highlight the need to coordinate with private providers in a more systematic manner. Additionally, the KHSDRP has established a model of contracting in specialists and contracting out PHC management. These models can be further scaled up to fill existing gaps in project districts, especially with blood banks and specialist providers. There are nine private facilities that provide both the C-section and blood transfusion facilities in the district.

In addition, any private providers participating in the Thayi Bhagya Scheme, which are then part of the referral network, should be made known to the government providers who would refer them. Tours of the facilities could be conducted, and lists of participating private facilities can be made available to government providers.

Human Resources Systems

HR management could be strengthened through a human resource information system (HRIS). Also, strengthen the programme management unit to help with human resources management, including supportive supervision and deployment. There is a need to strengthen the currently existing management information systems to track training needs at the district level to enable programme planners to address the needs through timely appointments, trainings and refreshers. This would also be an important support to the recently introduced counselling-based transfer policy.[23]

A merit-based career path could be created as a performance incentive: Create merit-based opportunities for training and promotion for providers at all levels, so there is an incentive to perform well. For MOs, abolish time-based promotions and make them merit/performance based.

Clarify roles between ASHAs, AWW and ANMs: While there is a need for ANMs, ASHAs and AWWs to work together on some tasks, clarity and clear lines of responsibility are required. Once clarity is established, a mechanism to relay this clarity to workers, through existing platforms such as the monthly meetings and

[23] M. Aiayappa, 'Medical Staff Transfers Through Counselling', *The Times of India*, 25 May 2011. Available at http://articles.timesofindia.india-times.com/2011-05-25/bangalore/29581082_1_transfer-policy-transfer-of-medical-officers-rural-areas (accessed on 8 February 2018).

supportive supervision is required. In addition, there needs to be clarity in roles between the first and second ANM.

Training needs to be skills based and followed up with supportive supervision: The service provider assessment reveals that despite a fair knowledge base, gaps exist in the skills and practice. This may indicate that the current system of trainings is focused on imparting knowledge, but lacks in providing follow up supportive supervision and mentoring to build skills. Trainings should be followed by supportive mentorship and follow up refreshers to reinforce the skills and practice. This is provided for in the State Integrated Health Policy. Additionally, coverage of training programmes is not high enough to have a sustained impact on health outcomes. Training needs to be delivered more widely, with priority given to high-volume facilities.

Induction training for all staff, including contractual staff and AYUSH doctors, could be expanded: Many staff who participated in the quality assessment, especially the recently employed contractual staff, had not received basic induction trainings. For example, ISDP training for ANMs, SBA training for SNs, BEmOC training for MOs/SNs of selected 24 × 7 PHC and IMNCI trainings. The trainings should follow an in-depth training needs assessment specific to the roles played by the care providers, and emphasize clarity of job roles and responsibilities. Training AYUSH doctors in key MNCH skill areas should be expanded as they constitute such a large part of the workforce.

Management and administration training for all MOs needs to be scaled up: A preservice finance and administration training programme is provided for in the 2004 State Integrated Health Policy, but does not appear to have a high level of coverage. The programme that does exist focuses on financial management, but MOs need skills on a variety of management areas. A revised programme with greater coverage could be provided to all MOs or a specific cadre dedicated to management and administration.

Procurement and Logistics

Data use for logistics and procurement: The 2002 National Health Policy and the 2004 State Integrated Health Policy both advocate rationalizing drug procurement and supply. The mapping data suggest that the systems could be further improved through using facility records for forecasting and procurement of drugs and supplies. A monitoring and indenting system to record and replace or repair non-functional equipment is required. Too frequently equipment is non-functional and is not replaced or repaired in a timely manner. This undermines the quality of care possible in facilities and creates an unpleasant environment.

Government Schemes

Increased awareness of all financial schemes is required: Linkages to the community such as ASHAs can be utilized to increase awareness of financial schemes.

The JSY scheme could be extended to all mothers: Applying for an income certificate (to receive benefits associated with BPL status) is currently an administrative burden to mothers and facilities, with many mothers applying more than once during the continuum of care. Almost 70% of mothers at public facilities have or are eligible for BPL cards. Thus, the JSY can be made available to all mothers in the project districts, reducing the administrative burden to both mothers and facilities without significantly increasing the cost burden to NRHM. Increase care components covered under JSY scheme. Inclusion of PNC and spacing of births would increase coverage of these services and practices, contributing to improved MCH outcomes.

Conclusion

The health system in Karnataka has achieved an unprecedented increase in facility-based deliveries. Two contributors to this success are the 'Number 108' Ambulance scheme and the Janani Suraksha Yojana (JSY) scheme. The 'Number 108' Ambulance scheme is a PPP which provides a comprehensive emergency response service, transporting pregnant women to facilities for delivery. The JSY scheme has led to unprecedented increases in institutional deliveries across the country and within the project districts. However, the coverage of these schemes has been low—only 14% and 34% of the exit interviews and community-survey respondents reported receiving any JSY benefit (respectively), despite over 60% of the sample being BPL. The exit interviews of beneficiaries of the incentive schemes also suggest that there is some delay in receipt of the benefits from both JSY and MK schemes. However, the targeted nature of the JSY scheme makes it cumbersome to implement, with the paperwork for certifying low-income status amounts to a burden to health workers and families. In addition, knowledge about the scheme is relatively low and the amount received and timeliness of the payments uneven. As it only provides an incentive for a facility-based delivery, other components of care are neglected (such as PNC and birth spacing). Therefore, while a success, there is some room for improvement.

The NRHM has managed to fill staffing gaps through contracting and employing AYUSH doctors as MOs. However, up-to-date information on human resources in the public system (vacancies and trainings) is not sufficiently available for accurate planning, making it difficult to prioritize vacancies, plan trainings or ensure even distribution of staff across the population. Across every care component, human resources need to be increased to ensure quality of care. In addition, the present system of facility referrals is not methodical and documentation practice is inadequate, with few facilities maintaining charts, registers or filling out referral slips.

Case Study 1B: Bagalkot District Assessment

Unlike the previous case study that focused on the state health system, this case study focuses on the district health system and shows how gap analysis and assessments can lead to greater insights on strengthening the health system and how it can inform the decision-making at district level.

To gather the required data for Bagalkot district, a series of assessments were undertaken, largely in 2010, including analysis of secondary data and collection of both qualitative and quantitative primary data. The data analysis consolidates these complementary data sources for decision-making and planning. The summary of results on Bagalkot district is presented further.

In Table 1b.1, key service utilization, outcome and impact indicators for Bagalkot district are shown alongside indicators for the state and the project districts (in northern Karnataka). The differences between the rates demonstrate the need for district-specific data for decentralized planning.

The summarized findings are presented further, first at the system level and then according to the care component, from ANC to essential newborn care (ENC).

The service delivery framework

The rate of institutional deliveries has increased with the JSY scheme, but still rates in Bagalkot district are lower than in the project districts (northern Karnataka) or in the state as a whole. Unfortunately, providers at the PHC level do not have the skills or supplies to treat complications (such as eclampsia or postpartum haemorrhage) and refer to higher-level facilities, creating system inefficiencies. To increase access to care, PHCs need to be strengthened to offer comprehensive intranatal care, particularly ensuring adequate numbers of providers with competencies to offer skilled birth attendance.

In terms of infrastructure, a lack of piped clean water, soap and waste management practices undermines the quality and safety of care provided in facilities.

Unsafe abortion accounts for 8% of all maternal mortalities in India. Household survey data on pregnancy termination is not

Table 1b.1	Key Maternal and Newborn Health Indicators for Bagalkot District		
Indicator	Bagalkot District	Project Districts (Bellary, Bidar, Bijapur, Gulbarga, Koppal, Raichur, Yadgir)	State
Fertility and family planning			
Average number of children:			
For 20–24 year-old age cohort	3.9	2.0	1.7
For total rural population	4.2	3.5	2.8
Contraceptive prevalence rate	52.9	52.5	61.8
Permanent method—sterilization %	50.9	50.3	56.8
Spacing methods %	1.3	1.8	4.0
Unmet need %	18.7	19.3	15.7
Pregnancy and birth			
3 or more ANC visits %	62.9	65.2	81.3
Institutional deliveries %	47.1	45.7	65.1
Home deliveries %	52.0	53.6	34.1
Newborn visit within 24 hours %	64.2	50.4	64.2
PNC visit within 48 hours %	53.6	51.5	65.6
Newborn and child health			
Breastfeeding: Initiated within one hour of birth %	38.5	40.2	46.5
Vaccination (full vaccination) %	58.5	62.1	76.7
Mortality			
MMR (per 100,000 live births)	395	408	294
IMR (per 1,000 live births)	61	67	51
Neonatal mortality (per 1,000 live births)	38.7	50.9	39.5
Under-5 mortality (per 1,000 live births)	71.8	91.7	64.1

Source: DLHS 2007–2008.

reliable, and for this reason, it is difficult to know the incidence of abortion in Bagalkot district. Provision of safe abortion services and post-abortion care is inadequate at all levels of the public system. In addition, post abortion contraceptive counselling and provision of contraceptives is poor.

NRHM investments in the elevation of regular PHCs to 24 × 7 PHCs (including increases in staffing, infrastructure, equipment and drugs and supplies) have increased access to care for all care components. Some gaps still remain, especially in staffing and infrastructure. Despite NRHM's innovations in increasing human resources the distribution of staff across the population is uneven. Gaps in staffing lead to inequities in service provision. More staff need to be hired to fill such gaps, in particular, more ANMs need to be hired across the district, especially in Bilgi and Mudhol taluks. In addition, a lack of piped clean water, toilets, soap and waste management practices undermines the quality and safety of care provided in all facilities.

Service delivery in communities

Although over 80% of pregnancy registrations occur at SCs, less than 5% of the SCs are providing all elements of basic ante-natal services. Women need to visit a variety of facility types to receive comprehensive antenatal care, including private facilities. Ultimately, most antenatal care occurs in the private sector, even for disadvantaged groups, leading to very high costs. Gaps are observed in the availability of counselling services, BP measure-ment and lab tests. Birth planning is almost non-existent, and referral systems are inadequate. The availability of some of the equipment and supplies related to ANC provision is inadequate. A large proportion (60%) of the SCs caters to more than the stipulated 5,000 population.

Few women stay in the facility the requisite 48 hours after delivery. Additionally, postnatal follow up at the community level is ad-hoc, with inadequate provision of domiciliary visits. The percentage of children under three years old who received a check-up within 24 hours of birth in rural Bagalkot is 46%, low compared to the regional rate of 50% and with wide disparities between population subgroups. Except for the immunization services, most elements of newborn care were weak, particularly the day 2 and day 4 visits. In particular, newborn counselling has been inadequate and few women are familiar with danger signs. As these 48 hours represent a time where over half of maternal and neonatal deaths occur postnatal and newborn care needs to be strengthened.

Unfortunately, care for sick newborns is uneven, with very few providers following IMNCI protocols. Gaps have been observed in the delivery of child services at community level such as monitoring of growth and nutrition, immunization, management of non-severe cases of pneumonia and diarrhoea and referral services for severely sick infants.

There is a need to strengthen the provision of ANC, PNC, child health and family planning at the community and SC level to ensure that women can receive comprehensive care. Mobile testing vans and visits from MOs can provide the scans and tests that ANMs are not able to provide.

Knowledge of family planning in Bagalkot district is near universal. The contraceptive prevalence rate is 53% in the district, but use of spacing methods is low, at only 1.2%. Lack of spacing is a contributing factor to poor newborn and infant health outcomes. In service delivery throughout the continuum of care, there are many missed opportunities for family planning counselling and commodity provision. This needs to be strengthened at both the facility and the community level.

Community support systems and health education

The prevailing cultural practices, beliefs and decision-making process for health-seeking play an important role in creating demand at the community level. For this reason it is important to examine the beliefs and attitudes that prevent women from seeking care. Following are a range of reasons relating to different care components along the continuum of care:

- For rural women who do not deliver in institutions, the main reasons cited were 'not necessary' and 'not customary'. However, the high levels of reported delivery complications suggest a high need for institutional deliveries, and this needs to be communicated back to the community.
- At the community level, knowledge of newborn danger signs is low with only 18% of women knowing all the danger signs, compared to 5.8% in the project districts and 8.3% in the state.
- Use of spacing methods is only 1.3% and most women are sterilized by 23. This suggests that knowledge about the health and economic benefits of spacing births needs to be increased.
- A substantial proportion of community members use private facilities for MNCH services, largely governed by the perception of higher quality of services. Developing and building a positive perception of all available MNCH services and providers in public health system through effective branding can enhance utilization.
- Exit interviews and community surveys, conducted among recently delivered mothers reflected low awareness of incentive schemes such as the JSY and Madilu Kit MK among pregnant and recently delivered women in project districts.
- Breastfeeding is perceived as the most important practice for ensuring the health of the neonate, however practices vary. Many mothers avoid giving the child colostrum, and providers encourage this. Rates of early initiation of breastfeeding are low in Bagalkot at only 39%.

Antenatal care

Antenatal care is the first point of contact for a pregnant woman with the health system, and provides an excellent opportunity to build a facility–patient relationship that can endure through the continuum of care. This is an opportunity that can be better leveraged; although over 80% of ANC registrations occur at SCs, less than 5% of SCs provide all elements of basic ANC services. Providers at all facility levels lack the knowledge and skills to deliver complete ANC services, especially counselling and treatment of pre-eclampsia. Due to these service deficits, women need to visit a variety of facility types to receive comprehensive antenatal care, including private facilities. Ultimately, a large proportion of antenatal care is sought in the private sector, even for disadvantaged groups.

Disparities between population subgroups (on the basis of caste, wealth and residence) in receiving ANC are not great, but disparities in the comprehensiveness of care received are large. Inadequate quality of service provision compounds existing risk factors, for example; those with the highest risk factors for inadequate nutrition are also less likely to be counselled on good nutrition practices. Making antenatal care more comprehensive and accessible in the public sector, and at the community level, would likely reduce these disparities. ANC care (including scans and tests) is the most expensive component of care, at an average cost of ₹1,200, compared to ₹1,000 for a facility-based delivery and postpartum care. While this cost seems excessive, qualitative data captures the perceived importance of scan results in assuring parents a pregnancy is healthy.

Intranatal care

While the rate of institutional deliveries has increased with the JSY scheme, the rate in Bagalkot district is lower than in the state. For rural women who do not deliver in institutions, the main reasons cited were 'not necessary' and 'not customary'. However, the high levels of reported delivery complications suggest a high need for skilled birth attendance and the benefits of skilled attendance needs to be better communicated back to the community. Qualitative data found a general preference for delivering in the private sector, despite the higher expense. The reasons were perceived efficiency, more supplies and a cleaner environment. For those who delivered in the government sector, the reasons were to avail in incentives and because they could not afford to deliver in the private sector.

The elevation of PHCs to the level of 24×7 PHCs is a process that is not yet complete. Providers at this level often do not have the skills or supplies to treat important complications (such as eclampsia or postpartum haemorrhage [PPH]) and refer patients to higher-level facilities, creating system inefficiencies. To further increase access, PHCs need to be strengthened to offer compre- hensive intranatal care, particularly ensuring adequate numbers of providers with competencies to offer skilled birth attendance.

Postnatal and newborn care

Improving facilities to encourage women to stay the recom- mended 48 hours after delivery would better enable PNC to be delivered. After delivery and once women have left the facility, postnatal follow up at the community level is ad hoc and needs to be improved. Only 45% of women in rural Bagalkot receive postnatal check-ups within 48 hours of delivery. This com- pares poorly to 52% in project districts and 66% in the state. Disparities between population subgroups are large, for example, only 40% of the poor received a postnatal check-up compared to 65% of the non-poor. In Bagalkot, only 39% of women initiate breastfeeding within one hour of giving birth; an increase in SBAs would likely improve this.

Essential newborn care and child health

The percentage of children under the age of three years who received a check-up within 24 hours of birth in rural Bagalkot is 46%, very low compared to the rate in the project districts (78%) and with wide disparities between population subgroups. These two sets of indicators are a concern; if mothers do not know dangers signs and the child does not receive regular check-ups, problems are unlikely to be identified and acted upon. Even if the mother does receive a visit, care for sick newborns is uneven, with very few providers following protocols for the integrated management of childhood illness (IMCI).

Implications

The findings of the assessments carried out by the Sukshema Project have implications across four domains, namely, the system level, the facility level, service delivery at the community level and health education and community support systems at the community level.

Implications for health systems

With the advent of the NRHM, the health system in project districts has become more dynamic and increasingly responsive. With the huge challenge of reaching the NRHM targets of an infant mortality rate of 30 per 1,000 and a maternal mortality rate of 100 per 100,000,[24] a number of challenges remain:

- Clinical record-keeping needs to be improved to facilitate better clinical decision-making.
- A more structured referral system to streamline the flow of patients between facility levels is needed, allowing each level to specialize in different levels of care.
- Greater coordination is required with private providers to allow gaps in the public sector to be filled through partnerships and referral linkages with private facilities.
- An enhanced HRIS would strengthen human resource management, including prioritization of vacancies.
- Mechanisms for supportive supervision, mentoring and monitoring needs improvement—to build competencies and support quality of practice.
- A merit-based career path could be created as a performance incentive.
- Induction training for all staff, including contractual staff would ensure that everyone starts at the same level, as human resources are expanded.
- Management training for MOs is required.
- In-service training needs to be skills based and specific to job roles.

[24] GoI, 2005. NRHM Mission Document, 2005–2012.

- Clarity is required between the overlapping roles of ASHAs, AWWs and ANMs.
- Service statistics need to be used for forecasting and procurement of drugs and supplies.
- A monitoring and indenting system is required to replace all non-functional equipment.
- Increased awareness is required of all financial schemes.
- The JSY scheme could be extended to all mothers (above and below poverty line).

Implications for service delivery in facilities

Service delivery in facilities is central to any strategy for addressing MCH outcomes. While there have been many improvements in facility-based care, assessments performed by the Sukshema Project have identified a number of gaps:

- Data on the high incidence of pregnancy complications need to be communicated back to the community.
- BEmONC and CEmONC need to be established according to population norms.
- Training of SBAs needs to be scaled up, with an emphasis on identification, treatment and referral of complications.
- The quality of postpartum care needs to be improved, to encourage women to stay 48 hours after delivery. This would include improvements in sanitation, provision of food and ensuring a family-friendly environment.
- Provision of safe abortion services at PHC and higher facilities will help reduce maternal mortality.
- Many opportunities are missed for providing family planning along the continuum of care, especially postpartum intrauterine device (PPIUD) insertion and post-abortion contraceptive counselling. In particular, birth-spacing methods need to be better promoted.

Implications for service delivery at the community level

ANC, PNC, counselling and provision of contraceptives can all be provided effectively at the community and SC levels through

ANMs, ASHAs and AWWs. The Sukshema Project has arrived at the following recommendations:

- SCs should be strengthened to provide comprehensive ANC and PNC at the community level, and mobile-testing centres should be established to ensure that women do not need to visit multiple facilities for diagnostic services.
- Community-level diagnosis, management and referral of ANC, postpartum and newborn complications all need to be improved.
- Stronger linkages need to be forged between facility-based deliveries and ANMs to improve community-based delivery of PNC.

Implications for health education and community support systems

Here are the following implications based on the assessment:

- The importance on institutional deliveries needs to be promoted in a culturally appropriate way.
- Knowledge of antenatal, postpartum and newborn danger signs needs to be increased at the community level.
- Knowledge about the health and economic benefits of spacing births needs to be increased.
- A positive perception of government facilities needs to be promoted.

Case Study 1C: Facility Mapping in Uttar Pradesh

This case study provides an overview of how facility mapping was undertaken in Uttar Pradesh and gives insights and also practical applicability of concepts and assessments described in the chapter before.

The NRHM in Uttar Pradesh (UP) aims to tackle the high burden of maternal, neonatal and child morbidity and mortality in its rural populations by improving the availability of and access to quality health care for the people, especially those residing in the rural areas. In order to achieve these goals, the state had to first map all the public and private health care facilities according to the populations and geographies that they cover, documenting the infrastructure, human resource, drugs, equipment and supplies. Mapping helps to identify and plan for minimizing the gaps that exist in the availability and accessibility of critical reproductive, maternal, newborn and child health services. In this context, the University of Manitoba (UoM) and the Karnataka Health Promotion Trust (KHPT) carried out a mapping of all health facilities in the 25 high-priority districts of UP.

These 25 HPDs have a total population of 59 million, 29% being rural, organized into 294 blocks. Between June and October 2013, over 8,200 health facilities were mapped—6,358 SCs, 856 PHCs, 324 block primary health centres (BPHCs) or CHCs, 24 DHs and 731 private facilities (Figure 1c.1).

Methodology

Facilities were identified through lists provided by state and district officials. As these lists were not complete, snowballing was conducted to identify unlisted public and private facilities. Private facilities were defined as all private hospitals, nursing homes or clinics that provided delivery services. The mapping tools (specific to facility types) were developed largely in accordance with appropriate service guidelines and were finalized in consultation with a team of experts from the UP-NRHM and BMGF. The tools were designed to capture details of population/villages covering physical infrastructure, staff, drugs, equipment, supplies, services (antenatal, delivery, postpartum, postnatal, abortion, new born and child care), certain service statistics and use of facilities' untied funds.

The facility mapping team consisted of 125 field researchers and 25 data quality supervisors, grouped into 25 teams of 5 field researchers each and a data quality supervisor each. Five such teams were deployed in each of the five zones, each zone

Figure 1c.1 Twenty-five HPDs of UP

Source: UP TSU Proposal, 2013–2014.

consisting of about five districts. The field researchers were largely the individuals local to the zone who had completed—or were pursuing—master's in public health courses in local medical colleges/institutions or postgraduate degree in social sciences. The ANMs at the SCs, medical officers in-charge (MOICs) at the PHCs and CHCs and the chief medical superintendents (CMSs) at the DH were the primary respondents.

Findings

The available delivery points are grossly inadequate in relation to the need. The public facilities in the 25 HPDs of UP conducted only 39% of the expected number of deliveries in the quarter ending May 2013. A total of 429,315 deliveries were expected in these districts based on their population as per 2011 census and the 2011–2012 crude birth rate (CBR) as per the AHS. A total of 187,398 deliveries were reported for the quarter ending May 2013, as per the documents maintained at the facilities (Figure 1c.2). The 'missing' deliveries are most likely to occur at homes, at private facilities that are missed by the mapping and at facilities that did not maintain records for the deliveries conducted.

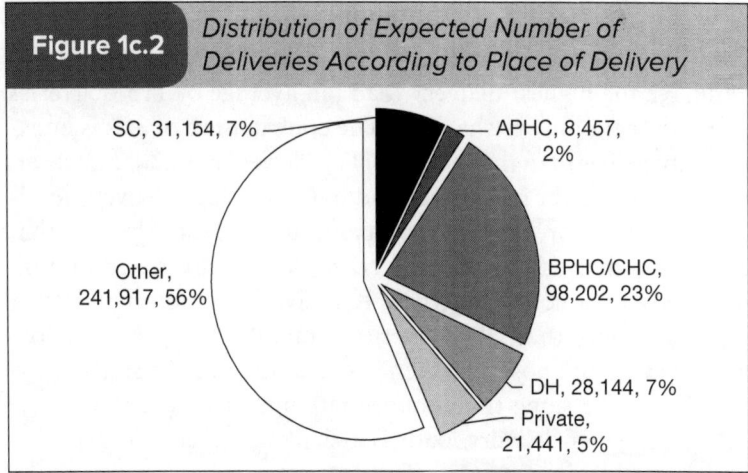

Figure 1c.2 *Distribution of Expected Number of Deliveries According to Place of Delivery*

SC, 31,154, 7%

APHC, 8,457, 2%

Other, 241,917, 56%

BPHC/CHC, 98,202, 23%

DH, 28,144, 7%

Private, 21,441, 5%

The low proportion of institutional deliveries, which is one of the major reasons for high mortality among mothers and newborns, is largely due to the fact that most facilities that are mandated to provide delivery services are not actually providing these services. Over 80% of the 856 PHCs do not provide delivery services. Similarly, only about 2% of the 4,000 SCs conduct deliveries. Although over 50% of the PHCs have labour rooms, a large majority of them do not have the sanctioned positions of SNs, the key personnel for conducting safe deliveries.

More importantly, there are far fewer health facilities per population in these HPDs than it is nationally recommended. For instance, the population covered by an SC in the 25 HPDs is about 8,000 on average, compared to the national recommendation of 1 SC per 5,000 rural population. Thus, there is a 40% shortage of the required 11,809 SCs. Similarly, there are only 856 PHCs in these HPDs against the recommended 1,968 PHCs, at the rate of one PHC per 30,000 rural population. On average, a PHC in these HPDs covers a population of 69,000, and these districts have only about 44% of the required number of PHCs. The average population per CHC is about 182,000 and 168 additional CHCs are required if we consider the national recommendation of one CHC for every 120,000 population.

Within the public sector health facilities, the BPHCs/CHCs contribute over half of the reported deliveries from institutions and have the highest delivery load (an average of 115 deliveries a month) next only to the DHs. The contribution of SCs is unexpectedly higher than that of the DH (17% versus 15%). However, the DHs are fewer in number and have very high delivery loads (390 a month, on average) compared to the SCs. The SCs that conducted deliveries had an average of 12 deliveries a month, with 63% conducting less than 10 deliveries a month and 10% reporting more than 30 deliveries a month. The generally low delivery volumes pose a challenge in maintaining the skills of the ANMs. At the same time, inadequate infrastructure in the few SCs with higher delivery loads is a challenge in ensuring quality of delivery services in SCs.

Table 1c.1	Distribution of 294 Blocks in the 25 HPDs of UP, According to the Reported Percentage of Deliveries in Public Health Facilities		
Percentage of Reported Deliveries in Public Health Facilities	Number of Blocks		Percentage of Blocks
<10	40		14
<25	122		42
<50	256		87
<75	287		98

The contribution of private sector in providing the delivery services seems to be an underestimate, as not all private facilities providing delivery services were mapped and not all of the private facilities mapped divulged the data on the number of deliveries conducted there. However, it is important to note here that in most blocks/districts, even the private facilities providing delivery services are very few and far between. The PHCs accounted for only 5% of the total institutional deliveries in these 25 HPDs.

Not all the 294 blocks in the HPDs have equal availability of delivery points, resulting in a disproportionately low percentage of institutional deliveries. There are not enough public health facilities that are conducting deliveries to meet the delivery needs in most of the blocks. For instance, in 40 (14%) blocks, the existing delivery points conducted only 10% or fewer of the total expected deliveries in that block. In 42% of the blocks, the existing delivery points in the block could conduct only 25% or less of the total expected deliveries in that block (Table 1c.1).

A total of 1,600–1,700 deliveries are expected in these two blocks per quarter, and the two delivery points in each block cater to less than half of the expected deliveries. It would be a challenge to increase the proportion of institutional deliveries without activating additional delivery points in these blocks as

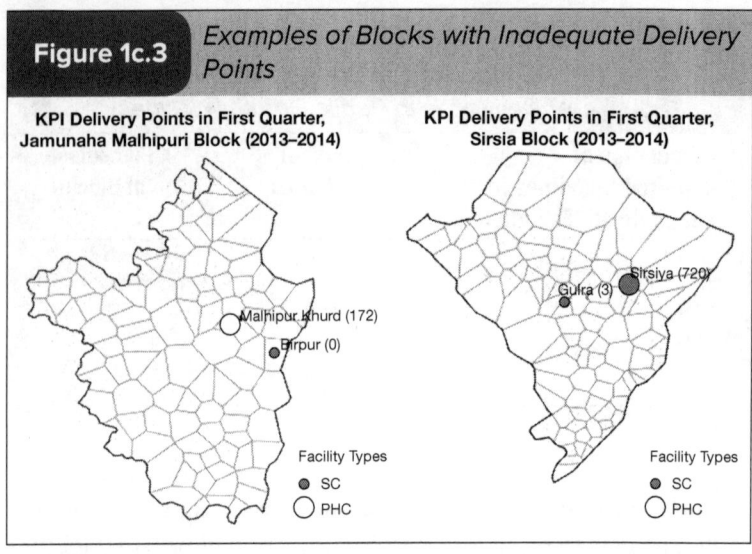

Figure 1c.3   Examples of Blocks with Inadequate Delivery Points

KPI Delivery Points in First Quarter, Jamunaha Malhipuri Block (2013–2014)

KPI Delivery Points in First Quarter, Sirsia Block (2013–2014)

the existing delivery points are already overloaded (each of the BPHC/CHCs conduct over 100 deliveries a month). Thus, the non-availability of adequate number and distribution of health facilities in general and of delivery points in particular seems to a critical gap in these HPDs of UP (Figure 1c.3).

The facility mapping in 25 HPDs also highlighted the gaps in the availability of CEmOC facilities. Based on the GoI's recommendation of 2 CEmOC facilities per million population, the 25 HPDs will require about 186 CEmOC facilities. However, currently, only 16 public health facilities are providing all the 9 signal functions of a CEmOC facility. The average distance from a CHC to a C-section facility (including private) is 32 km,[25] 34 km to blood bank, and intensive newborn care unit is 33 km. About 12% of the deliveries in DHs and less than 1% of the deliveries in BPHCs/CHCs were reported to be caesarean.

In sum, the supply of delivery points does not meet the need for delivery services per population or geography. The public

[25] If the facility itself allows for deliveries, distance is taken as 0 km.

health facilities are grossly inadequate in terms of infrastructure, human resource, the availability of essential services, equipment, drugs and supplies (EDS).

General infrastructure

The general infrastructure in the 328 CHCs in the 25 HPDs is quite good (Table 1c.2). However, almost 1 in 10 SCs in these

Table 1c.2	General Infrastructure at Public Health Facilities in 25 HPDs of UP		
	SC (N = 6,358)	PHC (N = 856)	CHC (N = 320)
Is the building owned by the govt?			
Yes	73.0		
No, rented	18.5		
No, building	8.5		
Source of water			
Tap water	6.6	27.0	76.3
Hand pump	68.9	67.8	91.9
Other	24.5	20.2	12.5
Waste disposal mechanism			
Burn in pit	20.2	40.4	48.1
Bury in pit	35.2	43.2	63.1
Thrown in common/open garbage	23.0	16.9	10.9
Outsourced	3.8	4.1	31.3
Thrown in premises	10.9	15.2	17.2
Other	6.9	4.8	4.7

(Continued)

Table 1c.2	*Continued*		
	SC (*N* = 6,358)	**PHC** (*N* = 856)	**CHC** (*N* = 320)
Boundary wall	64.8	76.1	85.0
Proper approach road	84.3	89.6	99.1
Electricity connection	21.8	65.4	97.8
Separate labour room	44.6	54.4	96.6
Separate laboratory		47.3	92.8
(Functional) Telephone connection		0.6	55.0
Functional computer		0.5	85.6
Internet connection			81.3
Does the ANM stay in SC HQ?	14.2		
Yes, in residential			
Quarters	18.9		
Yes, in rented house in HQ			
No	66.8		
# of available beds			
None		12.0	2.2
1–3		40.1	3.4
4–5		33.4	15.7
6+		14.5	78.7

districts does not have a building and 67% of the ANMs do not stay in the SC headquarters. Availability of safe and clean water in the SCs and PHCs is poor, as only 7% and 27%, respectively have access to tap water. Only 45% of the SCs and 54% of the PHCs have separate labour rooms. About one-third of the SCs and a quarter of PHCs do not have a boundary wall. Only 22% of the SCs and 65% of the PHCs have an electricity connection. Even in the CHCs, only 55% has a functional telephone connection, though 81% have an Internet connection.

Human resources

The availability of HR in the 25 HPDs of UP with regard to the ANMs in SCs is quite good; almost all the SCs have at least 1 ANM. Conversely, PHCs do not have adequate staff to provide most of the MNCH services because the staff in these facilities consist largely of only MOs, pharmacists, lab technicians, ward boys and Group-D employees. Alarming still, only 70% of the sanctioned MO positions in PHCs are currently filled. The PHCs do not have sufficient numbers of ANMs or SNs to provide delivery or other related maternal and newborn services.

The BPHCs/CHCs are relatively better positioned to provide basic maternal, newborn and child health services, but lack specialists to provide EmONC services. The BPHCs/CHCs have an average of 34 positions sanctioned, of which 80% are in position. The current staff availability in CHCs includes an average of 5 MOs, 3 SNs about 9 'other staff' including data entry operators (DEOs), BPMs and the like. The availability of specialists including obstetricians and gynaecologists, surgeons, anaesthetists and paediatricians in public health facilities in these districts is poor, largely because the required number of positions is not sanctioned. For instance, only 36 obstetrics and gynaecology (OBG) positions are sanctioned for these 320 BPHCs/CHCs and 58% of these positions are currently available. The DHs have almost all the sanctioned positions filled, although the number of sanctioned anaesthetists' positions remains low and there is no surgeon's position sanctioned in PHCs (Table 1c.3).

Table 1c.3 Availability of Human Resources at Public Health Facilities in the 25 HPDs of UP

Designation	SC (N = 6,358)		PHC (N = 856)					CHC (N = 320)					DH (N = 24)		
			Sanctioned		In position		Percentage in position	Sanctioned		In position		Percentage in position	Sanctioned	In position	Percentage in position
	Total	Mean	Total	Mean	Total	Mean		Total	Mean	Total	Mean				
ANM	7,016	1.1	368	0.4	276	0.3	75.0	210	0.7	194	0.6	92.4	16	16	100.0
MO			1,318	1.5	917	1.1	69.6	1,977	6.2	1,608	5.0	81.3	241	155	64.3
OBG								36	0.1	21	0.1	58.3	51	47	92.2
Surgeon								62	0.2	50	0.2	80.6	35	33	94.3
Anaesthetist								22	0.1	12	0.0	54.5	17	14	82.4
Paediatrician								33	0.1	27	0.1	81.8	28	27	96.4
SN			83	0.1	33	0.04	39.8	1,010	3.2	844	2.6	83.6	430	327	76.0
LHV			95	0.1	78	0.1	82.1	587	1.8	464	1.5	79.0	9	9	100.0
LT/LA			618	0.7	467	0.5	75.6	544	1.7	472	1.5	86.8	85	63	74.1
Pharmacist			856	1.0	762	0.9	89.0	710	2.2	650	2.0	91.5	120	109	90.8
BHW			96	0.1	81	0.1	84.4	438	1.4	205	0.6	46.8			
HS			86	0.1	71	0.1	82.6	533	1.7	370	1.2	69.4			
Group D			546	0.6	368	0.4	67.4	757	2.4	536	1.7	70.8	396	306	77.3
Ward boy			722	0.8	619	0.7	85.7	589	1.8	513	1.6	87.1	84	54	64.3
Other			626	0.7	484	0.6	77.3	3,378	10.6	2,758	8.6	81.6	422	334	79.1
TOTAL	7,016	1.1	5,414	6.3	4,156	4.9	76.8	10,886	34.0	8,724	27.3	80.1	1,934	1,494	77.2

Training

It is an SBA (safe birth attendance)-trained staff who is in the best position and most capable of delivering integrated intervention during the critical period of during and after delivery, for both the mother and the newborn. The staff are required to be able to skilfully deliver a set of critical services during this period and they need to be supported with systems and supplies appropriately. It is proven that SBA alone, without modern obstetric techniques that often require surgery, can save lives and treat complications. In the HPDs, though only 20% of the ANMs and 7% of the MOs are trained in SBA.

However, among the SCs that reported delivery in the quarter ending May 2013, very few of the ANMs were trained in SBA. If drastic reduction in maternal and newborn mortality is to be achieved, great priority needs to be given to training relevant staff in SBA.

Availability of equipment, drugs and supplies for delivery

A critical element of service provision is the EDS offered at a delivery point. Though shortfalls of critical requirements such as EDS do not entirely account for the partiality of service provision, they do undermine the ability of providers to offer comprehensive and quality care. Hence, drugs, equipment and supplies are needed for the provision of care through the continuum of care should be available as per the approved drugs and supplies list, without interruption, in each public health facility. Compared to the PHCs and SCs that conduct deliveries, the CHCs conducting deliveries in the district are relatively better equipped to provide quality delivery services (Figure 1c.4).

Even among the CHCs, however, only 42% has reported a current stock of Nifedipine tablets, which is a critical drug recommended to treat pre-eclampsia—one of the most common causes of maternal death. Uterotonics (including Inj. Syntocinon/Pitocin, Inj. Methergine/Methylergometrine, Tab Methylergometrine and

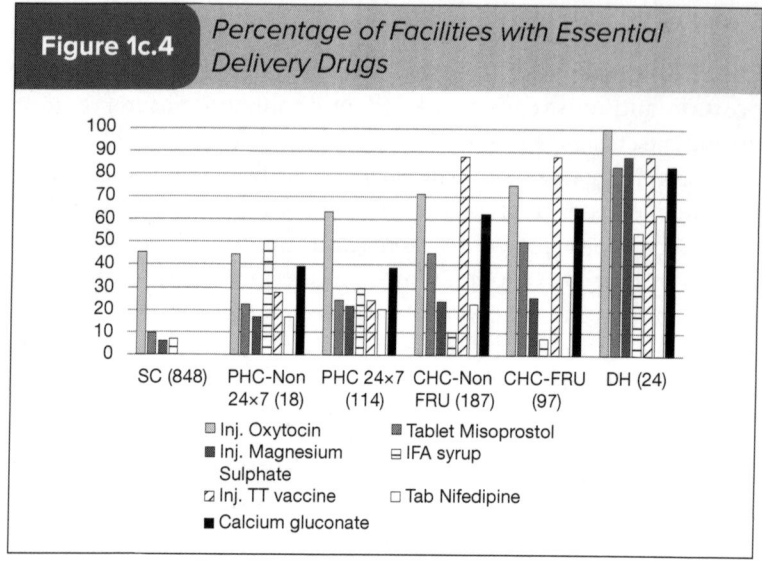

Figure 1c.4 *Percentage of Facilities with Essential Delivery Drugs*

Tab Misoprostol)—a group of critically recommended drugs to prevent and treat PPH, another major cause of maternal deaths—were available in only about 65% of the CHCs in the district (Figure 1c.5).

Other important EDS gaps at CHCs are found in the availability of fetoscope, gloves, neonatal bags and masks and disposable delivery kits. There is a need to strengthen the supply of almost all the equipment, drugs and supplies across facilities. None of the PHCs are currently equipped to conduct deliveries, although about 55% of them have separate labour rooms and neonatal corners.

The availability of drugs and equipment necessary for delivering essential new born care in SC and PHC facilities are especially poor. The key equipment not available in SCs and PHCs include radiant warmers (1%, 5%), mucous extractors (11%, 40%) and Ambu bags and masks (4%, 40%). The lack of critical drugs and vaccines at PHCs is particularly concerning. Some of these drugs—ampicillin, gentamicin—are not adequately available even in CHCs.

Figure 1c.5 *Percentage of Facilities That Have Essential Newborn Commodities in Public Health Facilities*

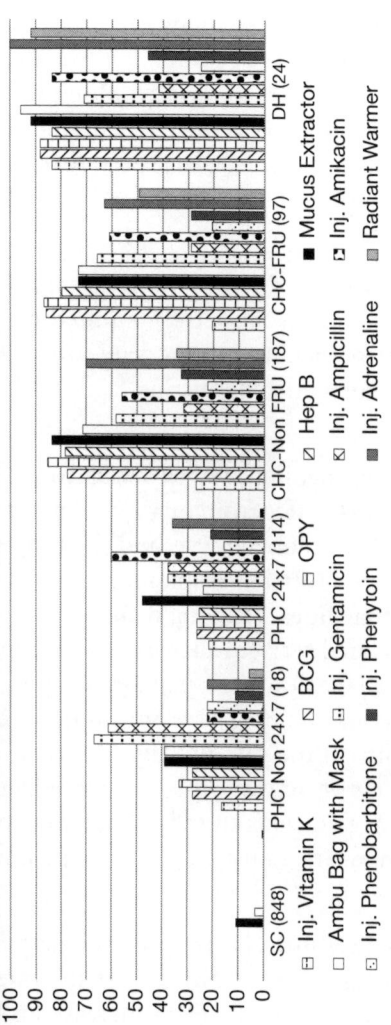

SC (848)   PHC Non 24×7 (18)   PHC 24×7 (114)   CHC-Non FRU (187)   CHC-FRU (97)   DH (24)

- ▦ Inj. Vitamin K
- ☒ BCG
- ▦ OPY
- ▨ Hep B
- ■ Mucus Extractor
- ⊡ Inj. Amikacin
- □ Ambu Bag with Mask
- ▦ Inj. Gentamicin
- ▨ Inj. Ampicillin
- ▤ Inj. Phenobarbitone
- ■ Inj. Phenytoin
- ■ Inj. Adrenaline
- ▥ Radiant Warmer

Staff	SC % (N)	PHC % (N)	CHC % (N)	Total % (N)
ANM	20.3 (7,016)	21.4 (276)	21.6 (194)	20.3 (7,486)
MO		6.5 (917)	7.2 (1,608)	6.9 (2,525)
SN		15.2 (33)	20.3 (844)	20.1 (877)

From analysis to planning

The information gathered during the mapping directly influenced the NRHM's planning process through its PIP. Facility mapping provided the government with an accurate and to-date situation analysis of the current condition of MNCH, along with a sense of status of key components such as HR, procurement, training and infrastructure. Most notably, the mapping revealed a wide disparity between UP's planned delivery load and the actual delivery need in the state.

The situation analysis allowed programme managers to assess all delivery points and focus on those that required greater support in two ways: by strengthening current delivery points and by activating facilities not currently conducting facilities as delivery points.

The purpose of strengthening facilities was to ensure that none of the delivery points suffer from quality-related gaps. The mapping provided (a) a situation analysis and (b) a gap analysis, and this helped the district officials in planning for the phasing in of 'strengthening' of facilities. Keeping delivery services at the fulcrum of planning, related services such as child health, family planning and adolescent health were planned only in delivery points, such that the continuum of care in the life cycle of an individual is accessibility in the same facility. Once a facility is chosen for strengthening or activation based on delivery needs of the district, all resources such as child health, family planning, human resources, training and construction were planned in the same facility.

Based on the gap analysis in 25 HPDs and the emerging pointers to the planning process, the UP NRHM, in its state PIP for the years 2014–2017 has proposed a 60% increase in the delivery points to meet at least 70–75% of the delivery needs of its population (Figure 1c.6).

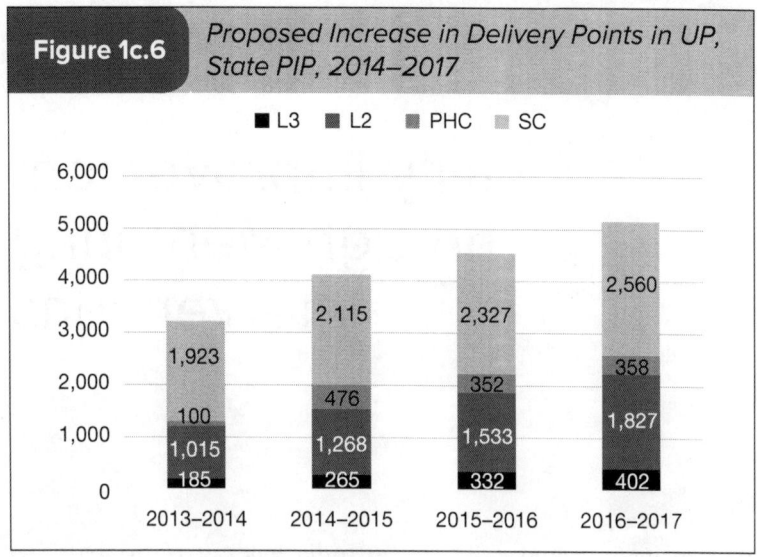

Figure 1c.6 *Proposed Increase in Delivery Points in UP, State PIP, 2014–2017*

Facility mapping and rapid gap analysis helped UP understand its current MNCH situation, isolate and analyse gaps from the state, district, block, facility and community levels and plan timelines for facility strengthening and activating.

2

Quality Improvement Through Mentoring Interventions

Rise in institutional deliveries in India has not translated into expected reductions in maternal and neonatal mortality because of the gaps in quality of care at the institutions. The national strategic document on RMNCH-A mentions that non-availability of basic reproductive health services, including contraceptives, pre- and postnatal care and EmONC results in delays in seeking institutional care. Moreover, the poor quality of care provided in the health facility contributes to maternal and child deaths. Therefore, NRHM recognized the quality of care as important and has set up quality assurance mechanisms in the states.

However, initial evaluations in a few states show positive changes in certain inputs and some process indicators, but do not show much change in related outcome indicators. The findings from these evaluations point to the need to strengthen supportive supervision of providers in order to change behaviours and practices that directly affect outcome indicators.[1] In addition, the national level bottleneck analysis of December 2012 of coverage of RMNCH-A interventions identifies the following major gaps:[2]

[1] http://kshsrc.org/quality-assurance-for-rch-services-the-karnataka-experience/
[2] SRS: Sample Registration System.

- Limited availability of skilled human resources, especially nurses
- Low coverage of services and of skilled staff posting among marginalized communities
- Inadequate supportive supervision of front-line service providers
- Low quality of training and skill building
- Lack of focus on improving quality of services
- Insufficient IEC on key family practices

The situation analysis in Karnataka and elsewhere has revealed the need to both improve provider competence in managing maternal and newborn care and to address facility-level factors such as drug stock-outs and lack of infrastructure that create barriers to providing quality MNCH services. There were no mechanisms in place for follow-up of staff after training to ensure good clinical practice and maintenance of skills or to facilitate system-level problem-solving. Also, weak referral processes and poor follow-up compromised the provision of continuum of care for mothers and newborns.

The assessments pointed to the following recommendations for delivering quality MNCH services:

- Need to comprehensively focus on quality, beyond just the infrastructural or competency issues
- Need to develop follow up support systems to MNCH providers (beyond one-time trainings) to sustain skills and competencies
- Need to promote use of job aids, checklists and protocols related to management of critical services
- Need to address gaps in facility-level systems such as referral, documentation, infection control and supply chain systems
- Need to create supportive environment in the facilities through fostering practices such as self-evaluation, teamwork, task shifting and attention to patient rights and dignity

Levels of Public Health System in India

Union and state governments in India have established a vast network of health facilities, through which free health services are provided to those in need. The network of public health facilities include SCs (one per 5,000 rural population without any in-patient facility, managed by an ANM, providing largely outreach services in terms of immunization, ANC, PNC and treatment of minor ailments), PHCs (one per 30,000 population with 5–6 beds and a labour room, managed by a trained medical doctor and a group of paramedics, providing primary care for all ailments and delivery care), CHCs (one per 120,000 population, managed by trained medical doctors and specialists, providing secondary care for all ailments and delivery care) and DHs (one per district, having multiple specialities, providing tertiary level care for all ailments and maternal, newborn and child care facilities).

Under the NHM, the public health facilities are categorized into three levels in accordance with the level of facility, specific human resources and infrastructure and service delivery criteria. The first level of service delivery is known as SC/Non-24×7 PHC, and the second and the third levels are known as 24×7 PHCs/non-FRU CHCs and FRU/CHC/SDH/DH, respectively.

Level-one MNCH facility: The level-one facility, most commonly referred as SC, is managed by one or two ANMs, depending upon the caseload. The SC normally covers 5–8 villages or a population of 5,000. The maternal health services provided by the SC are pregnancy testing, ANC, intranatal care and PNC. The normal deliveries are conducted here and referrals are made to the higher level in case any complications are observed. The SCs also provide newborn care, including resuscitation, immunization, breastfeeding support and initial management of complications before referral.

Level-two MNCH facility: It is commonly known as PHC and managed by one or two medical officers along with at least four SNs/ANMs, two lab technicians and equipped with minimum 6 beds and maximum of 30 beds. In terms of coverage, there has to be PHC for every 25,000. With respect to maternal health services, the PHC is responsible for assisted vaginal delivery, management of complication other than those requiring referral to level-three services, abortion services and management of reproductive tract infections/STIs. Regarding care of LBW newborns, phototherapy for newborns with hyperbilirubinemia, newborn sepsis and stabilization and referral of sick newborns with very low birth weight are available.

Level-three MNCH facility: The level-three facility is expected to provide all the maternal health services in the district, including taking care of referrals from other lower facilities. The district may have many level-three facilities in addition to DH, depending on the district population and geographic area. It is expected to have all the specialists, including gynaecologist/EmONC, anaesthetist/life-saving anaesthetic skill (LSAS) and paediatrician. It is also expected to have all the laboratory facilities to conduct labour function test, glucose tolerance test, platelet count, thyroid profile and blood storage unit. With respect to newborn care, it is expected to provide all the services for the sick newborn, follow-up of all babies discharged from the unit and high-risk newborns.

Defining Quality of Care

It is important to first understand 'quality of care' and appropriate performance standards[3] around critical RMNCH-A services that have highest impact in terms of reducing mortality. Focusing on the most critical aspects of services helps in achieving outcomes in the fastest possible way. First, we must recognize that there are different needs at different levels of the health care continuum. For example, the current national policy around maternal care is to increase the number of institutional deliveries, which requires that the quality of these services be enhanced. However, different efforts are required at the community level so as to increase participation and demand for quality and to assure good pre- and post-institutional care in the community. Nevertheless, although the approaches might be slightly different, the need for

[3] J. Raven, J. Hofman, A. Adegoke, and N. van den Broek, 'Methodology and Tools for Quality Improvement in Maternal and Newborn Health Care' *International Journal of Gynecology & Obstetrics* 114, no. 1 (July 2011): 4–9.

integration of these efforts and collaboration of stakeholders are the keys to overall success.

The term 'quality improvement' has within its scope multiple facets related to providers, clients and the health systems. All these factors need to be addressed in an integrated way. Providers should have opportunities to update their knowledge and skills in line with standard protocols and should have supportive job aids and tools to assist them in delivering care. Clients should feel respected and satisfied. Health systems should respond to the facility requirements in terms of adequate staffing, trainings, supplies, linkages and referral systems. Quality improvement itself is a continuous process and goes beyond one-time trainings or initial investments that are made to fix infrastructure. It needs approaches that are supportive, ongoing and provided on-site using checklists, aimed at enabling clinical, managerial, administrative and problem-solving competencies of personnel involved in care provision.[4] Many examples are available within the country, such as skills lab model that were tried in Bihar, supportive supervision of ANMs for improving SBA care in Jharkhand and onsite mentoring intervention to improve delivery and postpartum care in PHCs and emergency obstetric and newborn drills to improve quality of emergency care at first referral units in Karnataka. These need to be reviewed and assessed for potential scale-up.

Evidence for Planning

Literature review on the topic of quality of care gives us insights into various interventions around the world. Highlights of published findings related to mentoring, quality improvement and clinical guidelines are summarized further:

Mentoring interventions: Published literature on the application of MNH mentoring programmes at scale in developing countries

---

[4] J. Rhode, 'Supportive Supervision to Improve Integrated Primary Health Care', *Management Sciences for Health*.

is limited. Mentoring programmes have been established to improve delivery of HIV/AIDS care and such projects in India,[5] Uganda,[6] Zambia[7] and Botswana[8] have documented improvements in service quality. In Senegal,[9] a mentoring programme known as Tutorat strengthened nurse and midwife competence in family-planning counselling, skilled birth attendance and post-abortion care (PAC). In Jharkhand, India,[10] introduction of a supportive supervision programme in which MOs provided support to ANMs trained as SBAs contributed to improved use of active management of third stage of labour (AMTSL), partographs and increased access to drugs and supplies. In Ethiopia[11] a mentoring programme aimed at health centre managers reported improvement in management skills of hospital leaders in several management domains.

[5] Samastha project was implemented by KHPT/UoM in 15 districts of Karnataka and 5 districts of coastal Andhra Pradesh to develop a comprehensive HIV prevention, treatment, care and support programme between 2006 and 2012.

[6] G. Workneh, L. Scherzer, B. Kirk, H. R. Draper, G. Anabwani, R. S. Wanless RS, et al. 'Evaluation of the Effectiveness of an Outreach Clinical Mentoring Programme in Support of Paediatric HIV Care Scale-up in Botswana', *AIDS Care* 25, no. 1 (2013): 11–19.

[7] M.B. Morris, B. T. Chapula, B. H. Chi, A. Mwango, H. F. Chi, J. Mwanza, et al. 'Use of Task-shifting to Rapidly Scale-up HIV Treatment Services: Experiences from Lusaka, Zambia', *BMC Health Services Research* 9, no. 5 (2009).

[8] G. Workneh, L. Scherzer, B. Kirk, H. R. Draper, G. Anabwani, R. S.Wanless, et al. 'Evaluation of the Effectiveness of an Outreach Clinical Mentoring Programme in Support of Paediatric HIV Care Scale-up in Botswana', *AIDS Care*. doi:10.1080/09540121.2012.674096.

[9] IntraHealth, 'Tutorat: Improving Services Through On-the-Job Mentoring' (Chapel Hill, NC: IntraHealth International, 2011).

[10] IntraHealth, 'Improving Skilled Birth Attendance in Jharkhand Technical Brief', Vistaar Project (Chapel Hill, NC: IntraHealth International, October 2012).

[11] K. Hartwig, J. Pashman, E. Cherlin, M. Dale, M. Callaway, C. Czaplinski, et al. 'Hospital Management in the Context of Health Sector Reform: A Planning Model in Ethiopia', *International Journal of Health Planning and Management* 23, no. 3: 203–218.

Quality improvement interventions: There are several examples of team-based approaches to quality improvement that contributed to facility level improvements as measured by quality indicators. For example, an evaluation of COPE (team-based quality improvement approach) for Child Health in Kenya and Guinea examined changes in quality over a 15-month period at eight intervention and eight control sites and concluded that on almost every quality indicator, the intervention sites performed significantly better than the control sites, with most problems solved without outside assistance.[12] Health Care Collaboratives, in which coaches support quality teams from several facilities to address identified quality gaps, have improved services. In Uganda this approach was used in two districts to improve the provision of newborn resuscitation at government health centres.[13] In Malawi, health facility teams implemented a performance and quality improvement (PQI) intervention over a three-year period to improve reproductive health. Intervention facilities were more likely than comparison facilities to have the needed infrastructure, equipment, supplies and systems in place to offer reproductive health services. Observed quality of care was significantly higher at intervention than comparison facilities for PNC and family planning.[14]

Clinical guideline interventions: Evidence also supports the value of usable clinical checklists and guidelines. Checklist-based interventions can aid management of complex or neglected tasks and have been shown to reduce harm in health care. A pilot, pre-post-intervention study was conducted in a subdistrict-level birth centre in Karnataka, India between July and December

[12] J. Bradley, S. Igras, A. Shire, M. Diallo, E. Matwale, F. Fofana, et al., *COPE for Child Health in Kenya and Guinea: An Analysis of Service Quality* (New York, NY: EngenderHealth, 2002).

[13] Anne Casey, Presentation at American Public Health Association, 140th Annual Meeting, October 2012.

[14] B.J. Rawlins, Y. M. Kim, A. M. Rozario, E. Bazant, T. Rashidi, S. N. Bandaz, et al., 'Reproductive Health Services in Malawi: An Evaluation of a Quality Improvement Intervention', *Midwifery* 29, no. 1 (January 2013): 53–59. doi:10.1016/j.midw.2011.10.005.

2010 to evaluate changes in MNH health practices following the introduction of the WHO Safe Childbirth Checklist programme, a childbirth safety programme for institutional births incorporating a 29-item checklist. Delivery of essential childbirth-related care practices at each birth event increased from an average of 10 of 29 practices at baseline (95% CI 9.4, 10.1) to an average of 25 of 29 practices afterwards (95% CI 24.6, 25.3; $p<0.001$)[15] after introduction of the checklist. Other research explored use of clinical practice guidelines (CPGs) for maternal health in Burkina Faso, Ghana and Tanzania.[16] In all the three countries, the use of CPGs by health workers in practice was perceived to be limited. The cross-country study suggests the need to prioritize the format of guidelines to increase their usability and applicability.

In summary, the findings from the review suggest that a mentoring intervention should include components focused on the job provider training and support, user-friendly clinical job aids and team-based approaches to quality improvement. It is also imperative from the situation analysis that a quality improvement approach should comprehensively address issues related to the providers, clients and facility systems (Figure 2.1).

Designing Mentoring Interventions for Quality Improvement

Design of mentoring interventions entails answering many practical questions from a programme implementation perspective. They are:

[15] J.M. Spector, P. Agarwal, B. Kodkany, S. Lipsitz, A. Lashoer, G. Dgiekan, G. et al., 'Improving Quality of Care for Maternal and Newborn Health: Prospective Pilot Study of the WHO Safe Childbirth Checklist Program', *PLOS ONE* 7, no. 5 (2012): e35151. Epub: 16 May 2012. doi:10.1371/journal.pone.0035151.

[16] U. Baker, G. Tomson, M. Somé, B., Kouyaté, J. Williams, R. Mpembeni, et al., 'How to Know What You Need to Do: A Cross-country Comparison of Maternal Health Guidelines in Burkina Faso, Ghana and Tanzania'. *Implementation Science* 7, no. (13 April 2012): 31.

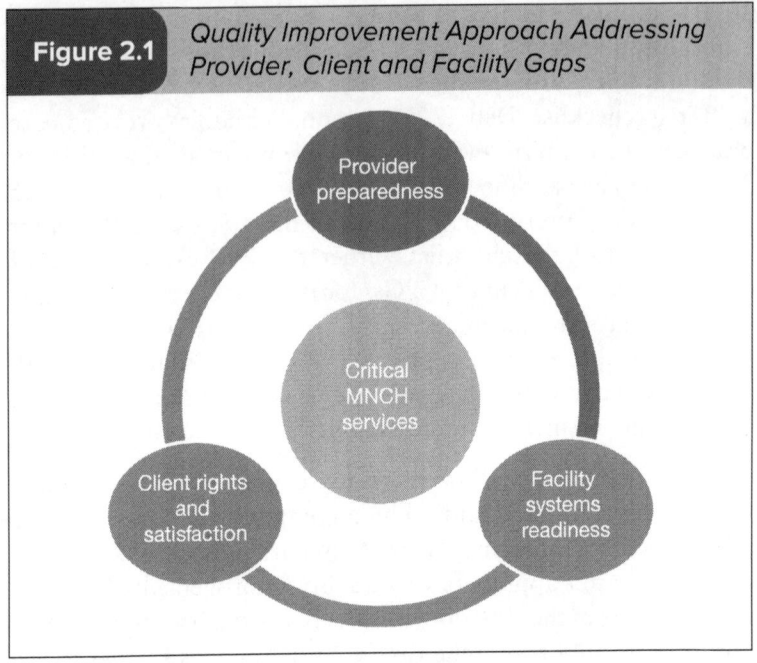

Figure 2.1 *Quality Improvement Approach Addressing Provider, Client and Facility Gaps*

- Who is the right person to assume the role of a mentor?
- What should be the scope/focus of a mentoring programme?
- How do we develop and equip the cadre of mentors?
- How often and for how long should the mentoring programmes be implemented?
- What review and monitoring mechanisms are required to track progress of mentoring programmes?
- What are the cost implications? Are the mentoring programmes scalable within the existing health systems?

Who is the right person to assume the role of a mentor?

The premise of the mentoring intervention is that it can complement in-service training to build competencies and confidence of providers on-site—that is, in the actual context where they are providing care. Evidence is pointing towards the effectiveness of peer-based models of mentorship. Considering the diversities at different levels of care provision, the choice of the mentor should align with the needs and requirements of a particular level of facility. In the context of PHCs, where institutional deliveries are on a rise over the last few years, hiring nurse mentors (NMs) seems advantageous for the following reasons:

- At PHCs, the SNs are primarily responsible for providing labour, delivery, postpartum and newborn care services. MOs are in charge of the PHC but only assist in labour and delivery as needed. Therefore, it is important that the mentoring intervention should largely focus on building the competence of SNs as SBAs.
- Because of the focus on SNs, it is advantageous to employ nurses as mentors as they would be mentoring their peers. A peer could be a more effective mentor than a MO or a specialist physician.
- It is very difficult to recruit MOs for the rural areas (as evidenced by the number of PHCs in the rural districts which do not have the required number of qualified MOs) and it is relatively easier to recruit experienced nurses for the positions.
- Turnover among skilled nurses may also be less than among MOs.[17]
- Utilizing nurses as mentors also present some cost advantages over MOs because of their lower salaries. This could be an important consideration in the overall cost of operating this programme at scale within the government system.
- Using nurses, who are most often women, as mentors also contributes to further the empowerment of female health workers in the health care system.

At the same time, it is critical to engage the facility leadership, that is, MOs who are the decision-makers to solve any problems

[17] Experience in working with MOs as technical support specialists in the Key Clinic private franchise model in Southern India found high levels of attrition as MOs often left for other opportunities including postgraduate work.

related to facility strengthening. Appropriate mechanisms have to be configured therein.

In the context of first referral units that are the higher-level facilities equipped with specialists and emergency services, mentorship models should consider a team of doctor (specialist) and nurses as mentors so that the teams are strengthened instead of individual providers with due emphasis on engagement of other stakeholders such as pharmacist, lab technician and support staff who may not be directly involved in care provision, yet play a role in overall quality improvement efforts (Figure 2.2).

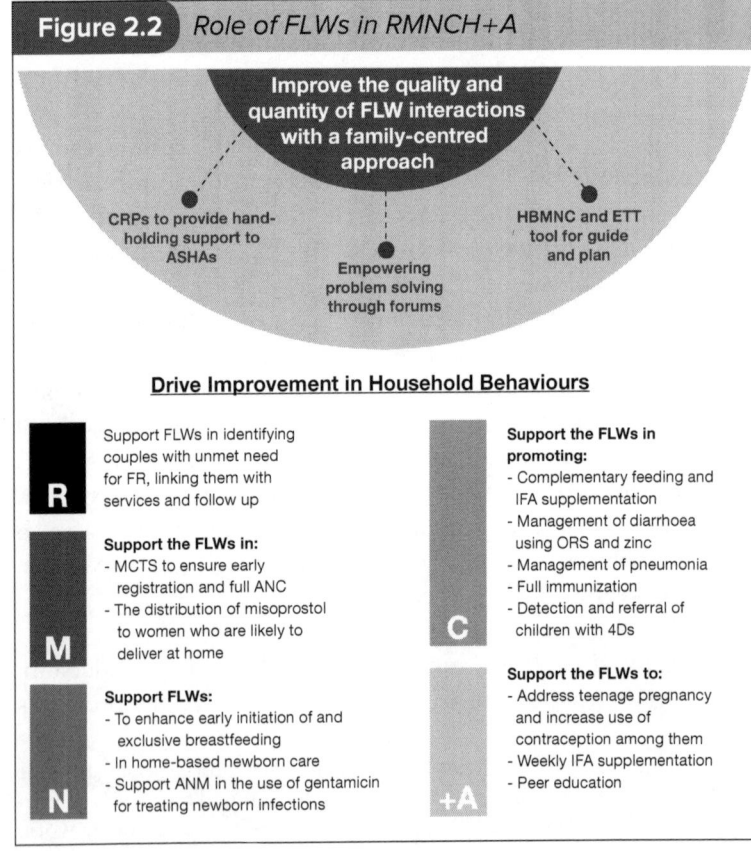

Figure 2.2 *Role of FLWs in RMNCH+A*

What should be the scope/focus of a mentoring programme?

In the past, programmes targeted at either only the clinical providers or the facility infrastructure has shown limited success. The mentorship programme aiming to improving quality of MNCH care in the facilities should meet the needs of providers, facility systems and client rights in a comprehensive way so as to sustain the gains made for long time. A systems approach committing to a culture of continuous quality improvement is critical. The goal of a mentoring programme should be to achieve optimum levels of facility readiness and provider preparedness so as to manage institutional delivery services with best outcomes and, at the same time, the clients and families feel satisfied and respected.

It is important for programme managers to note that it takes time and effort depending on the baseline situation of the facilities. Involvement and ownership of facility staff is critical. A planned and systematic approach to assess the situation, identify opportunities, develop and roll out mentorship plans and evaluate the progress made should be an integral part of the mentoring interventions.

How do you develop and equip a cadre of mentors?

Considering the large scale and coverage of government programmes, the mentoring programmes will require large number of mentors. The programmes may not have the luxury of utilizing services of readily available mentors, and hence it is prudent to invest resources in developing a cadre of mentors locally. The medical and nursing graduates may not be fully sensitized to the issues and quality gaps, or may not be equipped to solve them. A good induction programme will be worthwhile to help mentors realize the vision and scope of quality improvement, the requirements in terms of knowledge, skills and attitudes followed by actual trainings in relation to specific competencies. Trainings should be well balanced between clinical issues (obstetric and neonatal) and systems issues (facility infrastructure, drug supplies and the like) and, more importantly, should include sessions to build mentoring and problem-solving skills to address the gaps. Competency-based evaluations, demonstrations by experts, use of case studies, creating opportunities to observe and practise in the hospital wards will improve the impact of trainings. Supporting the trainings with job-aid (manuals for ready reference), encouraging peer-to-peer learning, practising use of tools and checklists for mentoring and problem-solving are important as well.

The trainings will be incomplete without a sound exposure to the government systems, the different cadres of facilities, linkages with the community and so on. Exposing trainees to ground realities and the unique requirements in the context of mentoring vis-à-vis routine clinical practice such as the need to travel, need to interact with administrative officers, need to work with staff of different backgrounds and experiences, need to wait for results that may take long time in some settings and so on helps in shaping the appropriate attitudes and perspectives among the mentors.

A one-time training may not be sufficient to develop effective mentors. Once the mentors start visiting the facilities, they will face issues and challenges that may be demotivating to the newly trained mentors. In the beginning, organizing reviews/exchange sessions with expert mentors, facilitating cross learning among mentors for peer-to-peer encouragement and learning will be critical. Particularly, the support by the expert mentors to the newly trained mentors on the ground can make a huge difference. The frequency and intensity of support will be high in the beginning. It is helpful to keep track of progress made by the mentors, in terms of their skill set and confidence during trainings and afterwards. This can inform the support required by the mentors.

Considering these requirements, it will be practical and cost effective to engage institutions to train and handhold mentors. Exploring teaching medical and nursing colleges or professional bodies (Federation of Obstetric and Gynaecological Societies of India [FOGSI]; National Neonatology Forum [NNF]) to support particular districts in implementing mentoring programmes can be a sustainable and collaborative model for quality improvement.

How often and for how long should the mentoring programmes implemented?

Experiences with regards to frequency and duration of mentoring visits vary with the scope and vision of the quality improvement and baseline status of facilities and staff.

Primary health centres tend to reach optimal status in a year's time whereas first referral units may require longer times. There is a need for fairly intensive and frequent mentoring visits in the beginning which tends to reduce as the facilities show improvement. In some context, the mentors take long to establish rapport with the facilities and the results may be slower; this could be due to issues inherent within the facilities (absence of MO, resistant SNs and the like) or the mentors (their skills and confidence). Some facilities will be very slow to respond due to prevalent wrong practices for long periods, high delivery volumes with limited number of staff and so on. Some aspects are quick to change (clinical skills related to active management of third stage of labour), but some aspects take long (neonatal resuscitation within the golden minute, partograph use, infection control practices and so on). Each facility will have unique issues and responds differently to the inputs of the mentors.

It is also possible that the issues being focused by the mentor are resolved completely, but there may be new clinical issues and challenges that emerge, or the staff-turn over and movements may bring back the facility to the baseline situation. Since the emphasis is to build a culture of continuous quality improvement, it is worthwhile to invest in this resource and have mentorship programmes that are lasting. An external objective resource helps to motivate facility staff to look at issues differently and solve problems, can respond to ongoing clinical mentoring needs and will also ensure ongoing monitoring of quality of care. A mentor once established can be an excellent vehicle to accommodate other areas of MNCH such as family planning, nutrition and even other priority programme areas as well.

What review and monitoring mechanisms are required to track progress of mentoring programmes?

Monitoring and evaluating quality of care in MNCH has its inherent challenges and opportunities. Many methods and tools have been explored, but each has its advantage and limitation. For example, clinical audit is a very effective tool to monitor and understand the compliance of the provider with standards of care. In effect, it may not actually reflect real-time practice as often the case sheets may be retrospectively filled or partially documented. Similarly, direct observation of staff practices helps to understand actual practices, but the presence of the observer itself may influence the staff and in effect what is being observed may not be routine practice. Specifically, complications are rare events and may not be available for observation. While it is feasible to track outputs (staff knowledge, skills), it is often a challenge to ascertain outcomes (mortality rates).

In this regard, it is good to configure a system of monitoring and evaluation that helps managers to track critical processes, outputs and outcomes using a mix of methods and tools as no one tool/method is completely helpful.

To measure provider knowledge, skills and practices, knowledge tests using case studies, objectively structured clinical examinations (OSCEs), case sheet audits and observations can be designed. To track progress in facility systems and its linkages, facility audits and referral audits will be helpful. Finally, to understand the client's experience and perspectives, exit interviews can be conducted. In addition to tracking changes in outcomes, case sheet summaries/abstracts that draw case-specific information from facility registers, case sheets and referral registers are very helpful; they can provide crucial information such as number of arrivals in a given time period, complication rates and case fatality rates, thus proving to be a rich source of outcome-level data. Systematic reviews of maternal and newborn deaths/near misses can provide crucial information related to lapses in care provision and delays that can shape quality improvement programmes significantly.

More detailed information related to monitoring and evaluation of MNCH services in facilities is provided in the chapter pertaining to data management.

Are there cost implications? Are these programmes scalable within the existing health systems?

From the stand point of government or donors, costs and scalability are important parameters. The impact gained due to mentoring programmes should weigh well against the costs incurred in implementing the programmes which is termed as cost effectiveness. Unfortunately, there are not too many mentoring models available or compared for assessing effectiveness in terms of outcomes and costs. The Karnataka experience of nurse mentoring programme for the PHCs showed that the nurse mentoring intervention when fully scaled up incurred additional 5.6 USD per delivery. For a district with an average population of 2 million, the programme incurred an additional annual cost of 58,413 USD which seems reasonable for the benefits in terms of deaths averted due to improved quality. These costs were expended by the pilot projects through dedicated staff; if the programmes were to be adopted by the government and the existing staff be used within the framework of existing training and programme management systems, there is potential for reducing the costs further.

The GoI has recently revised the quality assurance guidelines by bringing in structures and staffing dedicated for quality assurance at state and district levels. Principles of self-assessment, supportive supervision and participatory approaches for problem-solving and improving facility functioning are encouraged in the new guidelines. The GoI has also released guidelines for setting up skill labs; the skill labs are being set up in high priority districts, are staffed by doctors and nurses to function as trainers as well as mentors through onsite visits. The skill lab specifically focuses on critical and lifesaving skills during delivery and postpartum periods. These developments within the government health systems offer excellent opportunities to integrate the learnings from the mentoring programmes within the larger health systems. Since these two programmes are scaled up across the country with a priority focus in the high priority states and districts, scalability of mentoring programmes seems highly feasible through recognition of appropriate interfaces and convergence between the programmes.

Conclusions

The chapter highlights the practical considerations for designing mentoring programmes in settings in India. These learnings are informed by the emerging evidence related to implementing and measuring quality of MNCH care and more importantly by the direct implementation of large scale mentoring programmes in Karnataka and UP. As a continuation of this chapter, we present case studies from both Karnataka and UP that help the reader to visualize the practical aspects of design and implementation of mentoring programmes. It also throws light on how the programmes were similar in principles and approaches and yet different when it came to implementation, with due consideration of contextual differences.

Case Study 2A: The Karnataka Experience[18]

Context, evidence and intervention overview

In India, too many women and infants die from causes that are both preventable and easily treatable. Evidence points to the critical importance of ensuring high-quality care during labour, delivery, and the immediate postpartum and newborn period for saving maternal and newborn lives. This is the window in which

[18] Source: Mentoring Intervention Report, Sukshema Project.

more than half of maternal and newborn deaths take place. The ability of providers to manage normal deliveries according to best practice guidelines and to identify, manage and refer those patients with maternal and newborn complications can have a direct impact on MNH outcomes.

The Sukshema Project developed a mentoring intervention designed specifically to improve the quality of facility-based maternal and newborn care in 24×7 primary health care centres (PHCs) in northern Karnataka. By providing on-site mentoring for improved clinical care and service delivery, the project hypothesized that the quality of services and continuity of care would improve and that women and newborns would have better health outcomes.

Findings from situation analysis in project districts and evidence review

A situation analysis in eight project districts in 2011 revealed the need to both improve provider competence in managing maternal and newborn care and to address facility-level factors such as drug stock-outs and lack of infrastructure. The analysis showed that providers did not follow best practices such as active management of third stage of labour (AMTSL), use of partograph or ENC. Labour augmentation (not a recommended practice) was found to be very common. PHCs in particular often lacked the drugs and equipment to provide delivery services. The situation analysis also revealed a weak referral and follow-up system.

In designing the mentoring intervention, the Sukshema Project reviewed findings from similar interventions across a variety of settings and clinical areas. The evidence suggested that a mentoring intervention should include components focused on on-the-job provider training and support, user-friendly clinical job aids and team-based approaches to quality improvement.

Overview of intervention design

The Sukshema Project's MNCH mentoring intervention integrates elements of on-site clinical mentoring with facility-based quality improvement processes to support PHCs' abilities to deliver critical maternal and newborn care services. The project employed a new cadre of full-time NMs who were each responsible for mentoring staff in six to eight 24×7 PHCs. Since SNs are responsible for labour and delivery services in PHCs, Sukshema opted for a peer mentoring model and thus hired and trained qualified SNs to be mentors.

Project approaches and tools

The Sukshema Project introduced a quality improvement approach backed by tools to assess and track quality improvements.

AMMA quality improvement approach

Sukshema developed and promoted a quality improvement framework called AMMA that means 'mother' in Kannada. PHC teams were encouraged to use this quality improvement approach with individual patients and at the facility level (Figure 2a.1).

At the same time, the project introduced several tools such as case sheets, self-assessment tools and action-planning tools to operationalize quality improvement.

Case sheet: A key innovation of the mentoring intervention was the introduction of a newly developed case sheet for PHC providers that incorporated the AMMA (Assess, Manage, Measure, Advocate) approach. The case sheet served as a clinical record, a job aid and a teaching tool. The case sheet guided providers through the critical steps of patient assessment, labour monitoring and PNC and included a simplified partograph to monitor labour (Assess and Diagnose). The case sheet directed providers to complication case sheets that provided details on how to manage and

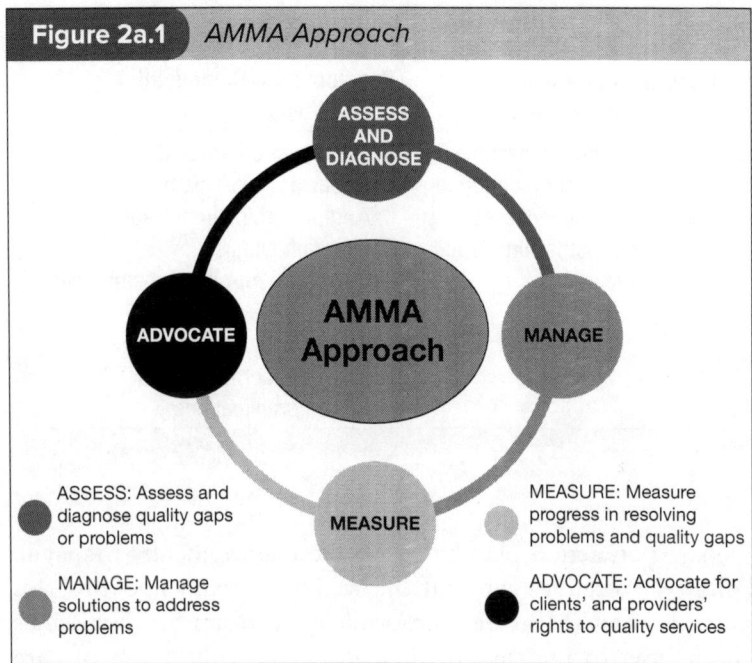

Figure 2a.1 *AMMA Approach*

ASSESS AND DIAGNOSE

AMMA Approach

ADVOCATE

MANAGE

MEASURE

ASSESS: Assess and diagnose quality gaps or problems

MANAGE: Manage solutions to address problems

MEASURE: Measure progress in resolving problems and quality gaps

ADVOCATE: Advocate for clients' and providers' rights to quality services

refer maternal and newborn complications (Manage). Providers used the case sheet to make clinical decisions aligned with SBA guidelines for PHCs. Mentors also used the case sheet to conduct case audits and monitor changes in compliance with SBA guidelines and as a teaching tool (Measure). Discussions about the case sheet led to wider discussions of how to improve quality of care for patients (Advocate) (Table 2a.1).

Self-assessment tools and action planning: The Sukshema Project developed self-assessment tools that mentors used with PHC teams to assess quality of care, identify gaps and examine causes of those gaps (Assess and Diagnose). The self-assessment checklist included questions for PHC teams to discuss and to decide whether the quality standard is met or whether there might be an opportunity for improvement. The checklists focused on patient and provider rights as critical aspects of quality. PHC teams

Table 2a.1	Case Sheet Components for 24×7 PHCs
Case Sheet for Normal Labour and Delivery	**Supplemental Complication Case Sheets**
Section 1: Initial assessment	A: Prolonged/obstructed labour
Section 2: Labour monitoring	B: Pre-eclampsia/eclampsia
Section 3: Delivery notes	C: Antepartum haemorrhage
Section 4: Postpartum period	D: Infection/sepsis
Outcome sheet	E: Premature rupture of membranes (PROM)
	F: PPH
	G: Newborn complications
	H: Other complications

prepared an action plan based on these assessments (Manage). Follow-up meetings with staff allowed for assessment of progress towards goals (Measure) and provided a forum for discussions about how to improve quality along the continuum of care (Advocate).

In addition to these tools, mentors brought mannequins, flip charts and other teaching aids to the sites to provide skills practice.

Hiring and training mentors

Recruitment and hiring: The Sukshema Project team crafted a three-tiered hiring strategy to identify the best candidates to be mentors. Because of the varied skills that mentors needed to possess, it was thought that a conventional hiring process of screening curricula vitae and interviewing candidates might not be sufficient to fully assess a candidate's capacities for the position. The project's need to hire many candidates at once also offered opportunities for more creative group-based assessment processes. An initial telephonic screening helped to assess educational qualifications and work experience, basic communication skills and readiness to work as mentor with its requirements to travel across facilities and working within health systems. The shortlisted candidates were invited to participate in selection process that included a series of assessments, that is, (a) at individual level to assess clinical skill and knowledge tests, (b) group work with case scenarios around specific problems plaguing health systems to understand problem-solving attitudes and leadership skills and (c) individual interviews to assess aptitude to work as mentor in health systems. The process followed for identifying and recruiting mentors worked well.

Training: The Sukshema Project developed a five-week induction training programme to equip mentors with the knowledge and skills needed to carry out their responsibilities. A combination of KHPT staff and faculty from St. John's Medical College Hospital (SJMC) trained mentors at SJMC in these skills. The training covered the following topics:

- Introduction and practice of applying self-assessment and quality improvement approaches
- Skilled birth attendance clinical content and hands-on training focused on skills to provide routine care, identify and manage complications and make timely referrals
- Exposure to PHC-level systems such as drug supply, referral, infection control, record-keeping and use of tools to help improve PHC systems
- Field visits to PHCs to practically apply the skills and tools

The project also provided ongoing capacity building of mentors using a combination of on-the-job support, refresher trainings and clinical postings.

Mentor visits in pilot districts: The project piloted and evaluated the mentoring programme in Bellary and Gulbarga districts with 11 mentors and 54 intervention PHCs in August 2012.

Structure of mentor visits: In the pilot districts, mentors were assigned six PHCs for mentoring and visited their assigned PHCs once a month initially and at longer intervals thereafter for a total of six visits a year. Each visit was expected to last two days, but later visits lasted 3–4 days. The time was extended to enable mentors to complete planned tasks, which was not always possible in a two-day visit given high outpatient loads and provider availability (Figure 2a.2).

The structure for the first mentor visit focused on establishing rapport and initiating the team-based quality improvement approaches through use of some of the self-assessment tools and development of an initial action plan. In subsequent visits,

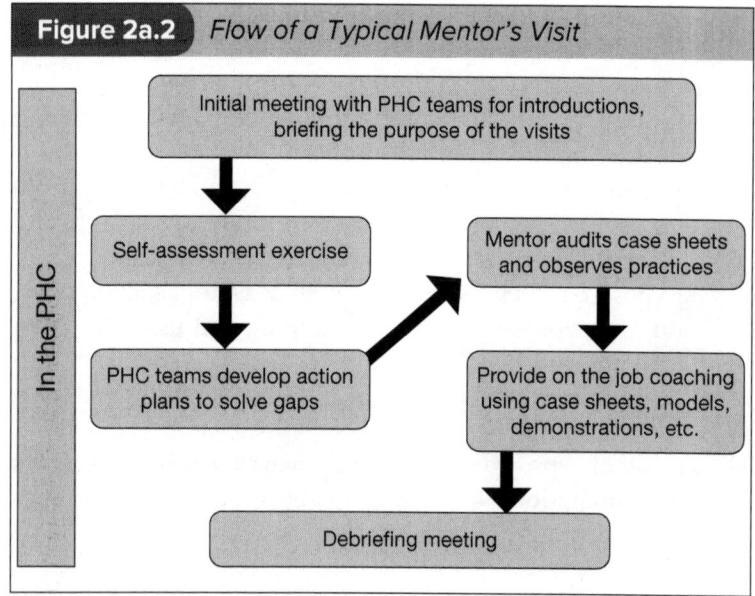

Figure 2a.2 *Flow of a Typical Mentor's Visit*

In the PHC

Initial meeting with PHC teams for introductions, briefing the purpose of the visits

Self-assessment exercise

PHC teams develop action plans to solve gaps

Mentor audits case sheets and observes practices

Provide on the job coaching using case sheets, models, demonstrations, etc.

Debriefing meeting

mentors continued to support PHC teams in using the self-assessment tools and developing and revisiting action plans, and provided individualized support to SNs on maternal and newborn topics. Mentors facilitated team-based problem-solving to address specific quality gaps such as equipment and supply logistics, infection prevention practices, referral practices, record-keeping, teamwork and staff attention to patient rights. Mentors also strengthened SN SBA skills through teaching, case reviews, case studies, demonstrations and modelling bedside patient care. All mentor visits included a review of the action plan, a case sheet audit and teaching.

Pilot district successes: Mentors in the pilot districts were able to work effectively with PHC teams to enact quality improvement processes and strengthen provider skills. Highlights include:

- **Rapport with PHC teams:** Mentors expressed and demonstrated confidence in building rapport with PHC teams and carrying out the mentoring visits.
- **Support for team-based quality improvement process:** The PHC staff were willing to engage with the mentors in quality improvement sessions. PHC teams remarked that they had rarely come together as a team before mentoring and welcomed the opportunity to do so. In some PHCs, teams initiated their own reviews and resolved their own problems in between mentor visits.
- **Value of self-assessment tools and action plans:** Mentors found that PHC teams were able to use the self-assessment tools and that these tools helped teams identify where they had problems.
- **Action plans addressed system strengthening:** Mentors noted that the process of reviewing and developing action plans was well entrenched as part of the mentoring visits.
- **Use of teaching models:** The training models provided to the mentors were used effectively to carry out demonstrations. SNs appreciated the opportunity to practise with newborn and pelvic models.

- **Case sheet acceptance and use:** Mentors indicated that with continued encouragement staff became more accustomed to the case sheet and appreciated its value as a job aid. Some staff initially resisted using the case sheet, perceiving it as a time-consuming documentation burden. Promoting consistent and correct use of the case sheet was a major undertaking for the mentors in all visits.
- **Opportunities for patient-focused teaching:** Mentors and project staff reported that they encountered pregnant women and recently delivered women in the PHCs so that they had the opportunity to provide bedside teaching and demonstration.
- **Customized support:** Mentors had a keen understanding of their PHCs and individual SNs and were able to objectively assess their strengths and shortcomings and develop individualized plans to support nurses.
- **Sustaining relationships with PHC teams:** Mentors became sources of support even between visits. Staff called mentors between mentoring visits to tell them about complications or ask for information (Figure 2a.3).

Pilot district challenges: Mentors encountered some circumstances that made it more difficult for the mentoring programme to achieve its objective of improving maternal and newborn care. Some of these challenges include:

- **PHC leadership engagement:** Mentors found it more difficult to facilitate change in PHCs that did not have a full-time MO or an MO who was engaged in providing strong leadership and support of the PHC teams. In these facilities, it was harder for the mentors to inspire a sense of teamwork and mutual accountability.
- **High-volume PHCs:** At some PHCs with high delivery and outpatient department volumes, it was hard for mentors to get time with staff. In busy PHCs, mentors found it difficult to retain the attention and focus of staff to provide teaching. Busy nurses sometimes had to deal with many

Figure 2a.3 *Nurse Mentoring in PHCs*

patients and were less likely to fill out case sheets or follow expected protocols.

- **Staff turnover, motivation and abilities:** Mentors also reported that there was a degree of staff turnover and they often had to bring new nurses up to speed. Another issue was that it was harder to consistently engage and have time with SNs who lived some distance away from the PHC. Other challenges included staff with poor attitudes or those who were slow learners.

PHC quality improvements: The use of team-based quality improvement processes combined with ongoing mentor support generated improvements in the quality of care in PHCs. Observations and mentor and PHC team interviews highlighted notable improvements:

- **Increased availability of drugs and supplies:** Mentors and PHC teams remarked that most pilot PHCs now had essential medicines and MOs were very supportive about getting needed drugs and supplies, usually using untied funds. Vitamin K, which was not available at all when the intervention began, was present in most PHCs. PHCs had acquired autoclaves, delivery sets and other equipment as needed.
- **Improved organization of labour room:** Mentors observed marked improvements in the organization of the labour room and its equipment, including separation of waste and increased cleanliness. Many PHCs now had kits readily available for emergencies. Many had posted guidelines on the walls and a list of essential drugs.
- **Decreased labour augmentation:** Mentors reported that nurses were no longer performing labour augmentation in most cases. Mentors observed that some senior nurses were reluctant to change practices.
- **Improved adherence to SBA guidelines for normal deliveries:** Mentors had been able to assist and observe deliveries and were thus able to assess how well nurses were handling

normal deliveries and complications. They reported that increasingly nurses were following the SBA guidelines, including using the partograph, practising AMTSL and providing improved general clinical care.

- **Increased capacity and confidence to manage maternal and newborn complications:** Nurses reported that they were now more comfortable and confident in handling maternal complications and were using the case sheets for guidance. Some mentors noted that nurses still needed some support in pre-referral patient management.
- **Improved referral processes:** Mentors and PHC teams reported that their referral processes were more systematic since the mentoring programme started. PHCs were now more likely to have referral directories and to call referral facilities in advance and follow up on patient outcomes.

There were a few areas that were slower to improve. They included the following:

- **Infection prevention:** While labour rooms were cleaner and sterilization had improved, there was still scope for improvement. PHC teams and mentors remarked that Group-D staff (who are responsible for general hygiene and cleanliness) were resistant to change.
- **Inadequate postpartum care:** Mentors reported that nurses did not properly monitor patients after delivery at the recommended intervals of every 15 minutes for two hours. Often this proved difficult for the nurses attending to other outpatient department functions. Mentors noted that the postpartum care section of the case sheet was often incomplete or incorrectly filled out.
- **Understaffing:** The blanket policy of three nurses for every 24 × 7 PHC results in staff in PHCs with high patient loads being overstretched and often unable to give sufficient time and attention to women in labour or during the postnatal period.

Scaling up mentoring programme: The mentoring programme was extended to the other six Sukshema districts starting in October 2012, and in September 2013 it was expanded further to include all PHCs in the pilot districts. As of July 2013, the mentoring programme covered 385 24×7 PHCs with a total of 53 mentors.

Programme refinements: The project made some changes to the mentoring programme design in the scale-up districts based on learning from the pilot districts. In the scale-up districts, each mentor was expected to cover 7–8 PHCs with three days set aside for each PHC visit from the start. Additionally, the project decided to intensify the mentoring support in high-volume PHCs and lessen the frequency and duration of mentor visits to PHCs that consistently reported low-delivery loads. Data indicated that 20 high-volume PHCs accounted for 19% of all PHC deliveries in the eight districts. For these high-volume PHCs, two experienced mentors together visited the PHC for three days every month.

Mentors in scale-up districts followed the established process for planning and carrying out PHC visits, which included preparatory work, periodic reviews after each mentor had conducted 1–2 PHC visits and a final review once each round of PHC visits was complete.

Lessons learned

Lessons learned in the scale-up districts emphasized the importance of creating an enabling environment, orienting providers to case sheets in advance of the intervention and the need to further strengthen referral processes. The high-volume PHC strategy worked well for PHCs in all districts. The pace and nature of quality improvements also followed a consistent pattern among PHCs, with improvements in the labour room and drug supplies being some of the first signs of quality improvement. Practices that were more resistant to change included infection prevention and PNC.

The scale-up experience demonstrated that the intervention could be replicated and applied in other districts. Systematically using the approaches and tools developed to implement the intervention resulted in a smooth and efficient implementation process and in just a five-month period the mentoring programme was extended to all eight project districts. Overall, mentors in these districts observed similar levels of staff engagement and improvement in their PHCs.

Managing the mentoring programme

The Sukshema Project developed a management structure and management processes to oversee implementation of the mentoring intervention. Overall guidance and support came from a core technical team based in Bangalore, consisting of the technical director, deputy director, quality improvement specialist and clinical specialist. These individuals routinely visited the project districts, advised on management processes and anticipated and provided troubleshooting as issues arose. At the district level, a district programme specialist (DPS) based in each district was responsible for managing and monitoring the mentoring intervention in that district. These individuals had a masters in public health degree with a medical background. As the principal liaison with district health officials, the DPS routinely informed them about the intervention and system-level issues that needed district-level attention. The Sukshema team also developed a set of tools to assist mentors in planning their mentoring visits and to assist DPSs in carrying out their supervisory and reporting responsibilities. A monitoring information system was also established to track intervention indicators (Figure 2a.4).

Voices of PHC and district staff

Interviews were conducted with four PHC teams and one DHO in May 2013 in pilot districts and with three PHC teams in scale-up districts and another DHO in October 2013 and April 2014

Figure 2a.4 *Organogram for Implementing Onsite Mentoring*

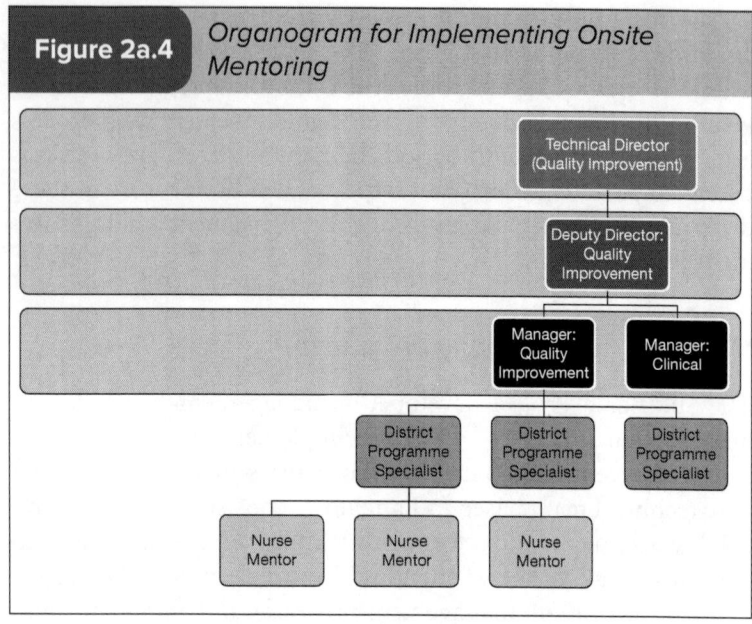

to assess their understanding of the mentoring programme and their own assessments of improvements since the programme began.

Nurses pointed out how mentors were helping them be more systematic and thorough in providing care. As one nurse stated, 'We didn't know much before and now the mentor tells us how to do each thing and explains why we do these things. The mentor reminds us about things we forget'. Nurses and other PHC staff praised the professionalism and interpersonal skills of the mentors. 'Mentors are very helpful and relaxed. Even if we are rude or stressed because we are busy they don't react and are always at ease with us which helps ease the tension'. An MO stated, 'mentors are very good and cooperative'.

Some PHCs had fully embraced the approaches the mentors used to strengthen systems. Several nurses interviewed appreciated the case sheet. Nurses and MOs nevertheless pointed out the challenges in filling out the case sheet, especially when staff were busy.

PHC teams also appreciated the mentoring programme for contributing to facility-level improvements. They commented on how the mentoring programme had helped them with managing stocks and coordinating with each other to ensure they had the drugs and supplies they needed. PHC teams described many improvements in their operations and their quality of care since the start of the mentoring programme.

Nurses and MOs felt the mentoring programme should continue. An MO noted, 'There is so much workload here that things sometimes fall behind so it is good to have the mentors to remind us and to keep coming often'. A nurse valued the intervention 'because mentors come with new information and they provide access to experts'. A DHO commented that nurses in PHCs rarely have someone available who can monitor their skills and support them and he felt that the mentoring programme was filling this important gap.

Coordination with community intervention

Sukshema Project's community intervention was designed to work on community-level issues through building the capacity of ASHAs, AWWs and junior health assistants (JHAs) to improve birth preparedness and maternal and newborn practices at the community level. The community intervention and mentoring programme coordinated together in each district to see how they complement each other in ensuring MNCH care continuum across levels of care. Each district held coordination meetings including the full community and mentoring teams and developed joint action plans. Infrastructure issues were a common concern that mentors and community coordinators tried to join forces to resolve. Other issues they discussed included preventing home births, encouraging women to come to the facility earlier in labour, follow up in the community after mothers and babies are discharged from the facilities.

The linkages between the two programme components evolved somewhat organically as the two teams got to know one another and found ways to work together.

Intervention results and costs

A more quantitative assessment of the mentoring programme's achievements was based on monitoring indicators and the pilot district evaluation findings.

Management information system (MIS) findings

According to MIS data, the use of case sheets increased over-time. As of March 2014, nurses had completely filled out a case sheet for more than 65% of all PHC arrivals compared to 12% in January 2013. The most frequently occurring complications related to prolonged labour, premature rupture of membranes or pregnancy-induced hypertension (PIH)/pre-eclampsia. The use of complication case sheets was also improving: the proportion of complication case sheets filled out as a proportion of total referrals reported (derived from the referral registers) was 42% in March 2014 up from 5% in January 2013.

Endline evaluation findings

The project corroborated its qualitative findings with an end-line evaluation of the mentoring programme and its impact on knowledge, skills and facility readiness to provide maternal and newborn services. PHCs in Bellary and Gulbarga were randomly assigned to either intervention or control groups. The endline study involved facility audits, provider interviews and interviews with postpartum women in the month after delivery in 2012 and again in 2013.

In terms of knowledge of management of labour and delivery, intervention and control sites both improved over the one-year period. There were improvements overall in knowledge of how to identify prematurity, AMTSL, eclampsia, sepsis, PPH, obstructed labour and foetal distress and how to manage neo-natal resuscitation. On almost every indicator, the intervention sites performed statistically significantly better than the control sites (Table 2a.2).

PHCs were much better equipped in 2013 than in 2012. Again, there were improvements overall in both types of sites; however, the intervention sites outdid the control sites and in many cases the differences were highly statistically significant. The biggest differences were observed with respect to drug availability and adherence to referral protocols; here intervention sites were far better equipped to manage all emergencies than were control sites in 2013 (Table 2a.3).

Mentoring was not able to affect more systemic problems such as staff shortages, the physical state of PHCs or services such as food, water and linens for postpartum women within the year's time.

Cost

The total start-up and annual cost of the intervention was 27,103,453 INR (467,301 USD) for all eight districts. For a district with an average population of 2 million, the programme incurred an annual cost of 58,413 USD. The additional costs incurred amount to 5.6 USD per delivery.

Summary of achievements and challenges

Qualitative and quantitative information[19,20] were all consistent in suggesting that the mentoring programme has been successful in improving many aspects of clinical care and helping PHCs be

[19] K. Jayanna, J. Bradley, P. Mony, T. Cunningham, M. Washington, S. Bhat et al., 'Effectiveness of Onsite Nurse Mentoring in Improving Quality of Institutional Births in the Primary Health Centres of High Priority Districts of Karnataka, South India: A Cluster Randomized Trial'. *PLoSONE* 11, no. 9:e0161957. doi: 10.1371/journal.pone.0161957

[20] E.A. Fischer, K. Jayanna, T. Cunningham, M. Washington, P. Mony, J. Bradley, and S. Moses. Nurse Mentors Catalyze Quality Improvement in Primary Health Centers: Lessons Learned from Implementation of a Pilot Program in Northern Karnataka, India. *Glob Health Sci Pract.* 3, no. 4: 660–675.

Table 2a.2 SNs' Knowledge About Diagnosis and Management of Complications in the Intervention and Control Facilities

Knowledge Parameter	Intervention 2012, (#/%) N=147	Intervention 2013, (#/%) N=136	Intervention 2012 vs. 2013 AOR, CI and p values	Control 2012, (#/%) N=148	Control 2013, (#/%) N=137	Control 2012 vs. 2013 AOR, CI and p values	Intervention vs. control 2013 AOR, CI and p values
Know all 3 steps of AMTSL	9 (6.4)	112 (82.4)	84.9 (36–200.4) p<0.001	14 (9.5)	49 (35.8)	5.3 (2.7–10.4) p<0.001	10.0 (5.5–18.2) p<0.001
Know all 3 signs for diagnosis of eclampsia	2 (1.4)	65 (47.8)	96.3 (20.2–459.1) p<0.001	3 (2.0)	23 (16.8)	10.3 (2.9–36.9) p<0.001	6.4 (2.9–13.9) p<0.001
Know correct dose of magnesium sulphate for eclampsia management	32 (21.8)	106 (77.9)	13.4 (7.0–25.4) p<0.001	23 (15.5)	65 (47.5)	4.6 (2.5–8.4) p<0.001	4.8 (2.7–8.9) p<0.001
Know 3 main signs for diagnosis of sepsis	5 (3.4)	64 (47.1)	28.3 (10.0–80.0) p<0.001	2 (1.4)	35 (25.5)	28.2 (6.3–126.7) p<0.001	3.3 (1.7–6.1) p<0.001

Knowledge Parameter	Intervention 2012, (#/%) N = 147	Intervention 2013, (#/%) N = 136	Intervention 2012 vs. 2013 AOR, CI and p values	Control 2012, (#/%) N = 148	Control 2013, (#/%) N = 137	Control 2012 vs. 2013 AOR, CI and p values	Intervention vs. control 2013 AOR, CI and p values
Know all 3 drugs for sepsis management	3 (2.0)	100 (73.5)	177.4 (42.8–734.4) $p < 0.001$	1 (0.7)	15 (10.9)	15.8 (2.0–123.4) $p = 0.009$	36.1 (13.6–95.9) $p < 0.001$
Know all 4 aspects of neonatal resuscitation	3 (2.0)	66 (48.5)	66.3 (16.5–266.7) $p < 0.001$	4 (2.7)	16 (11.7)	4.7 (1.4–15.1) $p = 0.010$	10.7 (4.6–25.0) $p < 0.001$
Know correct definition of LBW	117 (79.6)	119 (87.5)	1.7 (0.9–3.5) $p = 0.124$	102 (68.9)	115 (83.9)	2.3 (1.2–4.3) $p = 0.012$	1.4 (0.7–3.1) $p = 0.367$
Know 3 important aspects of LBW care	23 (15.7)	79 (58.1)	10.1 (5.2–19.7) $p < 0.001$	12 (9.1)	56 (40.9)	11.2 (5.0–25.0) $p < 0.001$	2.4 (1.2–4.7) $p = 0.010$
Know 2 drugs for newborn sepsis management	4 (2.7)	61 (44.9)	57.4 (15.6–211.1) $p < 0.001$	7 (4.7)	5 (3.6)	0.7 (0.2–2.5) $p = 0.577$	46.0 (12.2–173.8) $p < 0.001$

Notes: P values are based on Z-test using multilevel logistic regression model; OR—Odds Ratio; CI—Confidence Interval; N—Denominator.

Table 2a.3 *Facility Readiness to Deal with Maternal and Newborn Complications in the Intervention and Control Facilities*

Category	Intervention 2012 (#/%), N = 54%	Intervention 2013 (#/%), N = 54	Intervention 2012 vs. 2013 OR, 95% CI and p value	Control 2012 (#/%), N = 54	Control 2013 (#/%), N = 54	Control 2012 vs. 2013 OR, 95% CI and p value	Intervention vs. control, 2013 OR, 95% CI and p value
Gestational hypertension	0	19 (35.2)	—	0	3 (5.6)	—	9.2 (2.5–33.6) p = 0.001
PPH	16 (29.6)	29 (53.7)	2.8 (1.2–6.1) p = 0.012	13 (24.1)	12 (24.1)	1.0 (0.4–2.4) p = 0.999	3.7 (1.6–8.3) p = 0.002
Maternal sepsis	23 (42.6)	29 (53.7)	1.6 (0.7–3.3) p = 0.249	21 (38.9)	13 (24.1)	0.5 (0.2–1.1) p = 0.100	3.7 (1.6–8.3) p = 0.002
Obstructed labour	2 (3.7)	25 (46.3)	22.4 (4.9–101.5) p < 0.001	3 (5.6)	9 (16.7)	3.4 (0.9–13.3) p = 0.079	4.3 (1.8–10.5) p = 0.001
Neonatal complication	0	9 (16.7)	—	4 (7.4)	4 (7.4)	1.0 (0.2–4.2) p = 0.999	2.5 (0.7–8.7) p = 0.149
Referral systems	0	25 (46.3)	—	0	5 (9.3)	—	8.4 (2.9–24.5) p < 0.001

Notes: P values are based on Z-test using logistic regression model; OR—Odds Ratio; CI—Confidence Interval; N—Denominator.

better equipped and supplied to provide MNCH services. Key improvements are summarized further:

Clinical improvements	Physical improvements	Management improvements
• Knowledge and skills • Diagnosis and management of complications • Improved referral processes • Use of case sheet	• Availability of drugs and supplies • Labour room organization • Infection prevention in labour room	• Greater teamwork • Use of self-assessment tools • Action plans • Use of untied funds

Major lessons learned are listed as follows:

- The best mentors combine strong clinical and communication skills.
- A focused training programme combined with a strong system for ongoing training and support can prepare a capable and effective mentoring workforce.
- Self-assessment processes and team-based action planning are required to improve quality.
- The case sheet is a helpful tool but requires time and support to operationalize.
- Data use can drive programme improvements on many levels.
- PHC leadership is a critical factor in improving quality.
- High-volume PHCs require the most support.
- The DHO's role is vital to catalyse mentoring programme impact.
- Integration with government reporting forms and systems is needed for new formats.
- Extending mentoring to JHAs could reinforce linkages to community-based services.

Challenges that the mentoring programme cannot address stem from root causes that are at the community or system levels. The solutions will need to be addressed at these levels. For example, the issue of inadequate staffing or strengthening referral facilities requires district or state-level action. Behaviours such as untimely care seeking and short postnatal stays will require dialogue at the community level through ASHAs and local village leaders.

Overall, however, the mentoring programme has proven an effective intervention to improve the maternal and newborn services in PHCs. Mentors have been able to support PHC teams to identify and address quality gaps and to increase the capacity and confidence of SNs. In many PHCs, nurses say they are now providing care according to SBA guidelines and are better able to handle maternal and newborn complications. Facilities were also better organized, equipped and supplied to deliver quality services.

FRU mentoring

Encouraged by the success of onsite mentoring at 24×7 PHCs, the intervention was replicated in first referral units towards the last year of Sukshema Project. Here, the same is presented as a case study with results from the experience.

Background

In northern Karnataka, higher-level facilities, such as CHCs, THs and DHs account for about 40% of institutional deliveries. Most of these facilities are FRUs that are expected to be equipped with staff and facilities to provide EmONC. FRUs conduct a large proportion of deliveries, in addition to attending to referred complications from PHCs. However, only 32% of these higher level facilities offered caesarean section; 50% conducted assisted deliveries; 32% of providers at such facilities were able to interpret a partograph and only 41% checked for bleeding in postpartum mothers. Hence focusing efforts to quality improvement in these facilities was needed to enhance MNCH outcomes. The Sukshema Project has demonstrated that onsite mentoring at PHCs led to improvements in quality of care and referrals to higher facilities. Our hypothesis was that improving the quality of care at FRUs (CHCs, THs and DHs), in addition to the PHCs, would lead to further improvements in obstetric and newborn care practices and contribute to reductions in maternal and neonatal morbidity and mortality.

To test the feasibility of developing a mentoring programme at the FRU level, an intervention was implemented for 12 months in 16 FRUs across eight project districts. The following section describes the intervention and documents the process of implementation, highlighting achievements, challenges and opportunities.

Intervention design

Sukshema's FRU mentoring intervention integrated elements of clinical mentoring with facility-based quality improvement processes. The intervention specifically focused efforts on the most common maternal and newborn complications (PPH, hypertensive disorders, sepsis) and three newborn complications (LBW, asphyxia, sepsis) in addition to management of normal deliveries and postpartum care. Informed by Skills and Drills Intervention Model at FRUs in northern Karnataka and series of consultation with facility staff and government officials, the intervention adopted the following four components:

- Facility-based refresher training to bring facility teams up to speed on basic clinical knowledge and skills before initiating the mentoring visits.
- Instituting a quality improvement committee (QIC) to oversee improvements in facility systems and infrastructure.
- Emergency obstetric and newborn drills to enable facility teams to be prepared for handling an emergency.
- Regular visits by a team of specialists (an obstetrician and paediatrician) and two NMs facilitated by the district programme specialists to reinforce skills and practices as per the clinical standards.

This multidisciplinary mentoring team visited each FRU once per month for the first three months. Thereafter, visits took place every two months. The mentoring team provided clinical mentoring to SNs and site specialists and team-building and problem-solving support for all FRU staff that support MNCH services.

The mentoring team

The NMs for the FRU intervention were drawn from the pool of mentors Sukshema already employed for its PHC mentoring programme and DPS were already project staff. NMs and DPS received a two-week training at SJMC primarily focused on introducing skills that would be required at the FRU level for each of the common maternal and newborn complications. Obstetricians and paediatricians either affiliated with local medical colleges or in major public or private hospitals were recruited to serve as specialist mentors. The project signed contracts with medical colleges and in some cases with individual specialists to provide a total of up to 18 days of service (e.g., 2 days per FRU-mentoring visit) including training time and support to the FRUs they mentor over a 12-month period. These specialist mentors took part in a two-day standardization workshop to ensure that all specialists would follow the same guidelines and approaches during their mentor visits (Figure 2a.5).

Tools and approaches to support mentoring and quality improvement

The project developed a set of tools and approaches to support the FRU mentoring intervention. Key approaches and tools are profiled as follows:

Facility-based refresher training: Refresher trainings were organized for two days for all providers in the FRUs dealing with essential and EmONC to refresh their basic knowledge and skills before initiating mentoring visits.

Figure 2a.5 *Specialist Mentoring in FRUs*

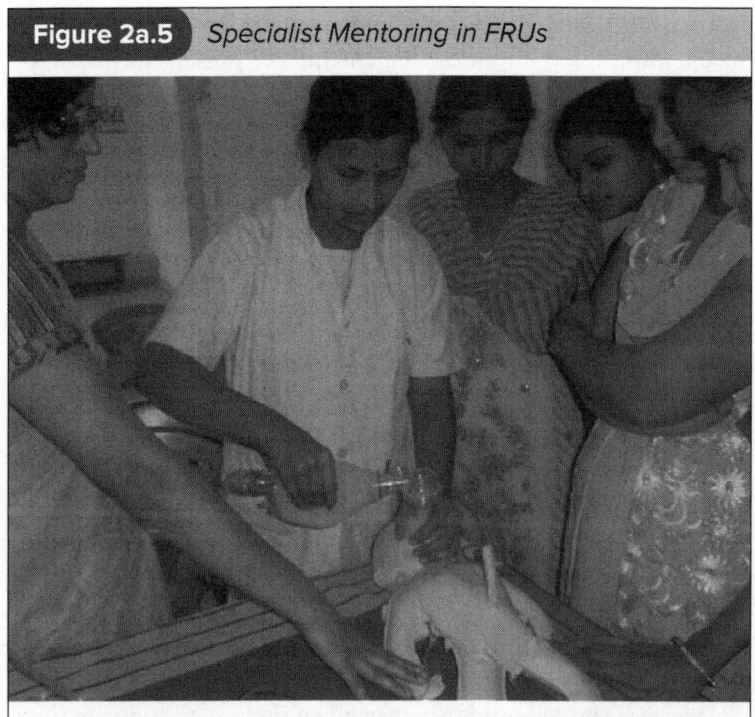

Quality improvement committee: FRUs participating in the intervention were requested to form a QIC comprised of the FRU chief medical officer (CMO), doctors and incharge nurses of obstetric and paediatric units, lab, pharmacy and housekeeping staff. The QIC met once a month and focused on problem-solving around all aspects of the provision of quality MNCH services. The DPS and NMs introduced self-assessment tools and action planning processes to the QIC to promote facility-based quality improvements.

Self-assessment tools: Checklists based on FRU standards of care were used by the QIC to assess whether they were complying with FRU guidelines. These tools were specific to the different stations that an FRU is supposed to have. Each tool required the QIC to evaluate the services, equipment, drugs and supplies and protocols for each station. QIC were expected to visit these areas once a month and check off if elements are present or missing.

The eight stations that are assessed include:

- Examination/OPD room/Area
- Pre-delivery observation room/Service area
- Labour room
- Newborn care corner/NBSU
- Post-delivery room/Area (until 2 hours after delivery)
- PNC ward (>2 hours to 48 hours after delivery)
- Eclampsia room
- Obstetric operating theatre (OT)/Blood storage/Laboratory/ Pharmacy

Revised case sheets: As in the PHC mentoring intervention a case sheet was introduced that served as a job aid, medical record and teaching tool. The basic case sheet, called a delivery record, was specifically designed for use in FRUs. Complication case sheets were expanded to reflect the treatment guidelines expected at the FRU level. Detailed guidance was given on how to manage these complications. In addition, the complication case sheet offered guidance and check points that informed providers' actions in varied circumstances at any given time in an FRU given that specialists were not always available. Complication case sheets were developed for the following conditions:

- Maternal complications
- Newborn complications
- PIH/pre-eclampsia/eclampsia
- Birth asphyxia
- PPH
- Newborn sepsis
- Sepsis
- LBW
- Others (e.g., anaemia, premature rupture of membranes, obstructed labour, cardiac)

Emergency drills: Drills are exercises intended to help FRU staff find out how prepared they are for handling emergencies. These are scripted role plays simulating real-life situations for which FRU staff should be prepared. All efforts are made to have the drills be as realistic as possible. Each mentoring visit included an obstetric and newborn emergency drill directed by the specialist mentor. The emergencies covered include PIH/eclampsia, PPH and newborn complications including birth asphyxia. The drills took place in the labour ward so providers could assess how they would handle an emergency situation with the resources and staff at hand. The entire session lasted for about 45 minutes to an hour including the debriefing session.

Skill stations: The mentoring team also introduced skill stations to expand training of FRU nurses. They would set up these skill stations in either a meeting hall or labour room depending on the skill. The skills station demonstrations used supplies and equipment readily available at the FRU and in some cases used the pelvic model and newborn mannequin that each mentor carried with her to the site. Mentors would use a specific set of skill stations aligned with the complications that were the topic of that particular visit. Therein a specialist conducted drills and discussed effective management of complications.

Specialists/mentors facilitate skill development through skill stations and there were 21 skill stations. Mentors ensured that all nurses participated in all skill stations during their visits.

Complications/Skill stations birth asphyxia

1. How to prepare NBCC—prepared before delivering a baby
2. How to check if an Ambu bag is working
3. How to perform initial steps of resuscitation
4. How to perform bag and mask ventilation
5. How to perform chest compression

Care of LBW infant

1. How to weigh newborn
2. How to perform kangaroo mother care (KMC)
3. How to assess oxygen saturation
4. How to wrap newborn
5. How to measure temperature
6. How to use radiant warmer

PIH, pre-eclampsia, eclampsia

1. How to measure BP accurately
2. How to conduct and interpret proteinuria test by dipstick method
3. How to prepare loading dose of intramuscular (IM) and intravenous (IV) of $MgSO_4$
4. How to assess patellar reflex

PPH

1. How to diagnose PPH based on blood loss
2. How to administer O_2 to a woman in sepsis/shock
3. How to perform controlled cord traction
4. How to exam placenta for its completeness
5. How to perform uterine massage till uterus is hard
6. How to perform Hb test using Sahli's haemoglobinometer

Schedule and structure of mentor visits

The project team prepared a mentoring visit plan that outlined topics to be covered in each mentoring visit. These topics were in addition to addressing need-based clinical and system issues that mentors observed during their visits or were included in action plans. Table 2a.4 summarizes the expected structure of each day of the mentor visit. The mentoring team had discretion in making adjustments to the sequencing of activities as required based on

Table 2a.4	Schedule of Topics to Be Covered in FRU Mentor Visits		
Visit	Clinical Topics— Maternal	Clinical Topics— Newborn	System Topics
1 and 4	Eclampsia	Birth asphyxia	Infection control and documentation
2 and 5	PPH	LBW	Supply chain
3 and 6	Maternal sepsis	Newborn sepsis	Referral system

the particular circumstances of each FRU. After the third mentor visit, the decision was made to extend the duration of the mentor visit from six days to as many days as needed for each FRU to enable mentors to reach all nurses in a facility. In total, the project contributed 2,031 days of mentor team support across all FRUs.

Structure of Typical FRU Mentor Visit		
Day 1 and 2	NMs	• Reinforce rapport • Be available as additional support staff in the delivery and postnatal wards • Encourage QIC to review and support implementation of action plans (with DPS)
Day 3	Specialist mentor (obstetrician) nurse mentors and DPS	• Specialist mentor interaction with FRU specialists and NMs and observations of practices, site tours and case sheet audits • Conduct emergency drill exercise • Provide support based on need through
Day 4	Specialist mentor (paediatrician), NMs, DPS	o Skill stations o Demonstrations o Case studies and protocols/guidelines

(Continued)

(Continued)

	Structure of Typical FRU Mentor Visit	
		o Case sheet reviews(For nurses, these happen on other days as well by the NMs. Since there are more numbers of nurses to cover at the FRU, NMs plan for these on different days. Specialist mentors focus on specialists and those SNs available during their visits.) • Debrief with FRU nurses and specialists to appreciate good work and summarize clinical action points
Day 5, 6 and all subsequent days	NMs	• Conduct skills stations (Visits 3–6) • Complete any pending tasks from days 1 and 2 • Provide additional support staff in delivery and postnatal rooms (including night duty nurses) • Review with CMO or QIC next steps and follow up visit plans • Alternate overnight shifts by NMs • Catch-up rounds with all FRU MNCH nurses

Management

Management support was provided by the district programme specialists and technical managers of the project at the state level. The district staff played an active role in introducing the mentors to the facilities, facilitating QIC meetings and in following up with the facility leadership in resolving issues. The technical managers and a deputy director, quality improvement supported the field teams during preparations and planning for the visits. They also reviewed the implementation through field visits and review meetings. The director, quality improvement provided the required technical stewardship. Clinical support through training and field support was provided by the experts from SJMC.

Achievements

Two to three months into the intervention, many improvements were already visible in the FRUs and continued improvements were observed over the duration of the intervention. Highlights based on site visits and interviews with mentors and FRU staff are noted:

Labour room equipment and supplies: Many of the improvements related to better equipped and organized labour rooms. All labour rooms had designated and equipped newborn care corners and emergency drug kits. Mentors and FRU staff related how labour rooms were now equipped with up to eight delivery sets so that instruments could be properly sterilized and autoclaved. Some FRUs acquired BP and stethoscopes for exclusive use in the in labour room.

Drugs: Drug indenting and supplies had substantially improved since the mentoring programme began. Mentors stated that all FRUs had improved indenting. They noted that before staff were indenting randomly and did not keep adequate buffer stock. FRU nurses explained how they were now indenting against a check-list which they posted on the labour room wall with quantities calculated. Mentors stated that drugs were in stock. There was a well-stocked and organized pharmacy in the labour rooms according to the essential drug list that the project had supplied to post on the labour room wall.

Infection control: Infection prevention protocols had improved. Mentors explained that in some cases staff knew what was to be done but were not doing it, while in other cases staff did not even know the protocols. Some FRUs did not have colour-coded bins for waste segregation. Mentors showed SNs and Group-D staff how to prepare and use chlorine solution. Staff were also advised on the need to autoclave all instruments and this had become a common practice. Prior to mentoring staff had only been steriliz-ing instruments but not autoclaving them.

In one FRU, staff explained how they were maintaining cleanliness now through cleaning the labour room 3–4 times a day where before they only cleaned it twice a day. They noted they had improved waste disposal. All FRUs are expected to have a sepsis room to isolate and treat infectious cases. Earlier this only existed in a few FRUs, however, where staff were able to designate a room for this use.

Improved management of normal labour and complications: The mentors and FRU staff concurred that knowledge, skills and practice in providing MNCH services had improved. As one CMO stated, 'Before mentoring, staff did not know guidelines or how to handle complications. Now they are much more informed and competent to provide care'. Mentors were able to cite examples of treatment protocols that had improved once staff were updated on guidelines. Over the course of the intervention, mentors found nurses had more confidence in handling complications. As one nurse explained, 'We used to manage cases earlier but now we are doing [it] more systematically'.

PNC counselling: Mentors encouraged FRU nurses to institute more standardized and consistent postnatal counselling. Several FRUs were assigned staff to do PNC counselling. For example, in one FRU the mentor advised that one nurse per shift spend one hour doing PNC counselling to reach all women. Staff used the home-based family-focused counselling (HBFFC) tool that the project had developed for its community intervention. Lack of staff is a major challenge when it comes to providing PNC care. In some FRUs, staff stated that it was hard for them to find time to do PNC counselling.

Improved documentation: Mentors and nurses found that documentation practices had improved. Much of this was attributable to the introduction and reinforcement of the case sheet. However, mentors also noted that documentation of parturition registers and referral registers had improved as well as documentation of QIC meeting proceedings. FRU staff also noted that improved documentation was an outcome of the mentoring programme. The quality and completeness of documentation continues to be a concern. Mentors and the monitoring and evaluation team noted that nurses are likely to start a delivery record for nearly all patients but do not fully complete it in a proportion of cases.

Improved cleanliness and patient amenities: The community element of the FRU intervention initially focused efforts around cleanliness and hygiene as that was an issue most readily acceptable and responded to as an identified need. In this way, the team was also able to leverage the interest created through the Swachh Bharat Abhiyan launched by Prime Minister Narendra Modi.

Challenges

Change takes time and the mentors and site visits confirmed some challenges that may be difficult to address in the short term. After one year of the intervention, mentors and FRU staff pointed out persistent challenges. These are highlighted further:

FRU leadership: Leadership is a key factor in the ability of the facilities to make improvements and achieve compliance with guidelines. Observations and mentor interviews confirmed that the leadership in some FRUs was very proactive and embraced the concepts of quality improvement and were supportive of the mentors' assistance. In other FRUs, the CMOs were ambivalent about wanting to make improvements or did not act on the recommendations articulated in the action plans. Some mentors expressed frustration at their inability to bring about improvements when the FRU leadership or staff were engaging in corrupt practices. Turnover among CMOs is also common and the mentoring team would need to build relationships each time there was a leadership change.

Lack of specialists: One characteristic common across all FRUs was the dearth of specialists in the facilities. FRUs are expected to have 24×7 coverage by obstetricians, anaesthetists and paediatricians (or at least MOs with supplemental training to perform C-sections) to provide EmONC. Very few FRUs meet this guideline. Among the 16 FRUs included in this intervention, none had the required number of specialists.

Staff shortages: Beyond specialists many FRUs do not have the required number of nurses or other positions as well. For example, one FRU had 58 sanctioned posts but only 19 staff. Staffing levels ran the gamut among the 16 FRUs. The two largest FRUs (DHs in Bijapur and Bagalkot) had 74 and 89 total SNs while at the other extreme some FRUs had just 9 nurses in the entire facility.

Lack of water and sanitation: Basic infrastructure such as water and sanitation is not available in some of the FRUs. Some facilities lack running water and must fill plastic barrels to have access to water in the labour room. Many facilities had no public toilets or drinking water available for patients or visitors. In some cases, the DCS was able to advocate that these larger infrastructure issues be taken up through reactivating the ARS.

Inadequate space and layout of facilities: Beyond the basic requirements of water and sanitation, the facilities designated as FRUs are not necessarily well designed to meet the guidelines called for by the government. FRU teams attempted to reorganize space to designate special rooms as per MNH guidelines for level-three facilities. The functionality of these rooms was uneven among facilities. Many of the labour rooms observed were small with multiple beds and limited or no provision for privacy. The labour room and newborn care corner were the most likely units to be compliant with guidelines.

What data has to say

Monitoring and evaluation data indicated improvements in FRU readiness to deal with emergency obstetric and neonatal care in many areas. Increase was evident in monitoring cervical dilatation and blood pressure (BP) monitoring. FRU SNs recorded substantially improved postpartum monitoring and recording of key indicators. Recording of newborn immunizations increased to over 78% among audited cases.

Direct observation of delivery was used to measure actual practice of provider and compliance to protocols (Figures 2a.6–2a.8).

Scalability and sustainability

The Sukshema project's tools and approaches have been adopted by Karnataka, Uttar Pradesh and other regions. Additionally, elements of the mentoring programme are being incorporated in recent GoI guidelines that call for the establishment of skill labs and training of NMs to provide on-site mentoring support to trained staff in maternal and newborn care. The most recent national quality assurance guidelines also include aspects of setting up quality improvement committees within facilities and use of self-assessment and action planning for addressing systems gaps of the same approaches that we found useful in the mentoring intervention. These developments are timely and acknowledge the need for quality improvement processes and on-site support in enhancing provider skills and performance and, ultimately, health outcomes. Growing recognition among India's health experts on the need for strengthening the capacities of nurses and midwives through ongoing support and mentorship and a focus on quality improvement offers promise for sustaining these interventions within the existing government health system.

Voices from FRU staff

In informal interviews, FRU staff expressed strong appreciation for the mentoring programme. They welcomed the mentors the need for quality improvement processes and skills they imparted.

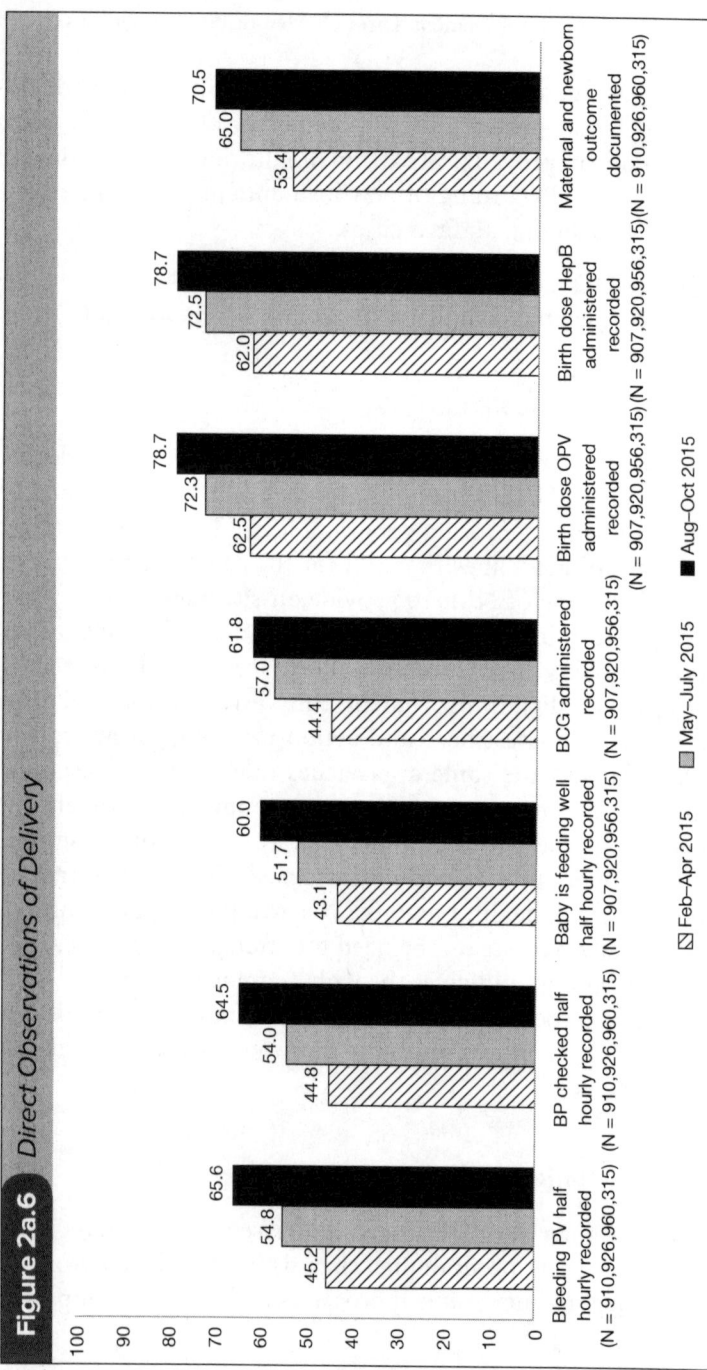

Figure 2a.6 Direct Observations of Delivery

Bleeding PV half hourly recorded (N = 910,926,960,315)
- Feb–Apr 2015: 45.2
- May–July 2015: 54.8
- Aug–Oct 2015: 65.6

BP checked half hourly recorded (N = 910,926,960,315)
- Feb–Apr 2015: 44.8
- May–July 2015: 54.0
- Aug–Oct 2015: 64.5

Baby is feeding well half hourly recorded (N = 907,920,956,315)
- Feb–Apr 2015: 43.1
- May–July 2015: 51.7
- Aug–Oct 2015: 60.0

BCG administered recorded (N = 907,920,956,315)
- Feb–Apr 2015: 44.4
- May–July 2015: 57.0
- Aug–Oct 2015: 61.8

Birth dose OPV administered recorded (N = 907,920,956,315)
- Feb–Apr 2015: 62.5
- May–July 2015: 72.3
- Aug–Oct 2015: 78.7

Birth dose HepB administered recorded (N = 907,920,956,315)
- Feb–Apr 2015: 62.0
- May–July 2015: 72.5
- Aug–Oct 2015: 78.7

Maternal and newborn outcome documented (N = 910,926,960,315)
- Feb–Apr 2015: 53.4
- May–July 2015: 65.0
- Aug–Oct 2015: 70.5

Feb–Apr 2015   May–July 2015   Aug–Oct 2015

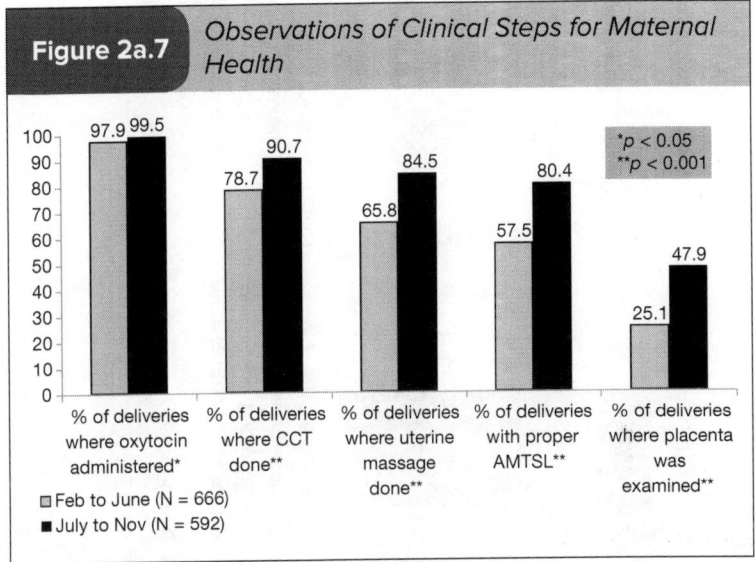

Figure 2a.7 *Observations of Clinical Steps for Maternal Health*

One CMO noted, 'Mentors are doing their job nicely.' Training and re-training are needed and mentors provide this.

Nurses at one FRU explained, 'The value of mentoring is the hands-on guidance mentors provide. They do not find fault. They observe and they advise'. They shared that 'Mentors can have friendship bond with nurses'. These nurses indicated that they had learned a lot from mentors and mentioned topics such as PPH, PIH and baby care. While all the SNs had been trained in SBA, NSSK and IMNCI, they explained, 'In training only lectures are given while here practically we do these skills with the nurse mentors to support us'. The nurses seemed eager and willing learners. As evidence, they shared how they call the NMs between visits when they have questions or need guidance. FRU leadership and specialists appreciated that their staff were getting this support. As one CMO (a surgeon) mentioned, 'Mentors have trained up nurses and now labour room is taken care of'.

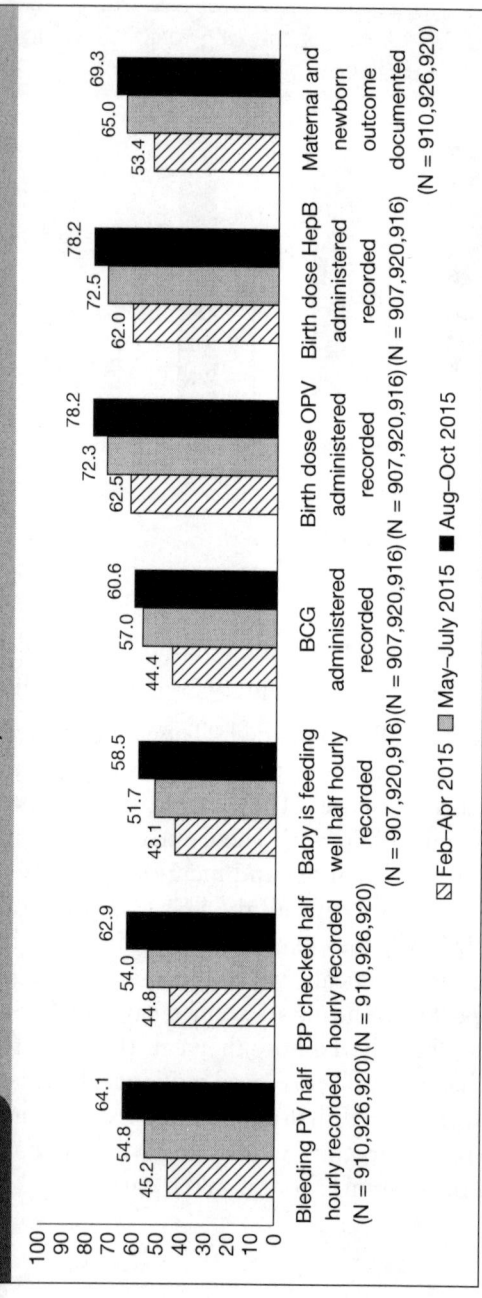

Figure 2a.8 *Observations of Clinical Steps for Newborn Health*

Bleeding PV half hourly recorded (N = 910,926,920)
- Feb–Apr 2015: 45.2
- May–July 2015: 54.8
- Aug–Oct 2015: 64.1

BP checked half hourly recorded (N = 910,926,920)
- Feb–Apr 2015: 44.8
- May–July 2015: 54.0
- Aug–Oct 2015: 62.9

Baby is feeding well half hourly recorded (N = 907,920,916)
- Feb–Apr 2015: 43.1
- May–July 2015: 51.7
- Aug–Oct 2015: 58.5

BCG administered recorded (N = 907,920,916)
- Feb–Apr 2015: 44.4
- May–July 2015: 57.0
- Aug–Oct 2015: 60.6

Birth dose OPV administered recorded (N = 907,920,916)
- Feb–Apr 2015: 62.5
- May–July 2015: 72.3
- Aug–Oct 2015: 78.2

Birth dose HepB administered recorded (N = 907,920,916)
- Feb–Apr 2015: 62.0
- May–July 2015: 72.5
- Aug–Oct 2015: 78.2

Maternal and newborn outcome documented (N = 910,926,920)
- Feb–Apr 2015: 53.4
- May–July 2015: 65.0
- Aug–Oct 2015: 69.3

Legend: ▨ Feb–Apr 2015 ▨ May–July 2015 ■ Aug–Oct 2015

Case Study 2B: The Uttar Pradesh Experience

In November 2013, the UoM entered into a contract with the BMGF to establish and manage the technical support unit (TSU) embedded within the Government of Uttar Pradesh (GoUP) and its NHM. The TSU is being largely implemented by UoM's India-based partner, the India Health Action Trust (IHAT). The newly established TSU's goal is to support the government to increase the efficiency, effectiveness and equity of its execution vis-à-vis the three platforms identified in the Foundation's ICO (India Country Office) strategy for integrated delivery: the government, the private sector and communities. On-site nurse-mentoring intervention was one of the key interventions that aimed at improving quality of MNCH services in the facilities of UP TSU focused districts.

The nurse-mentoring programme in UP was aligned with the Karnataka model with respect to quality improvement approach, principles, tools and measurement design and so on. However, the programme was adapted to suit the local requirements. For example, unlike in Karnataka, the UP facilities had overwhelming systems gaps in terms of poor availability of delivery points for the population catchment areas, poor availability of critical MNCH services in the existing delivery points. Hence, the mentors and the project staff also focused on activation of delivery points and activation of MNCH services in the facilities alongside quality-improvement work (Figure 2b.1).

The scale was much larger compared to Karnataka; the UP TSU covered 100 priority blocks across 25 HPDs. One hundred fifty NMs were recruited and trained to support close to 400 delivery points. The NM was based out of the block PHC/CHC for close to 7 days a month; here she also set up a mini skill lab for training the SNs and ANMs from the block. In the remaining three weeks, she visited the other facilities and the VHNDs where she mentored the ANMs and ASHAs in screening and management of high-risk pregnancies.

Figure 2b.1 Model for Provision of Quality Adolescent Care in UP

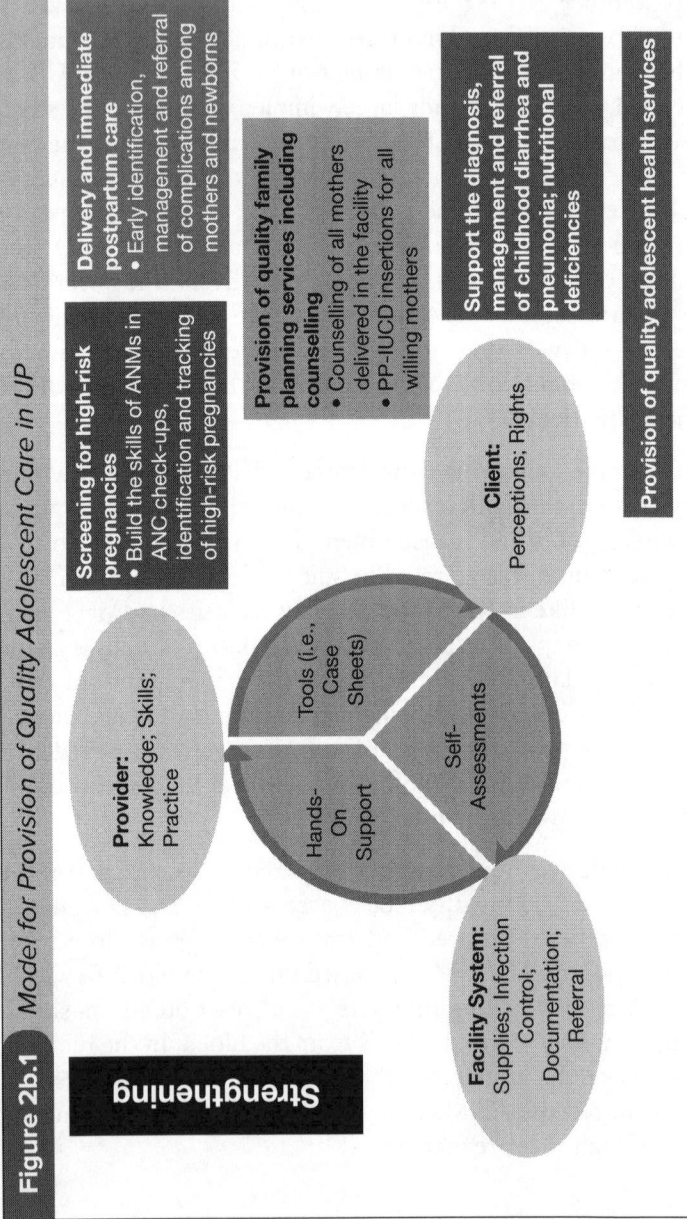

Strengthening

Screening for high-risk pregnancies
- Build the skills of ANMs in ANC check-ups, identification and tracking of high-risk pregnancies

Delivery and immediate postpartum care
- Early identification, management and referral of complications among mothers and newborns

Provision of quality family planning services including counselling
- Counselling of all mothers delivered in the facility
- PP-IUCD insertions for all willing mothers

Support the diagnosis, management and referral of childhood diarrhea and pneumonia; nutritional deficiencies

Provision of quality adolescent health services

Provider: Knowledge; Skills; Practice

Client: Perceptions; Rights

Facility System: Supplies; Infection Control; Documentation; Referral

Tools (i.e., Case Sheets)

Hands-On Support

Self-Assessments

With over two years of implementation on the ground, the GoUP has come forward to adopt the nurse-mentoring programme across all the 75 districts. The project is in discussion with the GoUP to scale up nurse mentoring across the state through using the senior SNs from within the system as mentors.

3

Interventions to Improve Utilization and Coverage

Evidence shows that to improve MNCH and reduce morbidity and mortality, efforts should focus on building capacities at individual, family and community levels to ensure appropriate self-care, prevention and care-seeking behaviour. In limited resource settings, community-level interventions can address this, since care-seeking behaviour is strongly influenced by the sociocultural environment.

The community interventions are designed specifically to enhance participation of community-level structures in supporting and monitoring the utilization and coverage of MNCH services using a continuum-of-care approach. This approach is globally viewed as a core principle for MNCH programmes as a means to reduce the burden of maternal, neonatal and child deaths. It promotes care for mothers and children from pregnancy to delivery, the immediate postnatal period and through the childhood. It recognizes that safe childbirth is critical to both maternal and newborn health and that a healthy start in life is an essential step towards a sound childhood and productive life. However, for such an approach to be successful, it needs to be linked to enhancing demand creation at community level, improving outreach services to promote good family care and care-seeking practices and strengthening linkages with primary health care services.

This is in line with the GoI NRHM whose main objectives are to reduce maternal and infant mortality rates through community-based strategies such as improving community access to health care by providing key MNCH services and building the capacity of community-based health workers called ASHAs who provide community outreach services and who serve as the first point of contact between communities and health facilities.

However, there needs to be a shift in viewing communities not just as 'recipients of services designed for their benefit' but as 'being active makers and shapers of services, exercising their preferences as consumers and their rights as citizens'.[1] In other words, communities are often passive recipients of government programmes and are not active in advocating for their rights to quality services or even know what to expect from government programmes. For example, one of the gaps identified by the NRHM is that communities are not aware of the role of ASHAs and do not know what to expect from this community-based volunteer. On the flip side, ASHAs report that they sometimes struggle to find acceptance in the community and to be seen as a credible source of information and support. Strengthening community accountability is promoted as a right in itself and to enhance quality of care, appropriateness of health service delivery for users and patient satisfaction and utilization.[2] Engaging the community in planning and monitoring health service delivery is central to enhancing the availability, accessibility, quality and use of the public health system.

The NRHM has positioned community ownership as central to its strategy, primarily through the VHSNCs. These are village-level bodies comprising key stakeholders in a village and serve as a forum for village planning and monitoring. VHSNCs were formed to ensure that no section of the village community is excluded from services, to prepare a village health plan to suit local realities and necessities, to provide monitoring and oversight

[1] Z. A. Bhutta, T. Ahmed, R. E. Black, et al., 'What Works? Interventions for Maternal and Child Under Nutrition and Survival,' *Lancet* 2008; 371, no. 9610 (2008): 417–440.

[2] H. Standing, *Understanding the 'Demand Side' in Service Delivery: Definitions, Frameworks and Tools from the Health Sector*. London: DFID Health Systems Resource Centre, 2004.

to all village health activities and to ensure that untied funds are appropriately used for improving maternal and neonatal health in the village.

In this chapter, the focus is on improving efficiency of FLWs—to change key behaviours in the households and for increasing utilization of services—and on improving community structures for monitoring and improving the accountability of the health system. The chapter starts with the current status of community behaviours and utilization of services as well as the current gaps in the capabilities of FLWs and community structures. Then interventions are suggested to enhance FLW performance—providing supportive supervision through community resource persons (CRPs) and block community supervisors (BCSs), developing job aids and methods and so on. It concludes with interventions to enhance community accountability mechanisms—VHSNC training and community-based monitoring tools.

Situational Analysis

Qualitative studies[3,4] conducted in Karnataka have revealed several deep-seated cultural beliefs around pregnancy and childbirth, women's lack of decision-making authority in key decisions around pregnancy and childbirth, low awareness/knowledge around immediate and exclusive breastfeeding and limited utilization of government schemes.

Women's lack of decision-making authority: The study revealed that the woman's family (her husband, her mother/grandmother and her in-laws) was the key decision maker in issues surrounding pregnancy and childbirth. Decisions around place of delivery,

---

[3] S. Bruce, A. Blanchard, K. Gurav, et al. Preferences for infant delivery site among pregnant women and new mothers in northern Karnataka, India. *BMC Pregnancy and Childbirth* 15 (2015): 49.

[4] A. Blanchard, S. Bruce, K. Jayanna, et al. An exploration of decision-making processes on infant delivery site from the perspective of pregnant women, new mothers, and their families in northern Karnataka, India. *Matern Child Health J* 19, no. 9(2015): 2074–2080.

care of a newborn and even nutrition during pregnancy and lactation were either made, or heavily influenced, by a pregnant woman's family.

Cultural beliefs around pregnancy and childbirth: The study identified several cultural beliefs around pregnancy and childbirth that could adversely affect the pregnant woman and her newborn. A number of cultural beliefs exist around nutrition during pregnancy, such as avoiding iron-rich non-vegetarian foods (meat, chicken and eggs) during pregnancy because they are 'hot foods'; avoiding sour and salty foods because they may cause excessive phlegm production; using particular herbs or foods to prevent infections and to reduce 'expansion of stomach'.

Lack of knowledge on immediate and exclusive breastfeeding: Many believed that colostrum was 'bad' for a newborn and a mother had to wait for a day or two until her milk 'comes in' before breastfeeding her baby. Some even reported that their doctors advised them to do so. Among them, there were such who believed that colostrum was bad for newborns, and many reported feeding newborns several pre-lacteal supplements such as cow's milk, herbal drinks and sugar water.

Limited utilization of government schemes: The study showed that while most respondents were aware of the government incentives and schemes around pregnancy and childcare, many reported not receiving any because of a number of reasons. An important reason for this was that they did not deliver at a government health facility or delivered at home and thus could not avail the incentives associated with public institutional delivery. Although many reported that cost was a major prohibitive factor in delivering at private hospitals, respondents felt that the additional costs were worth it since they perceived quality of care and the facilities themselves to be superior at private compared to that in government hospitals. Another drawback to choosing to deliver at home or at private hospitals could be that ASHAs and AWWs are unable to assist those families who are eligible to receive incentives but do not access government health care services, since all FLWs are linked to government facilities.

The evidence stresses the importance of designing community interventions that address these gaps in knowledge and shape demand for facility delivery as well as the need for communication messages that are family centric versus woman centric.

Findings from community-based interventions to improve MNCH outcomes

Home-based care of newborns: Indian studies

There are several publications on the SEARCH (Society for Education, Action and Research in Community Health), Gadchiroli field trials that assessed the effects of an HBNC package on neonatal and perinatal mortality in rural Gadchiroli in India. The package of interventions had a combination of both primary and secondary prevention interventions. The primary intervention focused on influencing mother's and caretakers' behaviours and the secondary intervention directly addressed management of sick newborn babies. The interventions were delivered to the communities through a cadre of village health workers trained in neonatal care who made home visits and managed birth asphyxia, pneumonia, premature birth or LBW, hypothermia and breastfeeding problems. They diagnosed and treated neonatal sepsis and pneumonia. Assistance by trained traditional birth attendants, health education and regular supervisory visits were also provided. The trials showed large reductions in neonatal and perinatal mortality rates and sustained gains at the end of the seven-year trial.

Similar reductions in neonatal mortality rates were observed in the rural communities of Shivgarh, UP in those homes receiving postnatal home visits along with a preventive package of interventions for ENC.

Other community-based interventions

Studies in Guatemala, Bangladesh, Pakistan and Kenya confirm that community-based interventions can positively influence MNCH outcomes, particularly with accompanied referral to nearby health facilities. The Kenyan study evaluated the effectiveness of the community health strategy in delivering community-based maternal and newborn care interventions as a means of influencing the adoption of essential maternal and newborn care practices among mothers with children aged 0–23 months. The results showed significant changes in ANC attendance, skilled deliveries and exclusive breastfeeding.

In summary, the findings from the evidence review suggest that the community interventions should include components focused on delivering maternal and newborn care interventions by means of community outreach via trained community health workers and timely referrals to available health services.

There is a need to focus on critical gaps in awareness, coverage and utilization of MNCH services and enhancing outreach practices for FLWs:

Coverage: Available data indicates that the coverage of target populations for MNCH services is poor and inequitable—there are unreached populations for many services, and those who are reached do not receive a complete package of services through the continuum of care from antenatal to newborn care.[5] Vulnerable populations, such as those belonging to SC/ST as well as migrants, seem to be left out of the registers maintained at the SCs. While the proportion of institutional deliveries has risen in recent years, only a small proportion of mothers stay for 48 hours after delivery in facilities.

Awareness: Currently, there is a lack of awareness in the community on healthy practices and available services for the mothers and newborns through the continuum of care. Often, existing cultural practices and beliefs, and poorly informed decisions, become barriers to access MNCH services. The ASHAs, being members from the neighbourhood, are the community resources to facilitate a positive change in awareness and practices around MCH through the continuum of care. Although ASHAs undergo

---

[5] NFHS, 2014, GoI; DLHS, 2012, GoI.

a fairly comprehensive initial training on roles and responsibilities, in practice, the training focus has been on referrals, or
bringing people to services—particularly for institutional delivery.
There has been very little emphasis and expectation from them as
'change agents' in influencing awareness and practices related to
critical MNCH services. There are no user-friendly interpersonal
communication materials and job-aids to facilitate ASHAs in
functioning as change agents.

There also is a need to focus on key MNCH issues that the
ASHAs need to emphasize while working with the community
to improve their awareness and practices. Similarly, AWWs
have been working on components related to nutrition during
pregnancy (anaemia) and childhood (exclusive breastfeeding
and timely complementary feeding). However, they lack effective communication skills, tools and job-aids to effectively bring
about positive changes in the awareness and practices around
nutrition issues.

PNC gaps: The first days following delivery are when women
and newborns are at greatest risk, yet it is often during this time
that the system breaks down. Due to constraints of workload
and travel, JHAs are not able to make timely PNC visits in the
community. One of ASHAs' roles is to visit mothers and newborns in their homes, yet many ASHAs do not know what they
are supposed to do during postnatal visits. According to the
national guidelines, the ASHA is supposed to weigh the newborn
as well as conduct a health check-up during each of these visits
and counsel on danger signs, if any, for mothers and newborns.
Despite PNC visits being incentivized for ASHAs, many recently
delivered women do not receive PNC visits from ASHAs and the
quality of those visits is often lacking.

Lack of simple and user-friendly tools for FLWs: The FLWs lacked
simple and user-friendly tools to be able to plan contacts and service delivery for their populations. The various registers used by
FLWs fulfilled the purpose of reporting and not really planning.

Designing Community-based Interventions

In order to address the aforementioned gaps, the various community interventions should target the FLW and community structures. The package of interventions will comprise tools, processes and support systems towards achieving the following objectives of community interventions:

1. To increase *the frequency and quality of interactions* between beneficiaries and FLWs
2. To ensure that all pregnant and postpartum women, newborns and infants *enter* into MNCH care continuum
3. To ensure that all pregnant and postpartum women, newborns and infants *continue* in MNCH care continuum
4. Enhance participation of community-level structures in *supporting and monitoring* the utilization and coverage of MNCH services

These objectives can then translate into improved utilization and coverage of the communities for critical MNCH services. The aforementioned objectives of community interventions can be achieved through broadly two strategies:

A. Improving management and delivery of outreach services and shaping demand: This requires a set of tools and job aids that equip FLWs (ASHAs, AWWs and JHAs) with competencies to improve the coverage for routine maternal and newborn services particularly for the SC/ST population and poor families, help them become better communicators with families about the importance of availing MNCH services and adopting healthy practices for pregnant women and newborns and help them screen, identify and refer danger signs, especially during the critical postnatal period. The tools include:

1. Family-focused communication (FFC) tools and materials to use along with families in order to influence awareness

and practices to support pregnant women and newborns; thus the focus of FLWs is the entire family, particularly the key decision-makers instead of only the women.

2. ETT/community demand list (CDL) for ASHAs to improve planning and coverage; this tool assists the ASHAs to prepare line list of her beneficiaries to be contacted during the month thus helping her to plan and prioritize her contacts. The list also assists her to get a snapshot of all her beneficiaries across the MNCH care continuum, thus helping her achieve better coverage of community for MNCH services.

3. An integrated maternal and newborn management tool (home-based maternal and newborn care [HBMNC]) to improve identification and actions for postnatal danger signs; this tool functions as a job aid to guide ASHAs in screen women/newborn comprehensively through a comprehensive history and examination during her home-visits.

B. Strengthening accountability: The following tools and methods are required to increase the capacity of the community structures to positively contribute to MNCH outcomes:

1. Supportive community monitoring tools (SCMTs) for VHSCs and ARSs: These tools are used by the VHSCs along with front-line workers on a regular basis to assess the overall health situation in the village, gaps in service provision and coverage. Through a consultative process, the reasons for gaps are explored and solutions discussed. The involvement of larger community in the health programmes is ensured and hence greater accountability and ownership of MNCH outcomes.

2. SC forum (Arogya Mantapa): The platform helps to bring the three FLWs together with an objective of forming a strong workforce and team to jointly address complex challenges faced on the ground.

Support systems for implementing community-based interventions

In order to ensure that the tools and processes are implemented effectively by the FLWs and VHSCs, a strong capacity building and support system is critical. Particularly, the scale of the community interventions needs to be considered while designing a project management and support system.

Trainings: The trainings for FLWs should focus on skills and competencies related to the roles (outreach, communication, service provision, community mobilizer and so on) and more importantly the aspects that empower and enable effective functioning (local cultural context, gender, caste and other structure-related inequities, soft skills such as communication, teamwork and problem-solving, use of tools and job aids while at work and so on). A TOT approach with an objective of creating a resource pool of trainers at district level will help in achieving the scale faster. Using peers as trainers and resource pool can go a long way in maximizing the impact of the trainings.

Mentoring support: While the trainings will help to inspire and instil confidence in the FLWs, the issues on the ground, particularly that relate to structural factors, can dampen their confidence. Use of the resource pool to support the FLWs on the field through regular review meetings can be helpful. These meetings help to take stock of the progress, identify challenges and solve problems and to build capacities of FLWs in the emerging areas.

Facilitating support from the VHSCs: The VHSC meetings will need hand-holding in the beginning to enable them to function supportively. Building a strong team of FLWs and VHSC members through appropriate capacity building and facilitation will help to gain long-term benefits for the village.

Monitoring and evaluation of community-based interventions

Since the community-based interventions involves rich processes and interactions between various stakeholders, the M&E systems should be well balanced to capture the critical process alongside critical outputs and outcomes.

Coverage of FLW trainings, home visits and use of tools need to be supported and monitored that help to get the interventions on the ground. Correct application of tools (that is, ETTs) and its translation into changes in coverage are critical indicators to be monitored regularly. The problems and gaps identified need to be solved at the earliest through appropriate support on the field or through refresher trainings. If the coverage gaps are due to resistant families/cultural norms, the same can be escalated to the level of SC platforms or VHSC forums to mobilize the support of other stakeholders. The ETT summaries help to monitor coverage of beneficiaries across the MNCH care continuum and hence can be a vital part of routine monitoring system. As the coverage gaps assist FLWs in planning outreach, the availability and use of the monitoring data in real-time planning should be systematized.

Community behaviour tracking surveys (CBTSs) that are regularly conducted or sample surveys of households can give rich information about the community behaviours and coverage at population level. This essentially gives an indication if the interventions are aligned towards achieving population-level impact, which are the desired goals of the large-scale MNCH projects. More details relating to M&E of community interventions can be found in the chapter on data management.

Conclusions

The details in the current chapter draws extensively from the available evidence and direct experience of implementing large-scale community interventions in Karnataka and UP. The case studies pertaining to the experiences in these two states are described as case studies in the subsequent sections of this chapter.

Case Study 3A: Experiences from Karnataka

The Sukshema Project focused on improving the availability, accessibility, quality, utilization and coverage of MNCH services. An important component of the project is to promote evidence-based decision-making at the district level in accordance with state and national guidelines. The project hoped that as data was made available and used for district-level decision-making to increase availability and accessibility of quality MNCH services, it would ultimately resulting in increased utilization and improved health outcomes.

The project adopted the following strategies for FLW support:

- Field test the methods and tools in two districts
- Support the FLWs through a new cadre of RPs
- Leverage the support from the government departments for rolling out the trainings in tools and methods
- Timely and regular review of the interventions' impact on key indicators towards improvement of MNCH
- Scale up the tools and methods to other districts based on the learning in two districts

The following steps were used for the design and implementation of FLW mentoring programme:

Developing of tools and methods

The major role of RPs in the project was to supervise and provide hand-holding support to ASHAs. RPs are provided with a number of supportive supervision and monitoring tools to guide their work.

- **RP analysis format:** This is an SC-level tool that RPs fill out each month. The tool has several key MNCH indicators that RPs track each month as well as a section for gap analyses.
- **SCMT hand-holding checklist:** This is a checklist for RPs to follow when SCMT/VHSNC meetings are conducted. RPs grade the meetings based on performance, using indicators such as adequately filling SCMT, member participation and functioning effectively without RP assistance.
- **ANM hand-holding checklist:** This checklist helps RPs assess AM meetings using indicators such as attendance by all members, gap analyses carried out at AM meeting, preparing monthly action plans and so on.
- **HBMNC checklist:** This checklist helps RPs assess the quality of interaction between an ASHA and her client (in this case, a pregnant or a postpartum woman) using indicators such as using appropriate counselling messages and tools, effective communication skills and scheduling follow-up visits.
- **RP reporting format:** This is a consolidated reporting tool for the RP to refer to as needed. It has five forms that need to be filled out by RPs:
  1. Day-to-day hand-holding reporting format
  2. Monthly ASHA grading format
  3. RP monthly hand-holding reporting format (abstracted version)
  4. SC-wise monthly progress format
  5. PHC convergence meeting report

As mentioned previously, providing hand-holding support to ASHAs was the main role of the RPs. They help build the capacity of ASHAs with on-the-job training. They use the checklists as guides to help them grade ASHAs based on their ability to adequately fill out the tools and to know what and who to focus on during the hand-holding process.

ASHA Diary

One of the problems ASHAs were facing in the field was maintenance of multiple registers. The Sukshema Project was able to solve this problem for ASHAs by developing the ASHA Diary and providing training on its usage. The purpose of ASHA Diary is to provide a comprehensive record for ASHAs that would encompass the ETT/CDL tools in addition to other relevant job aids and tools. It encompasses a daily activity record, monthly calendar with important days marked, a set of pictures for communicating key messages regarding care during ANC, delivery and PNC periods, contact numbers of key officials, tools for planning and tracking beneficiaries, tools for self-review and reflection, MNCH messages that serve as reminders, ASHA incentive list for her claims, expected date of delivery (EDD) calculation calendar as well as tools to record other services she provides such as HIV/TB. The diary serves as a job aid that has proven successful in providing a one-stop solution for most of the issues that the ASHA has been facing in the field. The Diary makes available all related formats for MNCH service delivery and follow up, local ASHA area-level data for reporting and planning, communication material for home visits, monthly calendar for planning activities and other essential information for ASHA both within and outside the MNCH context in a single record (Figure 3a.1).

Recruitment of RPs

In designing the community interventions, a key decision was to determine the profile of RPs. Sukshema's community intervention team created a hiring committee with team leaders. The hiring committee crafted a three-tier hiring strategy to identify the best candidates. Because of the varied skills that RPs need to possess, it was thought that a conventional hiring process of screening CVs and interviewing candidates might not be sufficient to fully assess a candidate's capacities for the position. Also, the project leads need to hire many candidates at once offered opportunities for more creative group-based assessment processes. This process

> **Figure 3a.1** *Cover of ASHA Diary*

is important owing to its priority on appointing local candidates, female candidates and people from backward castes.

More specifically, the hiring team decided the required qualifications of the RPs for initial screening as follows:

- RPs should be above 18 years and below 35 years (for suitable SC/ST candidates).
- The candidate should have a minimum educational qualification of secondary school-leaving certificate (SSLC).
- The candidate should be a resident of a village for the last five years of the district where the RP is employed.
- The candidate should be committed to work in all villages as per programme specifications.

In the second level of screening, the candidates selected in the first level were tested through the structured questionnaire that comprised questions related to a range of topics, including linguistic abilities, personal socio-economic details, emotional details and MNCH topics. Also, information on their participation in social activities within their communities was asked.

In the final level of screening, the selected candidates were invited to attend a two-day workshop that included discussions on rural health management, an exercise involving a group discussion, emotional creative expression tests, oratorical skills tests and team-building and communication tests. Checklists were used by the assessors to aid in objective scoring of the candidates across different competencies.

Training of RPs

The newly recruited RPs engaged in a one-month pre-induction profiling of their respective PHCs (1 RP: 1 PHC). RPs collected information on the number of SCs and ASHAs and engaged in other activities such as planning for training activities, sensitization and relationship building with the MOs and subdistrict health officers. There were several dropouts—initially as well as once roll-out had started. However, since there were two RPs who were shortlisted per cluster there was always an RP available to fill in vacant positions due to dropouts. Three-day induction training was conducted in three rolling batches.

The RPs included the technical leads and managers at the central office, district programme specialists and district M&E specialists. The training method included lectures, group works and role-plays. The training covered the following topics:

- Introduction to project Sukshema—goals, objectives, technical interventions and solution levers
- Maternal, newborn and infant care services during ANC, intrapartum, postpartum and postnatal periods
- Service delivery mechanisms
- Proposed interventions at the community level for the FLWs and community structures

On the last day of the induction training, all RPs were asked to plan for subdistrict-wise FFC based on their training. This is because the FFC intervention was planned strategically by the Sukshema Project to address the gaps seen among the FLWs in the field. For instance, a key gap that FFC aimed to address was that the womenfolk failed to engage with family members while trying to communicate healthy practices and accessing services during the pregnancy and childbirth. In addition to this, the ASHA, JHA and AWW seldom met together to discuss challenges and work together for a common objective.

Training front-line workers

As indicated earlier, one of the important interventions of the Sukshema Project for FLWS is FFC. This intervention comprised of activities to ensure that communication is effective and desired messages are transferred to the beneficiaries. Under this component of the intervention, keeping the woman and her family as focus, behaviour-change communication materials were developed and introduced to the FLWs. Thus, a need was identified for an intensive training that brings all the FLWs together and takes them through a process of critical thinking, reflection and evaluation of issues around MNCH with gender–social perspectives. It is also primarily intended to put into perspective how realities of gender roles, power structures and inequalities shape a woman's behaviours and practices. FFC training also emphasizes the coordination between all the three FLWs—ASHA, AWW and JHA—to avoid duplication of efforts and build an enabling environment where all three of them can work effectively through mutual support towards improving the health of mothers and infants.

The training first established an understanding among women about the social and gender contexts around the issue of MNCH through its initial sessions and moved on to build their communication skills and coordination functions not just as individual workers but as a team that has a common goal—to improve

MNCH. The FFC training was structured in such a way as to facilitate attitudinal changes and dispel individual misconceptions and roadblocks. It was so designed that the FFC training was the first training that all three FLWs attended in order to provide a good foundation for the project to start work. It has a three-day training module in place which addresses sociocultural and gender issues.

FLWs are taken through eight main topics over the course of three days. These are:

1. FFC concept and the need to focus on families
2. Conducting assessments and building communication skills
3. Status of women in society
4. Analysis of gender issues and their impact on MNCH
5. Health services for improving MCH
6. The need for coordination among FLWs
7. Roles and responsibilities of FLWs
8. Attitudes of FLWs

The training specifically focused on enhancing the ASHA's skill of communicating with the woman as well as her family members and trained her to plan her communication messages based on the need and the context within each family. For this purpose, two key FFC materials were developed and used in training by Sukshema—FLW reminder cards and birth-preparedness calendar for pregnant women.

1. Reminder cards could easily be carried and referred by the FLWs during the home visits to remind them about the key messages that need to be conveyed to the woman and her family members during home visits.
2. A birth-preparedness calendar for pregnant women consisting of simple storyline messages on birth planning and emergency preparedness. These calendars were provided to the pregnant women and were used by their household members.

Since the FFC training paved the way for the other interventions to be launched, the following points need to be kept in mind while planning them:

1. All the interventions need to be viewed holistically as a package rather than as individual activities at every stage of implementation.
2. The training sessions need to be linked ensuring that the messages of one session are connected to the session that follows. It is crucial to provide a sense of continuity, since the focus may shift and the outcome may be watered down.
3. Training needs to be followed immediately by hand-holding support so that the learning is immediately translated into actual action on the field.
4. FFC training needs to focus more on changing attitudes and perspectives rather than building FLW skills. Gender and social issues should dominate the content of the trainings.
5. Training methodology is critical for FFC. Participatory approaches and involvement of all the FLWs is essential for its success.
6. Linking the reminder cards to the HBMNC tool is useful in supporting the ASHAs improve the effectiveness of carrying out home visits.

Trainings on community demand list

One of the important task of ASHAs was to meet the community demands. In order to help ASHAs plan better on how to meet the demands, they were trained by the Sukshema Project staff on the guidelines for both the tracking tool and the ETT/CDL. The guideline for tracking tool (CDL 1) has definitions of all the important indicators while that of CDL 2 has information on how to define targets and achievements. The purpose of the guidelines is to maintain uniformity and have a common standard definition for all indicators used in the tools. This ensures that there is a shared common understanding among ASHAs while using the tool for planning and tracking.

The trainings for CDL did not focus on individual tools, rather on the CDL as one entire package with the three tools. For instance, ASHA is trained to record the names of all the women in her area who are either currently pregnant, or have a child under age 18 months, irrespective of whether she is a usual resident of her area or a visitor to her area (for pregnancy/delivery purposes). One row is allocated for one woman. Thus she will have, at any given point of time, about 60 women who are her current target groups (about 20 currently pregnant women, about 20 recently delivered women and about 20 women who have delivered in the previous year).

Every month, ASHAs with the help JHAs and RPs will use CDL to plan their outreach services. This planning will be done by identifying, from the CDL, who is due for what type of service during a given month, based on (1) whether a woman is due for a service as per the prescribed schedule for MNCH service delivery and (2) whether the woman has already received a service due for her in that month. Based on the target as well as the number of women receiving services, the ASHA will fill tool CDL 2 at the end of every month to carry out an assessment of her own performance on key indicators. ASHAs then fill out CDL 3, which is an abstract of CDL-2 and will submit it to the RP during the ASHA meeting that will be conducted on a fixed date of every month. It is important to note that CDL 1 is a visual tool that will help ASHAs list their target population (pregnant women, women who have recently delivered and newborns) in their allotted geographic area in a particular month, and track this population throughout the continuum of care, that is, pregnancy, delivery, 42-day post-delivery and 18 months of immunization of a child. It allows ASHAs to organize outreach information into six broad categories: identification details, antenatal care details, delivery details, PNC details and immunization details. Additionally, the tool has information on the identification details of the ASHA herself—the district, subdistrict, PHC, SC and village names as well as the estimated number of pregnant women in her area as per the community needs assessment (CNA).

Supportive community monitoring tool (SCMT)

As mentioned earlier, SCMT attempts to involve the community through VHSNC in planning and monitoring village health service delivery to realize the community participation and ownership of village health programmes as envisaged in the goals of NHM. It also strengthens community accountability towards village health in general and improved MNCH outcomes in particular, and provides opportunity for FLWs to be supported by the community in their efforts to improve MNCH outcomes (Figure 3a.2).

SCMT is used by seven chosen members: the ASHA worker, the president of the VHSNC, the member secretary, an SC/ST representative, an SG representative, a youth representative and an elderly village opinion creator with social concern at the village level. This is called the SCMT team. SCMT has the scope to bring about collective responsibility among community members in supporting FLWs and ensuring that sociocultural practices that directly and indirectly affect the village health, and more specifically MNCH, are curbed and managed well.

Ownership of tools and training

In order to generate ownership of the tool and its implementation in the Department of Health, TOTs were conducted not only for Sukshema RPs but also for staff from the GoK's Department of Health including senior JHAs, active ASHAs and ASHA mentors. In each subdistrict, the GoK health department staff were identified based on their earlier exposure as RPs for the HBNC training of the department, as mandated by the GoI. In addition to that, the health department staff had very strong clinical/technical knowledge about home-based care which needed to be tapped into for Sukshema's HBMNC training roll-out. The roll-out trainings were conducted at the PHC level by the GoK department staff and facilitated by the Sukshema RPs, with the GoK staff handling a major part of all the technical aspects of

Figure 3a.2 SCMT

Section 1
Services regarding ANC, PNC and Newborn child

Sl. No.		Indicators	Month					
1		ANC registration and distribution of *Thai card*	☺	☺	☺	☺	☺	☺
			☹	☹	☹	☹	☹	☹
2		TT injections	☺	☺	☺	☺	☺	☺
			☹	☹	☹	☹	☹	☹
3		Distribution IFA tablets	☺	☺	☺	☺	☺	☺
			☹	☹	☹	☹	☹	☹
4		ANC visits	☺	☺	☺	☺	☺	☺
			☹	☹	☹	☹	☹	☹
5		Institutional deliveries	☺	☺	☺	☺	☺	☺
			☹	☹	☹	☹	☹	☹
6		PNC visits	☺	☺	☺	☺	☺	☺
			☹	☹	☹	☹	☹	☹
7		Immunization of infants during the month	☺	☺	☺	☺	☺	☺
			☹	☹	☹	☹	☹	☹
8		Family Planning	☺	☺	☺	☺	☺	☺
			☹	☹	☹	☹	☹	☹
9		DOT service for TB	☺	☺	☺	☺	☺	☺
			☹	☹	☹	☹	☹	☹
10		IFA tablet distribution to school going adolescent girls	☺	☺	☺	☺	☺	☺
			☹	☹	☹	☹	☹	☹
Total Number of "smiley" faces ☺								
Total Number of "sad" Faces ☹								

HBMNC. Involving the department of health staff in the trainings and roll-out as the actual trainers, in contrast to the ETT roll-outs where Sukshema RPs were the trainers, created a sense of ownership in the GoK staff and helped make HBMNC implementation less challenging. Both the health system staff (JHA, LHV) and Sukshema RPs conducted the trainings together and this worked well because tapping into the GoK staff's technical skills with respect to home-based care also helped in a smoother roll-out of HBMNC.

Monitoring and evaluation

Community behaviour tracking survey (CBTS): This concurrent mobile phone (GPRS enabled)-based monitoring survey was used by the project to monitor changes in outcomes. ASHAs areas were the primary sampling units. In each district, 200 ASHA areas were selected systematically, and in each ASHA area, the investigator interviewed all women who delivered in last two months prior to the date of survey. Further, you will find data for both pilot districts (Bagalkot and Koppal) and remaining six districts where interventions were subsequently scaled up.

A progressive trend in coverage was observed of many critical indicators related to delivery and postnatal services. ANC check-up was always at a higher level, but substantially increased in the project period in all districts. Proportion of women who stayed for 48 hours after delivery and proportion of women who received all services across continuum improved slowly. What really influenced the change was stay in facility for 48 hours that was dependent on factors related to quality of care within the facility and also the health systems readiness in terms of safety and security, water and food availability, and provisions for accommodating family members. Though the increase in 48-hour stay between round 2 and round 7 in Koppal and between rounds 1 and 5 in other districts was marginal, these were significant, apart from ANC check-ups (Figures 3a.3 and 3a.4).

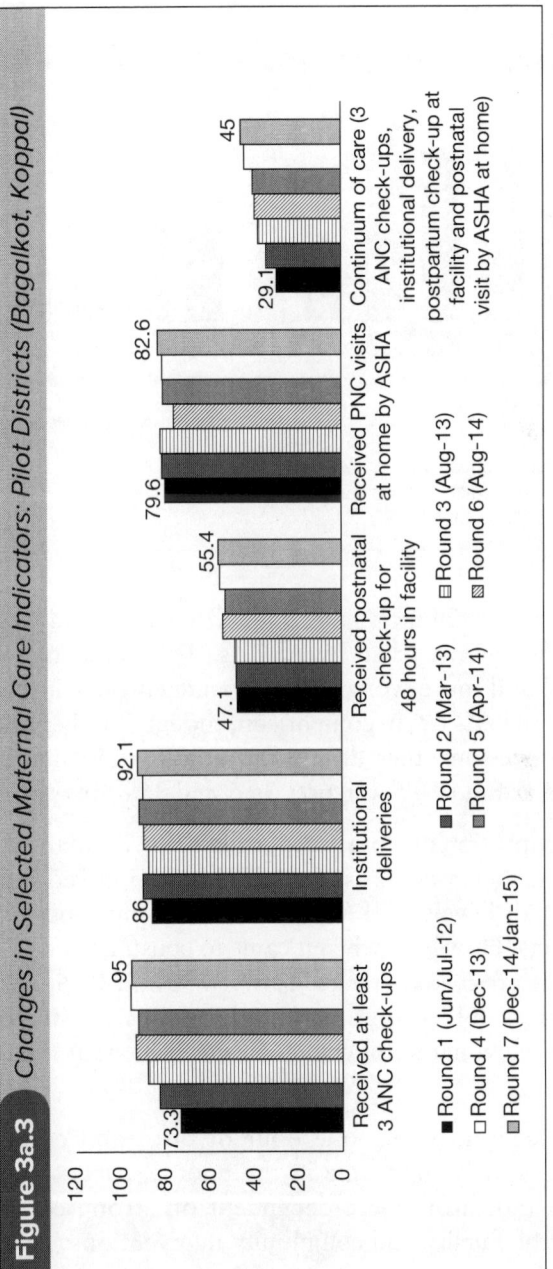

Figure 3a.3 Changes in Selected Maternal Care Indicators: Pilot Districts (Bagalkot, Koppal)

Received at least 3 ANC check-ups: 73.3, 95
Institutional deliveries: 86, 92.1
Received postnatal check-up for 48 hours in facility: 47.1, 55.4
Received PNC visits at home by ASHA: 79.6, 82.6
Continuum of care (3 ANC check-ups, institutional delivery, postpartum check-up at facility and postnatal visit by ASHA at home): 29.1, 45

■ Round 1 (Jun/Jul-12) ■ Round 2 (Mar-13) ▥ Round 3 (Aug-13)
□ Round 4 (Dec-13) ■ Round 5 (Apr-14) ▨ Round 6 (Aug-14)
▥ Round 7 (Dec-14/Jan-15)

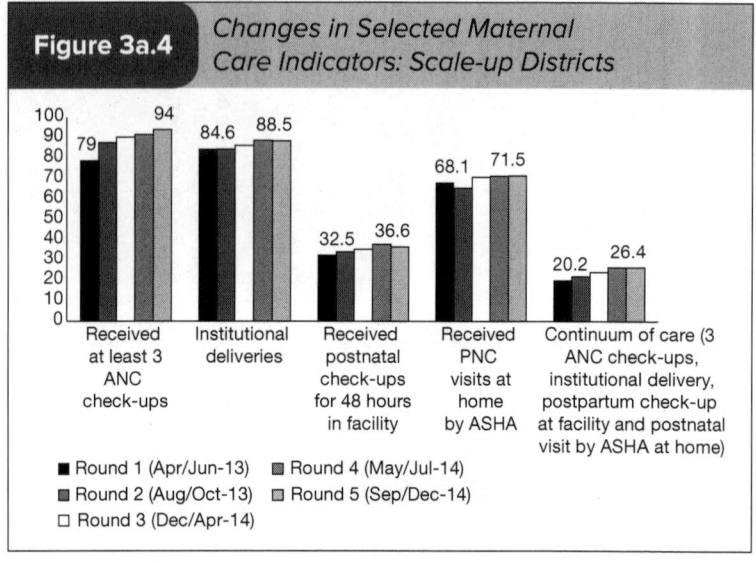

Figure 3a.4 *Changes in Selected Maternal Care Indicators: Scale-up Districts*

In terms of contacts, the pilot districts already had close to 90% women reached by ASHAs. The number of contacts increased and more women were contacted early in their pregnancy by the ASHA. In comparison, though number of contacts had improved in other districts, contact within first trimester remained around 50% (Figures 3a.5 and 3a.6).

The proportion of women reporting to have had three or more ANC visits increased. Provision of TT has improved in Bagalkot and Koppal. Levels of IFA distribution was around 90% in all the districts. However, when it came to consumption of 100 IFA tablets, the progression ranged between 30 and 40%. While there was progress in IFA consumption, the levels were still low, indicating the slow nature of change of this behaviour (Figures 3a.7 and 3a.8).

Breastfeeding within one hour of birth and cord hygiene improved slowly over time in the pilot districts significantly. Both the indicators were dependent on strong coordination between the facility and community interventions (Figures 3a.9 and 3a.10).

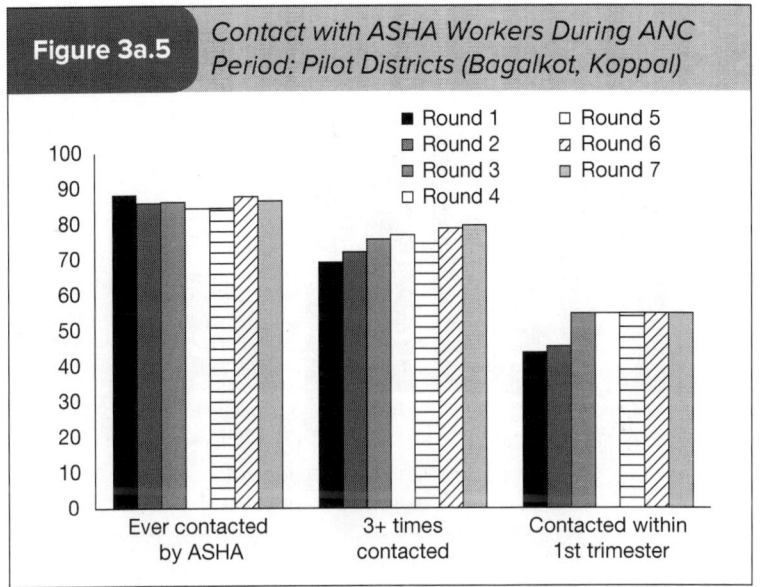

Figure 3a.5 Contact with ASHA Workers During ANC Period: Pilot Districts (Bagalkot, Koppal)

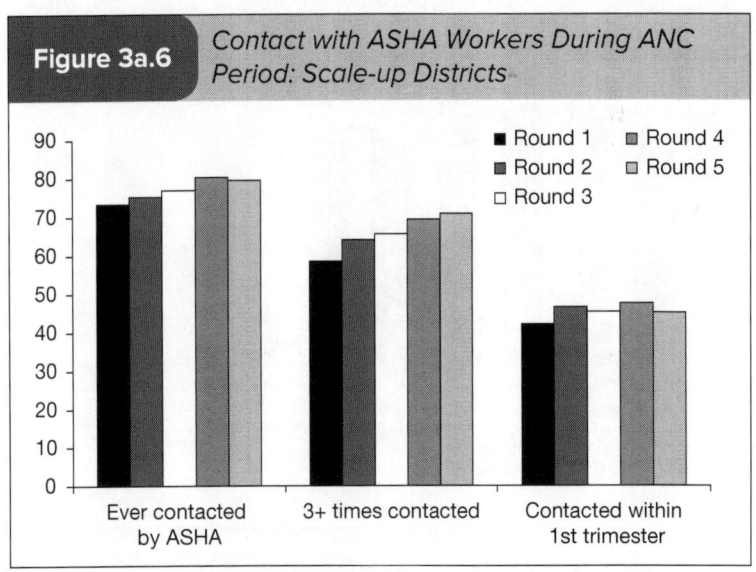

Figure 3a.6 Contact with ASHA Workers During ANC Period: Scale-up Districts

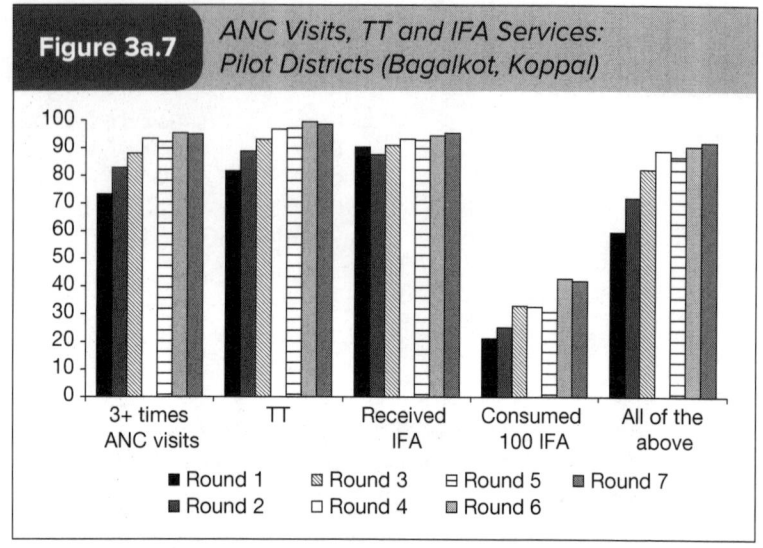

Figure 3a.7   ANC Visits, TT and IFA Services:
Pilot Districts (Bagalkot, Koppal)

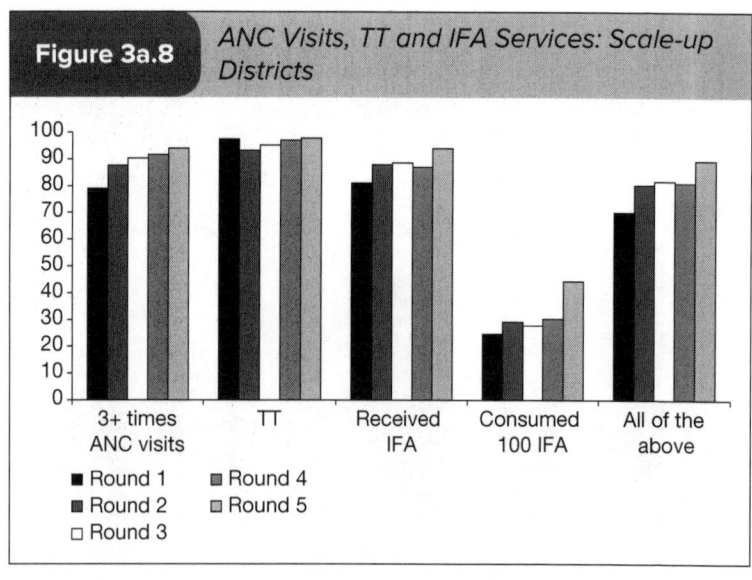

Figure 3a.8   ANC Visits, TT and IFA Services: Scale-up
Districts

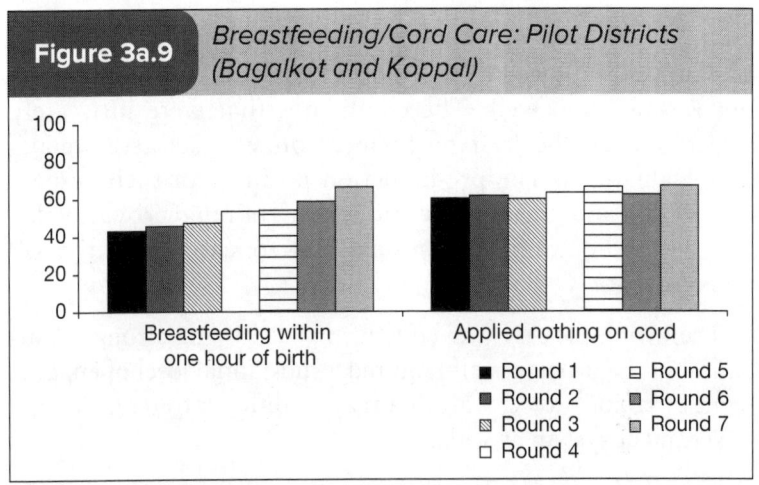

Figure 3a.9 *Breastfeeding/Cord Care: Pilot Districts (Bagalkot and Koppal)*

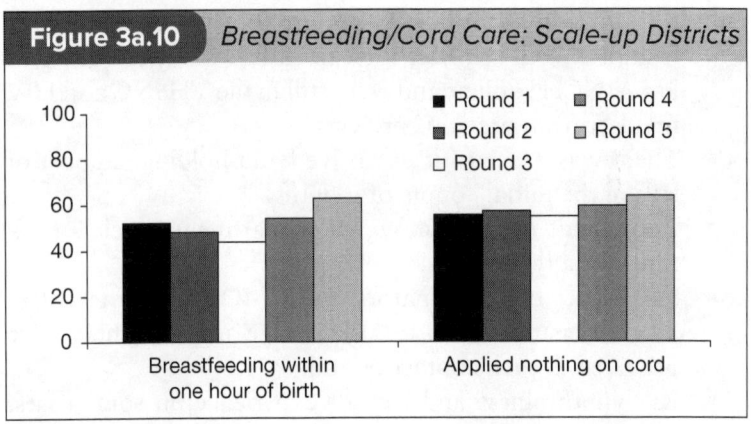

Figure 3a.10 *Breastfeeding/Cord Care: Scale-up Districts*

Challenges faced

The process followed by Sukshema for identifying and recruiting RPs worked well. The candidates that were ultimately selected were the best performers on various assessments and evaluations. The pre-induction profiling of their respective PHCs and their 5-day induction training proved valuable as candidates had additional time to learn about the job responsibilities.

The hiring process was effective in identifying strong candidates but the process itself required a substantial level of engagement of senior project staff that may be difficult to replicate in a government system at scale.

However, some of the challenges that were faced by the RPs are as follows:

- Initially, the transition from a community mobilization approach in the VHSNC project to a technical support task of MNCH project took time. RPs had poor grasp of key MNCH content and were still in the VHSNC and HIV mindset from previous projects.
- There was a need for extensive hand-holding support of RPs in the initial couple of months.
- Acceptance of RPs among the department officials took time initially.
- Subdistrict co-coordinators and CMOs had to translate all abbreviations into local language and refreshers were provided at each contact period.
- RPs youthfulness and lack of experience, in some cases, posed a challenge to their ability to establish credibility with the FLWs and more experienced PHC staff.
- Specific behaviours and practices such as breastfeeding and cord care continued to pose as challenges that needed more in-depth exploration and formative research to identify barriers.

Scalability and sustainability

By and large, the community interventions showed promise in improving utilization and coverage of critical RMNCH services in high priority districts of Karnataka. GoK scaled up front-line workers tools and processes as well as community monitoring interventions in the rest of the state. ASHA Diary, which was a consolidation of 13 different registers and greatly helped ASHAs in planning her work, was a great success story that was replicated in other high priority regions in India such as UP.

Case Study 3B: Experiences from Uttar Pradesh

In November 2013, the University of Manitoba (UoM) entered into a contract with the BMGF to establish and manage the TSU embedded within the GoUP and its NHM. One of the key objectives of the TSU was to improve the performance of front-line workers. The major thrust of TSU's effort was focused on achieving the goal of 'activating' the government system to improve interactions between FLWs and households and communities and improve the quality of care at first level clinics and referral units up to the district level.

Situation analysis

Assessments done in UP indicated that there was a lack of awareness in the community on healthy RMNCH+A practices and available services, and population-based coverage for these interventions was lacking. Available data indicated that the coverage of target populations for RMNCH+A services was poor and inequitable—there are unreached populations for many services, and those who are reached do not receive a complete package of services through the continuum of care from antenatal to newborn care. For instance, as per the AHS of 2012–2013, while 84% of pregnant women received TT injections, fewer than 7%

received the full set of ANC visits. Only 36% of recently delivered mothers were screened for high BP. On the other hand, 78% of recently delivered women received PNC visit within 48 hours of delivery.

Moreover, there was a lack of awareness in the community on healthy practices and available services for the mothers and newborns through the continuum of care. Often, existing cultural practices and beliefs, and insufficiently informed decisions were barriers to accessing RMNCH+A services. Often the practices related to pregnancy, delivery and PNC, as well as the decisions to seek care, were institutionalized within the family. The elders in the family, particularly the mothers-in-law and the mothers, as well as the husband, played an important role in decisions on seeking care as well as in perpetuating unhealthy practices.

There were no tools and methods available for FLWs to map and track pregnant women and children to enable them to monitor and plan outreach for services through the continuum of care. The existing tools for the FLWs did not present an integrated approach to the health of the mother and the baby, nor help her be a change agent to encourage improved RMNCH+A practices in the community. Finally, there was a need for innovative tools that can aid FLWs in screening for danger signs among mothers and newborns and be able to quickly link them to skilled care when needed. ASHAs in UP lack effective planning and monitoring skills. Current documentation methods include multiple registrars that lack cohesion.

Given this scenario, ASHAs needed to be strengthened and supported to be able to identify critical gaps, solve problems and prioritize. An important method to address these issues was to provide ASHAs with the tools that will assist her:

1. In identifying high-risk pregnancies and at-risk newborns.
2. In tracking pregnant women/new mothers and their newborns in her community to ensure that they have received

adequate care and health teaching (including 4 ANC appointments, TT injections, IFA tablets, the appropriate screenings, newborn care, immunizations, teaching on breastfeeding, the recognition of danger signs, etc.).
3. In organizing registrars so that women and newborns can be followed in a continuous and precise manner.
4. In creating action plans for her community.

Intervention approach

The approach adopted was to provide technical support to the NHM, the district health systems and the Department of Women & Child Development to develop and implement enhanced training programmes for front-line workers, implement improved field level processes such as enumeration and tracking, and develop systems for peer-to-peer learning and supportive supervision. The intent was for these systems to be implemented by the state NHM, with technical support at the state, district and block levels from the TSU. Since most FLWs have already been recruited and have received basic training in the state, quality improvements in their work was of focus.

In addition to shaping demand, the project also worked closely with the NHM and allied systems to improve the quality of RMNCH+A service delivery by FLWs. The focus was on the quantity and quality (content, format) of interactions between FLWs (e.g., ASHAs, AWWs and ANMs), and women and their families, through enhanced training and job-based supports (including ETTs and job aids). The TSU also supported the GoUP at block, district and state levels to recruit and train an adequate number of FLWs per population and geography, as per GOI norms under the RNMCH+A strategy.

The key strategies of the UP TSU under this objective were:

1. Develop and implement a clear plan to complete the training of ASHAs in modules 6 and 7.

2. Develop and implement simple to use tools/job aids and methods/processes to improve quality and quantity of interactions.
3. Develop and implement an FLW mentoring and supportive supervision system.
4. Design and implement appropriate communication and messaging to communities.

Training of FLWs

The TSU supported GoUP in completing the training of ASHAs in module 6 and 7, which is critical to promote postnatal home visits by the ASHAs (only the ASHAs trained in modules 6 and 7 were eligible to receive the incentives related to postnatal home visits) and the promotion of home-based newborn care. The training on modules 6 and 7 was skill-based and was implemented in two rounds. The trained ASHAs were provided with drug and equipment kit. In UP, 136,094 ASHAs were selected in year 2007–2009, of which 128,611 received induction training (modules 1–5). The ASHA trainings in modules 6 and 7 in the state were conducted in two phases: first 17 districts and then the remaining 58 districts. By the end of September 2013, 55% (16,725) of the targeted 30,398 ASHAs received round 1 of modules 6 and 7 training, and 21% (6,467) had completed the round 2 of the training as well. During the year 2013–2014, the state had the approval from the NHM to train 64,905 ASHAs in 58 districts.

In total, 56 state level trainers against the target of 80, and the district trainers in the 58 districts were identified. The TSU developed a detailed joint work plan with the community processes team of the state project management unit (SPMU), the Directorate and the SIHFW with an objective of completing the modules 6 and 7 training as committed to the GoI. Most trainings were expected to be implemented and funded by the GoUP, with the TSU providing only technical, planning and quality assurance inputs. However, in the case of select capacity building on innovations being introduced by the TSU, trainings were conducted by the TSU until the funds were secured through GoUP. In the case of modules 6 and 7 trainings of ASHAs, the TSU supported the GoUP in (a) planning and monitoring training execution and (b) training of trainers; creating a cadre of master trainers from the existing government training institutes—SIHFW, for example. In the month of September, the TSU has supported the GoUP in the organization of the training of master trainers for modules 6 and 7 in the state.

The UP TSU, with the assistance of Engender Health, supported the GoUP in providing focus on family planning in FLW and household and community interactions. The ASHAs in selected blocks were oriented on FP to improve the FP messaging provided at the community level. Educational videos on family planning methods were used for orientation to ASHAs. Orientation was provided on social marketing of condoms and pills. The ASHAs were supported further, in the field, for achieving higher coverage for FP in the community.

Tools and job aids

In order to Improve the management and delivery of outreach services and shaping demand, the TSU supported the GoUP in the development and implementation of simple-to-use tools/job-aids and methods/processes for the FLWs. These tools/job aids and methods/processes were to equip FLWs (ASHAs, AWWs and ANMs) with competencies in improving the coverage for routine RMNCH+A services, particularly for the most vulnerable/marginalized SC/ST and poor families and the most at risk individuals (high-risk pregnancies, under-/malnourished children, sick newborns and infants), to help them become better communicators with families about the importance of availing RMNCH+A services and to adopt healthy practices for preventing maternal, newborn, child and adolescent morbidities and mortalities and to help them screen, identify and refer danger signs, especially during the critical postnatal period. The tools/job aids included the following:

1. Village Health Index Register (VHIR) or ASHA Diary that includes tools for ETT for ASHAs to improve planning and coverage.
2. Home-visit checklists for ASHAs—an integrated maternal and newborn management tool—to improve identification and actions for postnatal danger signs.
3. Family-focused communication tools and materials to use with families to influence awareness and practices to support pregnant women and newborns.

The methods/processes that the TSU supported the FLWs with for improving coordinated organization of supply of services and problem-solving included:

1. VHNDs for improved service delivery
2. AAA (ANMs, ASHAs and AWWs) forum for better coordination and problem-solving
3. VHIR and ETT

The TSU has supported the development and implementation of VHIR or ASHA Diary that includes among other items:

1. Line listing of the 1,000 names within the ASHA area
2. ETT for pregnant women and their children age 0–59 months as well as eligible couples with unmet need for family planning
3. Monthly community need (due) lists for various services
4. The monthly item-wise summary of achievements

The VHIR is being printed by the GoUP with the approval from the National Health Systems Resource Centre (NHSRC), New Delhi, on the model of ASHA Diary that is being used in Karnataka.

The ETT allows ASHAs to organize the outreach information in six broad categories: identification details, ANC details, delivery details, PNC details and immunization details. Additionally, the tool has information on the identification details of the ASHA herself—the district, taluk, PHC, SC and village names as well as the estimated number of pregnant women in her area, as per the household survey.

Every month, the ASHAs, with the help of ANMs and the CRPs, use the ETT to plan their outreach services. This planning is done by identifying, from the ETT, who is due for what services in that month, based on (a) whether the woman is due for the service as per the prescribed schedule for RMNCH service delivery and (b) whether the woman has already received the service due for her in that month. Based on the target as well as the number receiving services, she prepares a monthly community need list or due list for each of the services. The monthly abstracts from the ASHAs were discussed at the AAA forums to identify and facilitate reducing the gaps in service coverage and utilization through the continuum of care in the population covered by the SC.

Home visit checklist: In order to improve the quality of interactions between the ASHA and the pregnant/recently delivered woman and the newborn during the antenatal and postnatal periods, the UP TSU supported the GoUP in the development of a tool/job aid to help ASHAs to remember to seek certain information from the mother about herself or the newborn, so that she can screen for any complications during pregnancy or during the post-delivery period in either the mother or the newborn. This checklist was used by ASHA in each of her home visits to a pregnant woman or a woman in the postnatal period (42 days after delivery), for screening and linking them to appropriate services.

Family-focused communication

Under this component, keeping the woman and her family as focus, the TSU supported the GoUP in the introduction of behaviour-change communication materials to the FLWs. The following behaviour-change communication materials were introduced:

1. Mobile Kunji in collaboration with BBC Media Action: Mobile Kunji is a multimedia service developed by BBC Media Action to enhance the immediate impact of CHWs' counselling of families. It is an interactive voice response (IVR)-based mobile service that has a printed deck of cards on a ring. The Kunji cards have been designed to look like a mobile phone, with illustrations, supporting arguments and key messages about MCH. Each card has a unique mobile short code printed on it, which corresponds to a specific audio health message. When a health worker dials the number, they can play the health message.
2. Other materials that were adopted included from the areas of family planning (adopted from Urban Health Initiative), exclusive breastfeeding, timely and complementary feeding (in collaboration with Alive and Thrive) and so on.

Community participation and monitoring

Village Health and Nutrition Days (VHNDs): The TSU supported the GoUP in the development and implementation of revised guidelines for improving the scope and quality of VHNDs. The state-level consultations were completed and the revisions in the guidelines were undertaken.

AAA forum meetings: The TSU supported the implementation of AAA forum meetings that aim at improving the coordination, planning and problem-solving at the SC level. One of the critical gaps that were addressed through AAA forum meetings was that the three FLWs did not have a formal forum to discuss their issues and challenges to help them follow up and take proactive decisions and actions. AAA is a platform for FLWs to come together to discuss and share common issues, experiences, concerns and thoughts. The AAA forum was also used as a platform to review the progress through the summary of VHIR. It offers an opportunity for FLWs to come together for reasons beyond just work. Entertainment and other creative programmes were organized. The AAA forum meets on the last Friday of every month for about 2–3 hours at the SC.

FLW mentoring and supportive supervision system

With a goal of enhancing the household behaviour change, the UP TSU will provide on-site mentoring and supportive supervision for AAA in each of the 100 focus blocks, through a dedicated cadre of CRPs (3 per block) and BCSs (1 per block).

A total of 80 district and zonal TSU members were trained in community processes for five days during 21–25 May 2014. These were the RPs for the training of the BCSs and the CRPs. The BCSs underwent a two-day induction training during 15–16 May 2014. Subsequently, they were trained along with the CRPs in community processes, for 16 days during 10–30 June in 11 batches at five zonal locations. The CRPs in the first round of village visits oriented the FLW on the VHIR and the community level information necessary for prioritizing the mentoring visits.

Communication campaign

In shaping demand, the TSU sought to understand and address barriers and constraints on the demand side, including the knowledge, attitudes and practices of rural women and their families, and the mix of financial barriers and incentives that influence demand for and utilization of services. The TSU also supported the GoUP in designing and implementing mass and mid-media strategies to influence behaviours.

The TSU leveraged and guided the GoUP's recently launched campaign, Hausla. The campaign which was launched by the chief minister of UP in a high profile event in July 2013, has the goals of galvanizing state health systems to deliver high-quality, accessible health programmes and services, while also increasing awareness and utilization of services by families and communities around the eight priority household behaviours. The campaign focuses on mother and child health.

Priority household behaviours addressed through Hausla campaign are:

1. Birth preparedness and safe delivery
2. Exclusive breastfeeding and complementary feeding
3. Birth spacing and limiting family size
4. ANC
5. Thermal care for newborns
6. Immunization
7. Vitamin A
8. Diarrhoea treatment

Where appropriate, initiatives of the TSU were branded under of the Hausla umbrella. For instance, Hausla aims to promote priority behaviours (birth preparedness and safe delivery, nutrition: exclusive breastfeeding and complementary feeding, family planning: birth spacing and limiting, antenatal care, thermal care, immunization and Vitamin A and diarrhoea treatment) which were well aligned with the TSU's and the foundation's objectives. The TSU ensured consistency of messages delivered to the relevant audience through Hausla and its own activities. Working closely with the Hausla campaign fostered continuing political ownership of the project.

In addition to the earlier, the TSU supported the GoUP in the following:

(a) Revising the ASHA incentives.
(b) The development of differential funds allocation strategy for RKSs and VHSNCs.
(c) In the development of guidelines for the AAA forum (at the SC level), VHSNC and Rogi Sahayata Kendra (Citizen's

Help Desk). The TSU had organized a three-day consultation workshop for a group of 38 ASHAs, AWWs and ANMs in Lucknow in May 2014 to get their inputs to the TSU's tools and methods.

Results framework

A key aspect of this objective is the periodic measurement of behavioural changes in the target populations to detect gaps in implementation and strategies. The TSU supported the GoUP in designing and implementing such periodic rapid and short population-based surveys. The TSU assumed that the GoUP was willing and able to devote sufficient resources to implement communication plans to shape demand, and was also willing to adapt innovative strategies that have proven successful in other states/settings to enhance the skills of FLWs.

Using the concurrent monitoring processes such as the CBTS and internal monitoring processes, the TSU tracked the results and activity milestones as given in Table 3b.1.

Key results

CBTS showed that percentage of women receiving any ANC has increased between survey rounds and the percentage receiving any ANC in VHNDs has also increased in 20 poorest performing blocks (Figure 3b.1).

Greater proportion of ASHA areas had ALL pregnant women receiving any ANC in Round 3 compared to the previous survey rounds in 20 blocks (Figure 3b.2).

Inequities in any ANC by socio-demographic characteristics have also been reduced between survey rounds in 20 blocks (Figure 3b.3).

The quality of ANC services has also improved between survey rounds (Figure 3b.4).

Table 3b.1	Results Framework for UP TSU Objective 1		
Result		**Baseline**	**Target (%)**
Improved FLW skills, capabilities and performance, including: • Improved FLW use of data, communication methods, attendance, quality of contacts and quantity of contacts • Increased percentage of blocks conducting regular mid-media communication activities to influence household behaviours around RMNCH		TBD	80
Improved use of mass/mid-media by the GoUP to improve behaviours and consumer awareness of schemes and incentives		TBD	80
Percentage of women receiving critical contacts from pregnancy until the child is one year of age—at least two contacts in the last trimester of pregnancy, contact within 24 hours of delivery or returning from the facility, three contacts in the first week after delivery, at least one monthly contact in the first three months post delivery and one between 5 and 8 months.		TBD	80
Percentage of women receiving the full ANC package.		TBD	80
Improved facility usage and services • Percentage of all births delivered in BEmONC facilities • Percentage of weak newborns identified			
Family planning • Percentage of mothers receiving FP counselling during pregnancy and within six months after delivery • Percentage of women informed about side effects of FP methods • Percentage of women given FP information when visited by FLW • Percentage of women with knowledge of method mix		TBD	

Result	Baseline	Target (%)
Institutionalization of good approaches for sustainability—Percentage of 'successful innovations' approved for funding by the GoUP/GoI, e.g., 3A platform, job aids for FLWs, trainings for ASHAs		

Critical milestones
1. All ASHAs are using tools and methods to improve and measure achievements (within 18 months).
2. The GoUP implemented communication materials and methods for FLWs to influence the individual's/family's utilization of critical RMNCH and nutrition services in the 25 districts (within 24 months).

At least 85% of the FLWs are meeting minimum performance standards in delivery of the critical RMNCHN intervention package (within 36 months).

Activities
1. Support the GoUP in the design and implementation of a clear training plan at state, district and block levels to complete the training of FLWs with all ASHA modules.
2. Support the GoUP to develop and implement simple-to-use tools and job aids for FLWs to increase utilization of critical RMNCHN services through improved antenatal and PNC home visits and improved family-focused communication in project districts and blocks.
3. Support the GoUP at state and district levels in the design and implementation of mentoring and supportive supervision systems, including tools and methods, for FLWs.
4. Support the GoUP at state and district levels to design and implement appropriate communication and messaging to communities (e.g., mass and mid-media efforts).

Support the GoUP to identify and to adapt the successful innovations for scale-up in the blocks and districts that are not the focus of the TSU, and finance the implementation of these innovations through the PIP process within and beyond the project period.

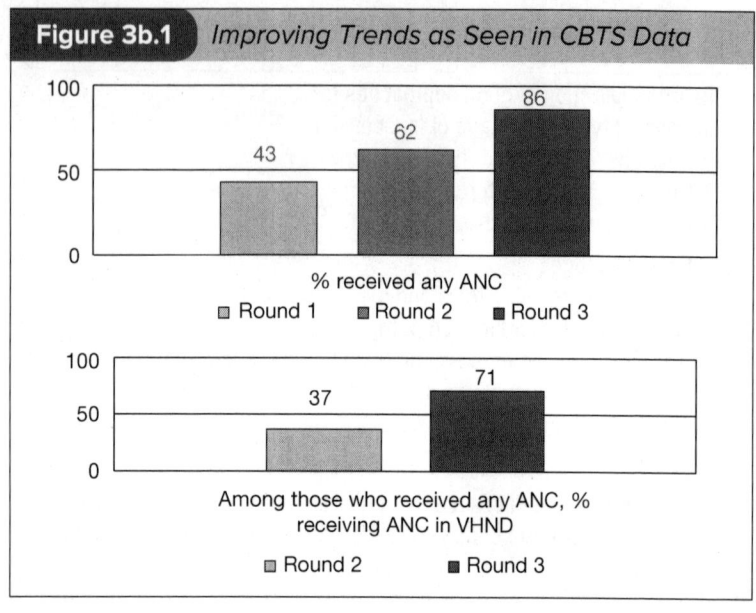

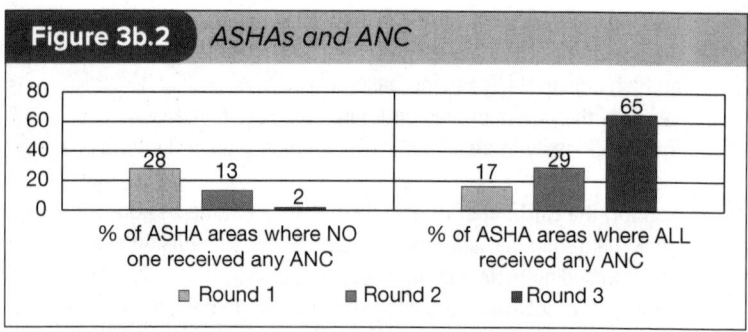

Check up within 48 hours of delivery (in facility or in the community) has increased by place of delivery between survey rounds 2 and 3 in the 20 blocks (Figure 3b.5).

Early initiation of breastfeeding has increased in all facility types except the private facilities in 20 blocks (Figure 3b.6).

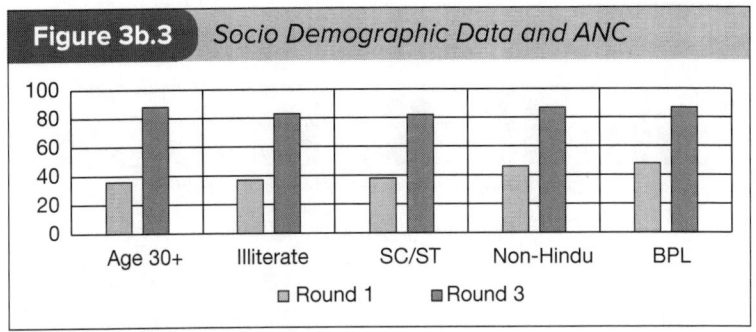

Figure 3b.3   *Socio Demographic Data and ANC*

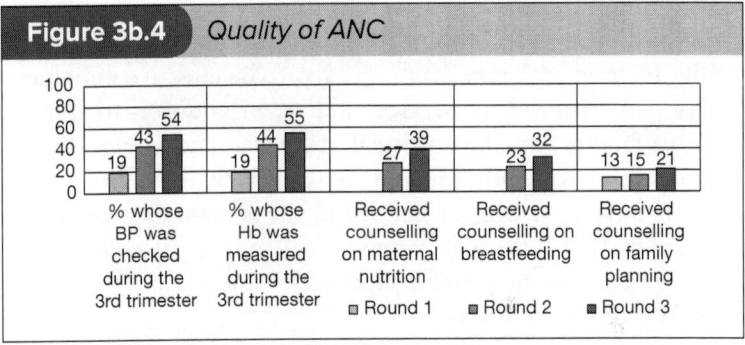

Figure 3b.4   *Quality of ANC*

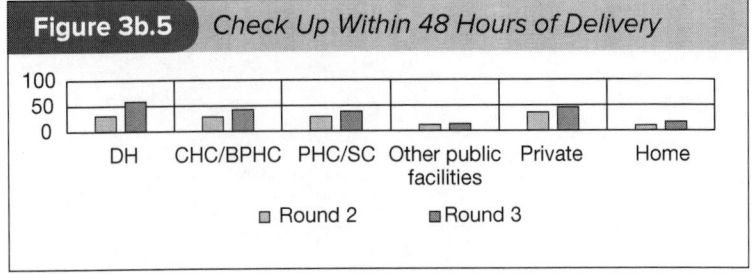

Figure 3b.5   *Check Up Within 48 Hours of Delivery*

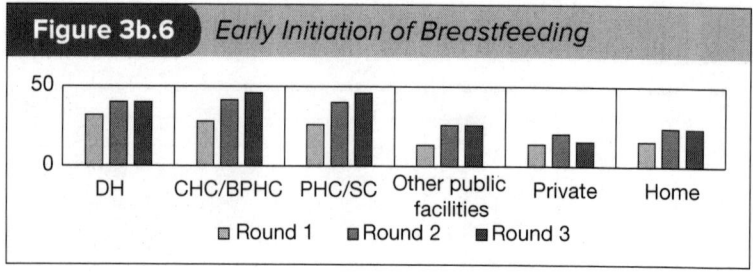

Figure 3b.6 *Early Initiation of Breastfeeding*

Conclusions

The community interventions enabled strengthening FLW platform in the state of UP and thereby improved coverage of critical MNCH services. The various tools such as VHIR, ETT and family-focused communication proved to be effective in helping FLWs plan and deliver services better, in addition to linking them to facilities for institutional and emergency services. The interventions originally focused in 100 blocks of high priority districts have now been scaled up in the remaining blocks and districts by GoUP through a new set of supportive cadre called ASHA Sanghinis who provide supervisory support and mentoring to ASHAs in the fieldwork.

4

Strengthening Data Management and Use

Health information systems have been identified as by the WHO one of the six key building blocks of a well-functioning health system.[1] Health information systems are critical for decision-making in many aspects of health workforce, governance, service delivery, financing and access to essential medicines. High quality health information, which is the foundation of health systems, is critical for addressing RMNCH+A challenges in India and building strong public health systems. It is essential for monitoring programme objectives and activities, guiding evidence-based programme management and resource allocation.

Routinely collected M&E data can provide important information related to RMNCH+A service delivery when the data is of high quality. Data management encompasses multiple dimensions, including accuracy, reliability, timeliness and completeness. Health information systems rely on multiple sources of data such as HMIS, MCTS, logistics management information system (LMIS), household surveys, census and routine M&E of health services. Yet, in many resource-limited settings, such as

[1] World Health Organization, Monitoring the Building Blocks of Health Systems: A Handbook of Indicators and Their Measurement Strategies (Geneva: World Health Organization, 2010).

India, ensuring data is of sufficient quality for evidence-based decision-making remains a challenge.

While collecting and disseminating data is important, there is a need to examine the underlying factors within the health system that influence data quality. By doing so, we can establish best institutional mechanism and implement relevant interventions for improving data quality. There are five main components of data management which encompass a health system and help in producing quality information for decision-making:

1. M&E structures, functions and capabilities
2. Indicator definitions and reporting guidelines
3. Data collection and reporting forms and tools
4. Data management processes
5. Links with the national reporting system[2]

Understanding the strengths and issues with various functional components within the national and state health systems can help to improve data quality through data strengthening activities. To better understand the factors that influence data quality within the routine RMNCH+A systems in India, an overview of data management and reporting systems is provided in this chapter, which include capturing and transferring of health data from the point of generation at the health facility or community level to the point of incorporation into national HMIS.

Existing Data Structures

In order to understand current situation of mother and child health by using health information system in India, it is imperative to look at the various data sources that are available in the country. The national health surveys often have hundreds of

[2] K. Hardee, 'MEASURE Evaluation: Data Quality Audit Tool: Guidelines for Implementation'. Available at: http://www.cpc.unc.edu/measure/publications/ms-08-29 (accessed on 2 November 2017).

indicators that serve to monitor the implementation of the mother and child programmes. In addition, specific health and diseases programme plans also have their own indicators and targets. Data collection for the indicators must draw upon the full range of data sources. Each indicator needs to be linked to some data sources in order to compile consistent estimates of the indicators. Data can be from surveys, administrative/secondary sources and programme sources.

Charu Garg in his paper 'Availability, Quality and Data Gaps in Health Statistics in India' gives a succinct overview of various surveys, including the indicators they capture, the frequency, the focus and the like.[3]

Survey data sources

Census: Census is conducted every 10 years for monitoring vital events such as birth rates, death rates and several other social factors. It is a complete enumeration of population statistics on important demographic variables down to the district level. Most of the information is available by regions, gender and castes scheduled in the Constitution. The last census was conducted in 2011. These demographic indicators along with cause-of-death statistics are also monitored through civil registration systems, demographic surveillance sites or hospital statistics. Data is available at state and regional levels and can be disaggregated by social categories.

Sample Registration System (SRS): SRS is a large-scale demographic survey for providing reliable annual estimates of birth rate, death rate and other fertility and mortality indicators at the national and subnational levels by place of residence and gender. The Office of the Registrar General, India is the responsible agency. It is a continuous enumeration of births and deaths

---

[3] C.C. Garg, 'Availability, Quality and Data Gaps in Health Statistics in India' (New Delhi: Ministry of Statistics and Programme Implementation, GoI, 2015).

in selected sample units by resident part time enumerators, generally AWWs and teachers, and an independent survey every six months by SRS supervisors. At present, SRS is operational in 7,597 sample units (4,433 rural and 3,164 urban) spread across all States and Union territories and covers about 1.5 million households and 7.27 million population. Latest SRS data is available for 2012.

District Level Household Survey (DLHS): DLHS-1 (1998–1999), DLHS-2 (2002–2004) and DLHS-3 (2007–2008) are household surveys of MoHFW conducted by its nodal agency International Institute for Population Sciences (IIPS), Mumbai. In DLHS-3, the survey covered 611 districts in India, with 1,000 to 1,500 households chosen from each district. The focus of DLHS-3 is to provide health care and utilization indicators at the district level for the enhancement of the activities under NRHM. It estimates the coverage for ANC and immunization services; extent of safe deliveries; contraceptive prevalence; unmet need for family planning; awareness about RTI/STI and HIV/AIDS; utilization of government health services and users' satisfaction. It also provides information on newborn care, PNC within 48 hours, role of ASHA in enhancing the reproductive and child health care and coverage of JSY. An important component of DLHS-3 is the integration of Facility Survey of health institution (SC, PHC, CHC and DH) accessible to the sampled villages.

National Family Health Survey (NFHS): NFHS is a large-scale, multi-round survey conducted in a representative sample of households throughout India. Three rounds of the survey have been conducted: NFHS-1 (1992–1993), NFHS-2 (1998–1999) and NFHS-3 (2005–2006). NFHS-4 has been implemented in 2014–2015 and combines aspects of DLHS, covering all 640 districts and 568,000 households. These are conducted by IIPS, Mumbai under the stewardship of MoHFW, with some financial and technical support from international agencies during the earlier surveys. The survey focuses on data on health and family welfare for policy and programme purposes. It provides state and national information on fertility, infant and child mortality, the practice of family planning, MCH, reproductive health, nutrition, anaemia, utilization and quality of health and family planning services. NFHS-4 additionally covers perinatal mortality, adolescent reproductive health, high-risk sexual behaviour, safe injections, HIV, tuberculosis, malaria, non-communicable diseases and domestic violence.

Annual Health Survey (AHS): AHS is a three-year (2010, 2011 and 2012) longitudinal, demographic survey of nine high-focus states—Assam, Bihar, Jharkhand, UP, Uttarakhand, Madhya Pradesh, Chhattisgarh, Odisha and Rajasthan—conducted by Office of Registrar General & Census Commissioner, India (ORGI). It is one of the largest population-based surveys. The second round of the AHS drew a representative sample of 20,694 primary sample units, covering 4.28 million households and 20.61 million people from the 284 districts in these nine states. The objective is to yield benchmarks of core vital and health indicators at the district level and to map changes therein on an annual basis. State level bulletins contain vital indicators, namely, crude birth rate, crude death rate, infant mortality rate, neo-natal mortality rate, under five mortality rate, maternal mortality ratio, sex ratio at birth, 0–4 years and all ages. District-level fact sheets contain 161 indicators on fertility, mother and childcare, family planning practices, mortality, disability, marriage and so on. Data were released in 2011 and 2013 by ORGI.[4]

Civil Registration System (CRS): CRS records vital events and characteristics thereof, as a unified process of continuous, permanent and compulsory registrations as provided through the legal requirements of the country. The registrar of births and deaths appointed by state government collects information in prescribed forms from health facilities, midwives and other medical and para-medical persons who attend a birth of a child outside health facility, keepers

---

[4] Office of the Registrar General and Census Commissioner of India (2013), Annual Health Survey of India, Uttar Pradesh, 2011–12, New Delhi.

of crematoria and burial grounds and from those who are in the knowledge. The Office of the Registrar General of India (ORGI) is the agency coordinating the process with local Registrars. While data on birth and death rates are updated until 2012, a report on medical certification for cause of death is available for 2009.

Programme data sources

Health management information system: During the Eleventh Five-Year Plan, a web-based HMIS application software has been developed and made operational for online data capture at district and subdistrict levels on RCH service delivery indicators. National web-portal (nrhmmis.nic.in) has data uploaded by all the states and districts across the country. National Health System Resource Centre (NHSRC) conducts analysis of this data and has updated information state-wise for some major indicators. However, each state can develop and use the date for their specific purposes. For instance, Tamil Nadu Government conceptualized the system to provide critical health data across the health chain for quick and timely intervention by the health directorates. Similarly, the government of Gujarat has envisaged the system to help the administrators to have better monitoring and control of the functioning of hospitals across the state using decision support indicators and assist the doctors and medical staff to improve health services with readily reference patient data, work flow enabled less-paper process and parameterized alarms and triggers during patient treatment cycle. On the other hand, the government of Andhra Pradesh intended to use the system for evidence-based policy making and undertake effective monitoring, leading to improve accountability and effectiveness at all levels of the health system.

In short, HMIS helps with the following:

- Follows the nationally developed standard list of indicators and formats for reporting, and is computerized in the nationally implemented web-based HMIS portal.

- Data are collected by facility the events and services occurring in all government health facilities are reported every month.
- Captures about 120 indicators on average at each facility, covering a large number of programme areas, with the focus on MNCH.
- Facility-wise reporting started in all districts in April 2010, but complete data are available from August 2010 onwards.

Mother and child tracking system: The MCTS was developed jointly by the MoHFW and National Informatics Centre (NIC) and launched by the GoI in collaborations with states and union territories in 2009. The purpose of this is to have a name-based tracking system whereby pregnant women and children can be tracked for their ANC check-up and immunization along with a feedback system for the ANM and ASHA to ensure that all pregnant women receive their ANC check-ups and recently delivered women their PNC, and further children receive their full immunization and generates work plan for ANMs and ASHA for VHNDs. All pregnancies and births are expected to be captured irrespective of where the ANC check-ups are being given or the place of delivery. Thus details of all deliveries taking place either at home, public or private institution is to be captured irrespective of the fact whether the mother is a JSY beneficiary or not. This is an IT-based management tool plan to deliver and monitor quality MCH services, track dropouts and ensure complete service delivery through work plans and analysis of performance and message alerts, thereby reducing IMR and MMR.

The highlights of MCTS are:

- A mobile phone SMS-based data-feeding process, where the ANMs send information on services that she provides.
- Implemented in all districts of the state since January 2011.
- All services provided to women and children, starting with ANC registration until the child is given full immunization,

are captured in the system for each mother and child pair, along with nature and date of service.

- A portion of the Thayi Card that is issued to pregnant women during ANC registration is computerized to provide the profile of the pregnant woman as well as a unique identification number.
- Subsequent services are registered in the web-based server through SMS from the ANM.
- At the end of the registered pregnancy, the child portion of the Thayi Card is filled and computerized to provide the profile of the child or the pregnancy outcome as appropriate.
- Subsequent services provided to the child are registered on the web server through SMS from the ANM.
- The ANMs receive monthly work plans on their mobile phones from the server to remind them which women/children are due for services.

Specifically, there are 58 fields in the MCTS data set that can be classified into following domains:

- Location detail: District, blocks, facility, mother's village and contact details
- Demography: Mother's ID, name, husbands name, date of birth, age and caste
- Providers detail: ANM's contact details, name of the facility where delivery is planned
- ANC and service details: Last menstrual period (LMP), ANC date, TT, IFA, anaemia, ANC complications and RTI/STI
- Delivery history: Place, type, complications, date of discharge and abortion
- PNC details: PNC home visit, PNC complications, PNC check-up
- Family planning: Postpartum contraception methods
- Child details: Sex, weight, breastfeeding and immunization

The actual MCTS process is as follows:

1. ANM makes first contact with pregnant woman/child—in village or VHND—and records details in MCTS register.
2. ANM brings updated MCTS register to BPM/MCTS DEO on weekly basis.
3. BPM/DEO enters data on MCTS portal where a unique ID is generated.
4. MCTS portal automatically generates a work plan for the ANM.
5. ANM directs ASHAs to mobilize community members due for services based on work plan.
6. Work plan includes due services for ANC, delivery, PNC and immunization.
7. ASHA mobilizes beneficiaries to VHND.
8. ANM provides due services at VHND and updates MCTS register.
9. ANM brings register to BPM/DEO to update on MCTS portal.

Limitations of Existing Data Structures

The availability of data sources, clear and specific indicators, regularity of the information flow both bottom-up and top-down are important for any information system to function well. Garg in his review of data sources writes that the system of health statistics in India presents a mixed-bag scenario in terms of the quality of data:[5]

---

[5] C.C. Garg, 'Availability, Quality and Data Gaps in Health Statistics in India' (New Delhi: Ministry of Statistics and Programme Implementation, GoI, 2015).

Survey data

In order to conduct any socio-economic analysis, one has to rely on surveys as facility-level data does not contain this level of dis-aggregation. The irregular frequency of the surveys and inferences on the basis of old data is often misleading in the context of the health sector in the country witnessing reform measures such as the NRHM and other state-level initiatives. Apart from the large surveys, recent statistics on MCH, for example at the district level, is mostly from the AHS and HMIS portal. While this is a remarkable milestone to have key indicators on MNCH outcomes for all districts within the high-focus states in the country on a regular basis, wider and more effective use could be propagated through better data dissemination, such as making unit record data available for disaggregated analysis.

Also, socio-economic variables should have a full coverage at geographic (national, state, district and so on) and popula-tion levels (income, social classes, gender and so on) and should cover all sectors—public and private. Surveys are costly, and for countries of India's size and diversity routine data flow regard-ing health statistics cannot solely rely on periodic surveys or data from national health programmes.

A standard format for reporting diseases and related informa-tion on the patient and the treatment in formal health establish-ments from both public and private sector holds lot of promise. Regular facility level information can provide routine information on health scenario, utilization and financing patterns. Further regular monitoring of facilities also provides service availability and readiness. Independent assessments at regular intervals will be necessary to ensure quality.

Under primary impetus from the stipulations under NRHM, and the corollary technical support by development partners and non-governmental agencies, there has been a sudden spike in the amount of data being collected at the primary care level, aggregated at the districts and passed on thereafter. There is little standardization across states, making the data being reported of little practical use, and much of the data generated is not easily disseminated. Also, data from primary sources is not used for facility assessments.

Data analysed should also flow back to the producers of data for monitoring the performance and accountability to the population. A systematic, structured approach is required to streamline both collection and reporting of data and real-time updating by leveraging on technological advancements and capabilities.

Programme data

The main problem with HMIS is facility-wise data uploading. For instance, a study in UP especially in high priority districts shows only 95% facilities uploaded report on regular basis but not on timely basis and nearly 5% facilities uploaded zero data on HMIS portal. Similarly, on an average 58% data elements, including zero, were reported by the facilities as per HMIS format; average 27% data elements, excluding zero, were reported by the facilities as per HMIS format. Additional PHCs, some public health facilities and medical college hospital data was not uploaded on the HMIS web portal and private facilities data was not uploaded on web portal on a regular basis. There were also other problems with the data set associated with validation and consistency. As per the GoI recommendation, 30 validation rules are available on HMIS web portal. As per the analysis of data available on portal for April–August 2014, on an average 93% facilities were proving the validation checks, resulting in unreliable data being uploaded on portal.

There are also other data quality issues. For instance, along with underreporting, the HMIS also suffers from frequent double counting. For example, if a woman goes to a variety of facilities to seek care, she is registered again at each facility, resulting in double counting. At the facility level, there is not a consistent understanding of what constitutes a registration. For example, some facilities report the number of IFA tablets distributed under the indicator 'number of women given 100 IFA tablets'. This could be due to the complexity of the system without adequate capacity building of the staff. It captures about 120 indicators, on average, at each facility, covering a large number of programme areas, with the focus on neonatal and child health. Indicators are poorly defined and understood, resulting in inconsistencies in recording. Indicators do not directly relate to programme goals and objectives and are not linked to management decisions that need to be made. Monthly meetings are used to review data but are frequently a platform for punitive action, rather than as an opportunity to identify and solve problems. The root cause of the problem is that the data providers at the SC level, such as ANMs, generally lack understanding of the system or the potential utility of the data for their work. In UP, only 6% of ANMs in HPDs are trained on HMIS formats and process in terms of data collection, coalition of data and preparation of report and definition and validation of data elements. Also, only 18% of ANMs are getting feedback on HMIS data to improve the quality from facilities such as CHC and PHC. Only 6% of ANMs are trained on HMIS formats and process in terms of data collection, data elements definition, validation and report writing.

There are also other problems associated with infrastructure and human resources. A comprehensive study conducted in 117 facilities including CHCs, PHCs and SCs by the UP TSU staff using supportive supervision checklist found the following gaps:

Availability of infrastructure and HR: There are 62% facilities having separate computer system for HMIS data uploading and only 38% having the computer operator; and out of available computer operators 73% are trained on HMIS system. Initially, block development administrative assistants were hired for uploading data on portal, but as of now they have upgraded as block account manager, and hence they refuse HMIS uploading work.

Availability of broadband connection and power backup: Nearly 70% facilities/data entry points have power backup but it was observed during regular check-up visit that power backup was not regular for HMIS and MCTS data entry and only 34% facilities were found to have functional broadband connection at the time of visit. In spite of this, the problem was not discussed in the monthly review meetings as such meetings were conducted in only 17% of the facilities including CHCs and PHCs.

Availability of printed HMIS format: Only 44% facilities have printed appropriate HMIS formats and only 42% reported in the prescribed format, according to block HQ authorities. Most of them are using old photocopies of HMIS formats for reporting.

Reporting period: Reporting period for HMIS is not uniform among the districts and blocks: for 66% of the facilities reporting period is 20–21 of each month, for 19% facilities reporting period is 15–16 and 15% facilities have different dates than mentioned earlier.

Availability and updating of registers: There is a list of essential registers maintained at facilities and from these HMIS data is collected in HMIS reporting format. The TSU has reviewed some of the registers and following was observed:

- 90% facilities maintained these registers; in 88% of the facilities the registers were prepared manually. May be because of this only 52% facilities' registers were matching with HMIS format fields and only half of them were updated correctly.
- Delivery registers were available in 54% of delivery points and only 42% of these facilities updating the registers correctly. Similarly, the JSY registers were found in only 33% of delivery points and updated correctly.
- It is also found that there were multiple reporting systems such as monthly performance review (MPR), routine immunization and front-line worker, and these were very similar to HMIS reporting formats leading to duplications of efforts by ANMs not in data collection and report writing.

Although MCTS is an important initiative to improve data availability, assessments have identified a number of critical gaps in data availability and data quality at various levels of the MCTS. To begin with, data collection process is a vicious cycle. For instance, date reporting is incomplete because there are not enough registers. Similarly, data entry system is also problematic as data is not submitted for data on time and not only there are not enough DEOs but also they are not well trained. Moreover, electricity supply is irregular. This will affect delays in data entry and in turn impede work-plan generation and work plan does require high volume of printing. Besides, due to lack of appropriate software, individualized data is not easily accessible and system is not user friendly, resulting in lack of data usage for programme planning. It is important that the field functionaries are to be constantly encouraged to capture information of all children and pregnant women, so that they can monitor the progress of service delivery to the target beneficiaries.

Currently, the MCTS suffers from incomplete data capture. For example, only about 40% of women registered in the HMIS are also entered into the MCTS database, and the coverage of children is only 13%. This relates to omissions in registration and data entry, and ANMs generally lack understanding of the system or the potential utility of the data for their work. There is a lack of standard protocols for downloading, organizing and analysing the HMIS and MCTS data, as well as poor data analysis skills. Although there is a data analysis manual for programme managers, there is a need to further demystify the analysis by providing simple step-by-step protocols. Stronger skills in analysis may help link data to management decisions. Indicators do not directly relate to programme goals and objectives and are not linked to management decisions that need to be made. Monthly meetings are used to review data but are frequently a platform for punitive action, rather than being an opportunity to identify and solve problems.

Strengthening HMIS and MCTS

When a maternal death or near miss is not reported, the system can not address the gaps that allowed the death to occur.[6] For this reason, a functional health information system is a central component of any strategy to address maternal mortality.

[6] P. Setel, S. Macfarlane, S. Szreter, L. Mikkelsen, P. Jha, S. Stout, and C. AbouZahr, 'A Scandal of Invisibility: Making Everyone Count by Counting Everyone', *Lancet* 370, no. 9598 (2007): 1569–1577.

Accurate, relevant and up-to-date information is essential for evidence-based decision-making at all levels of the health system to promote good governance, transparency and accountability.

Recommendations to strengthen HMIS

1. For complete coverage, enrolment of all the health facilities should be made mandatory on web portal.
2. The system should ensure that printing and distribution of formats and registers is done, including the HMIS data elements, as per the requirements of all the health facilities.
3. Comprehensive guidelines should be issued to conduct district- and block-level monthly review meetings to discuss HMIS data quality, sharing for use and implementation. The following should be observed:

    a. Timeline for data uploading and forwarding
    b. Responsible person to conduct meetings at district and block levels and record of the minutes of the meetings and any action taken
    c. Providing sufficient power backup to computer system for uploading the data
    d. Availability of functional broadband and data card
    e. Data uploading from block level
    f. ANM/facility should keep copy of a report submitted to the block level.
    g. Assign the data uploading responsibility to block account manager

4. Hand-holding of DEOs on HMIS formats, data definition, validation, consistency and data analysis.
5. Provide orientation and regular hand-holding of ANMs in accurate recording of information in registers and transferring it to HMIS formats, data element definition, validation and its importance.

In addition to the issues discussed earlier, other observations are made to improve HMIS and possible solutions are suggested as given in Table 4.1.

Table 4.1 *Issues and Solutions for HMIS*

Issues	Possible Solutions
1. Reporting from health facilities not mapped and/or enrolled in HMIS	• Government order should be issued for the identification and enrolment of remaining public and private district-wise health facilities (e.g., medical colleges, Employees' State Insurance Corporation [ESIC], railway and army hospitals, private nursing homes registered with government) on HMIS portal. • Orientation should be conducted to these new facilities to report in HMIS system.
2. Printing and distribution of formats and registers as per the need of the health facilities which include the HMIS data elements	• Standardized formats and registers should be distributed to district health facilities including the new ones with instruction to be uploaded on NHM state portal. • Budget for printing should be released on timely basis. • Need-based printing and distribution should be ensured up to facility level.
3. Duplication of reporting system such as MPR, universal immunization programme, KPI and others at district level with similar fields as per HMIS	• There should be guidelines for single reporting format with detailed instructions as to which data field or data element from where can be collected (e.g., name of register/format/person). • Protocol should be established for HMIS data use in review meetings for planning purposes.
4. Absence of SOP and guidelines for HMIS process, implementation, data use in monthly review meetings	• Comprehensive guidelines should be issued to conduct district- and block-level review meetings and HMIS data sharing for use and implementation including: • Timeline for data uploading and forwarding. • Responsible person to conduct a meeting at district and block level and preparing the minutes for action taken and/or to be taken. • Providing sufficient power backup to computer system for uploading the data.

		• Availability of functional broadband and data card. • Data uploading from block level only. • ANM/facility should keep copy of report submitted to a block. • Assign the data uploading responsibility to block account manager.
5.	Capacity of data use and analysis at different level	• Should introduce HMIS bulletin by highlighting performance and quality issues and establish protocol to use and provide feedback to districts on monthly basis. • Should upload HMIS dashboard and bulletin on NHM portal. • Plan for hand-holding and orientation of district- and block-level officials on HMIS data analysis and use. • Introduce HMIS data analysis software and orient district and block officials to analyse and use the data at district and block level.
6.	Capacity of ANMs and reporting person on HMIS formats regarding data definitions, validation and completeness and importance	• Plan for supportive supervision of ANMs and reporting person on HMIS through data-element reference manual, validation and completeness. • Plan for data use at ANM level for programme planning.
7.	Underreporting of data on death in HMIS	• Should build confidence to report death data in HMIS formats. • District-wise analysis of frequency of meetings held at district level should be monitored. • Compilation of causes of death at district and state levels, and it should be followed by supportive supervision visits at concerned health facilities for ensuring corrective measures.

Recommendations to strengthen MCTS

Build capacities of stakeholders so that they understand the indicators and the simplified data capture formats. They should also be trained in simple data analysis and management and in programme review protocols and presentation. Key to building capacity will be to increase the perceived utility of and commitment to maintaining the MCTS for everyone's job role.

Protocols should fit neatly with the systems context, taking advantage of existing platforms and processes. There has to be standard protocols for downloading, organizing and analysing the MCTS data. Establishing protocols and building capability for data quality checking, analysis and use should result in improved evidenced-based planning and management.

There has to be a specific action plan to make sure that the whole system works. For instance, the state-level authority should advise the district CMO; the district CMOs should hold regular meetings of the block MOs to sensitize them on this initiative and the block MOs would need to hold meetings of the ANMs/ASHAs/block-level officials/block programme management unit/lady health visitor (LHV) to apprise them of the details and decide on the modalities for getting the primary information on name-based tracking of pregnant women and immunization of children.

ASHAs could play a vital role in gathering information for the ANMs. After the ANM has captured the base information for the name-based tracking of pregnant women and immunization of children and passed on to the block PHC, she should be reporting the services delivered to the children and pregnant women based on the stipulated dates as per the ANC and immunization schedule each month. Each child/pregnant mother record will then result in the generation of a unique ID with which the child/pregnant mother can be tracked subsequently. This process of supervisory checks may be carried out as per the flow chart given in Figure 4.1 to ensure correctness of primary data and services delivered.

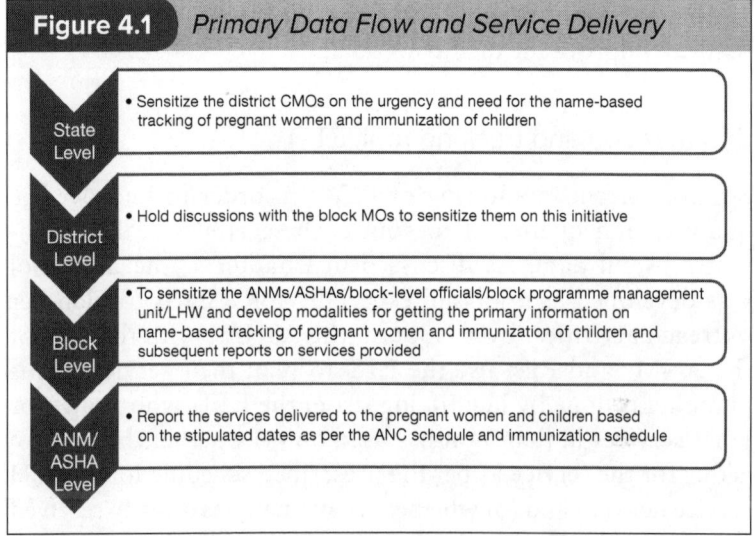

Figure 4.1 *Primary Data Flow and Service Delivery*

State Level
- Sensitize the district CMOs on the urgency and need for the name-based tracking of pregnant women and immunization of children

District Level
- Hold discussions with the block MOs to sensitize them on this initiative

Block Level
- To sensitize the ANMs/ASHAs/block-level officials/block programme management unit/LHW and develop modalities for getting the primary information on name-based tracking of pregnant women and immunization of children and subsequent reports on services provided

ANM/ASHA Level
- Report the services delivered to the pregnant women and children based on the stipulated dates as per the ANC schedule and immunization schedule

Concurrent Monitoring

For the quality of data to improve significantly, along with the aforementioned suggestions, concurrent monitoring should be seen as a critical component. This activity should establish processes through the FLW mentors and block supervisors to aggregate critical indicators of service provision, on the basis of tracking tools, which should be aggregated further at higher levels to understand the trends in various indicators at various levels of implementation and the gaps in quality and use of those indicators. In addition, data that are already collected as part of the HMIS/MCTS should be used to measure key indicators of scale and coverage. The initiative should design and implement periodic short surveys to monitor coverage of key interventions at population, facility and FLW levels. In addition, the coordination with the external partners should use data from DLHS and NFHS surveys to explore change in project outcomes, subject to their being conducted in a timely fashion in relation to project activities.

The following are some of the suggested tools and techniques that can improve the quality of data:

Enumeration and tracking tool (ETT)

For concurrent monitoring of FLWs in order to improve the quantity and quality of the outreach services, the ETT generates useful data. As discussed in Chapter 4, the ETT tool was developed as a job aid especially for ASHAs to plan her outreach activities. Every month, the ASHAs, with the help of the ANMs and RPs, use the ETT to plan their services. This planning is done by identifying, from the ETT, who is due for what services in that month, based on (a) whether the woman is due for the service as per the prescribed schedule for MNCH service delivery and (b) whether the woman has already received the service due for her in that month. Based on the target as well as the actual number of women receiving services, she prepares monthly abstracts. These monthly abstracts from the ASHAs are summarized at the SC level by the ANM and are discussed at the Arogya Mantapa to identify and facilitate reducing the gaps in service coverage and utilization through the continuum of care in the population covered by the SC. The targets and achievements using standard definitions are provided in Table 4.2.

Village health index register (VHIR)

Available data indicate that the coverage of target populations for RMNCH + A services is poor—there are unreached populations for many services, and those who are reached do not receive a complete package of services through the continuum of care from adolescent, reproductive, maternal, newborn and child health. For last few years no tools and methods available for ASHAs to map and track adolescent, reproductive age group women, pregnant women and children to enable them to monitor and plan coverage

Table 4.2 Guidelines for Defining Targets and Achievements Based on ETT

Indicator	Target	Achievement
ANC registration	This is a constant number every month: Estimated number of pregnant women as per the recent CNA/12, rounded off to the nearest integer	Number of pregnant women issued Thayi Card in the reporting month, based on the date of registration in ETT
TT injection	• Number of pregnant women who have not received any TT injection so far irrespective of the month of pregnancy PLUS • Number of pregnant women who had received the first TT a month ago AND have not received the 2nd TT	Number of pregnant women who received TT injections (either TT1 or TT2 or TT Booster) in the reporting month
IFA 100	• Number of pregnant women in their fourth to ninth month of pregnancy who have so far received <100 IFA tablets PLUS • Number of severely anaemic pregnant women in their fourth to ninth month of pregnancy who have so far received <200 IFA tablets	• Number of pregnant women who reached a cumulative of 100/200 IFA tablets in the month
ANC check-up	• Number of pregnant women in their third to sixth month of pregnancy who did not receive any ANC check-up from a medical doctor (either in a government or a private facility) PLUS	Number of pregnant women who received ANC check-up from a medical doctor (either in a government or a private facility) in the reporting month

(Continued)

Table 4.2 Continued

Indicator	Target	Achievement
	• Number of pregnant women in their seventh to eighth month of pregnancy who received <2 ANC check-ups from a medical doctor (either in a government or a private facility) PLUS • Number of pregnant women in their ninth month of pregnancy who received <3 ANC check-ups from a medical doctor (either in a government or a private facility)	
Delivery	Number of pregnant women who are due for delivery in the reporting month, based on the EDD	This has two parts: • Number of women who delivered at home in the reporting month • Number of women who delivered in a facility (government or private) in the reporting month
PNC visits	Number of delivered women who have received <6 PNC visits (based on PNC visit dates) within 42 days of delivery (based on date of delivery)	Number of delivered women who received 6+PNC visits in the reporting month

BCG	Number of children age <12 months who did not receive a BCG vaccination	Number of children age <12 months given BCG vaccination in the reporting month
OPV (can be given anytime within 5 years of age)	• Number of children under age 15 days who have not received OPV birth dose PLUS • Number of children age 45 days and above who have not received the first dose of OPV PLUS • Number of children age 75 days and above who have not received the second dose of OPV PLUS • Number of children age 105 days and above who have not received the third dose of OPV	Number of children age <12 months given OPV vaccination in the reporting month
Hep B [Can be administered only during the first year of life and should only be given along with DPT; thus if a child age <12 months has already received three doses of DPT but missed any dose of Hep B, the child cannot be administered Hep B and would move out of target]	Number of children within 24 hours after birth who have not received Hep B birth dose PLUS • Number of children age 45 days and above who have not received the first dose of Hep B • Number of children age 75 days and above who have not received the second dose of Hep B • Number of children age 105 days and above who have not received the third dose of Hep B	Number of children age <12 months given Hep B vaccination in the reporting month

(Continued)

Table 4.2 *Continued*

Indicator	Target	Achievement
DPT [Can be administered till attainment of two years of age]	• Number of children age 45 days and above who have not received the first dose of DPT • Number of children age 75 days and above who have not received the second dose of DPT • Number of children age 105 days and above who have not received the third dose of DPT	Number of children age <12 months given DPT vaccination in the reporting month
Pentavalent vaccine	• Number of children age 45 days and above who have not received any dose of pentavalent vaccine and any dose of Hep B,DPT and OPV	Number of children age <12 months given pentavalent vaccine in the reporting month
Measles	• Number of children age 9 months and above who have not received measles vaccine	Number of children age <12 months given measles vaccination in the reporting month
Family planning	• Local resident women listed in the ETT who are not currently using any family planning methods	Number of local resident women who are currently using any family planning method, separately for permanent and temporary methods

of services through the continuum of care. The previous tools for ASHAs also do not represent an integrated approach to the health of the mother and the child, nor help her to be a change agent to encourage improved RMNCH+A practices in the community. Therefore, there is a need to develop a tool which can combine their documentation needs as well as help them in planning and prioritizing the services to be provided and also help ASHAs in screening for danger signs among mothers and new-borns and be able to quickly link them to skilled care when needed.

VHIR is designed to address the gap analysis and raise opportunity in outreach services and to create demand mechanism for services, thus moving towards a solution. This VHIR will not only help in identification of critical gaps from service delivery side but also from utilization perspective, hence empowering ASHAs to raise both side issues in AAA forum as well as in VHSNC meetings. This will help ASHAs in clearly defining support areas for VHSNC, AWW and ANM and thereby helping her to increase coverage of services as well as improving her own performance. VHIR will also help ASHAs in the tracking of incentives received for different services rendered by her through keeping section-wise record of beneficiaries and entering the data in payment sheet. She can also claim to verify services or activities based on documentation in ASHA Diary. Drug supply can also be tracked through the current VHIR as it has provision of quarterly replenishment of drugs and supplies mentioned in one of its sections.

Some of the problems in the old tool are:

- Earlier tool had mother and child registration as well as service delivery in different section, which sometimes resulted in lack of newborn registration update after delivery. It was also observed that a newborn registration is done in child health section without mother being registered in ANC section. This results in delayed service delivery.
- Due to non-availability of a printed tool (VHIR), ASHAs were purchasing blank registers from the market, spending almost ₹300 to 400 per year. Without guidance, they were

drawing columns as per their own understanding, which resulted in different formats as well as increased time spent on drawing lines in a blank register.

- Since no one from government was guiding ASHAs, they kept planning, recording and reporting formats drawn in blank registered as per their own understanding and ease. This resulted in different types of formats in field. Most of the ASHAs kept details of child immunization and delivery status of pregnant women, which left little room for ASHAs to plan ANC and PNC care.
- ASHAs had to refer many registers to give information of various services provided to a single beneficiary.

The uses of the new VHIR tool are:

- Earlier tool did not have comprehensive information on family planning (unmet need), adolescent health (weekly iron and folic acid supplementation [WIFS] and sanitary napkin), community-based management of NRC and SNCU discharged children. Hence, rollout of RMNCH+A strategy was very difficult. New VHIR has been framed in such a way that it addresses the planning and service delivery issues of all RMNCH+A strategy related services.
- It was observed in field, in a VHND session, that only immunization register was with ASHA and when she visited facility with a pregnant woman she carried only delivery register. Now, a single register with all information related to mother and child is available to her. This would provide all information at one place at any point in time.
- New tool is designed in such a way that even the least educated ASHA can also fill it with ease. She has to write minimum content and most of the information is either in marking ticks or in digits form.
- It will help in tracking timely health service delivery to all target groups, especially migratory population, socially and geographically excluded groups, and those who have low service acceptance level.

- It is observed that most of the ASHAs get paid only on JSY, immunization and Polio Programme. But now, with availability of new VHIR, it helps her to create opportunity and encourages her to work on different sections to increase her income. This will also help her to crosscheck with incentives received from block and actual claims received against her work.
- It was observed that during VHSNC meetings, ASHA usually sit silently. Now, with the help of VHIR she can identify and raise issues where she need help form VHSNC members, AWW, and ANM and others to increase coverage. She can ask for help in persuading families in accessing services. She can ask ANM to arrange service delivery as per the community need. She can ask AWW to jointly visit a malnourished child for NRC admission and follow up with an NRC discharged child. She can help VHSNC in preparation of village health plan as she has details of diseases prevalence in her assigned area.
- Since all the target group population is registered in different sections of VHIR, a list for the same can be prepared by ASHAs that will enable them and service provider in planning of services for underserved, hard to reach population and high-risk cases.

Facility data-case sheet

To achieve the goals for reduction of maternal mortality and morbidity, the GoI has commitment to provide quality antenatal, postnatal and intranatal care during pregnancy and childbirth by skilled birth attendant. Timely identification and management of obstetric complications is the key to the survival of mothers. To achieve this, PHCs and CHCs should be operated with proficiency for providing basic and emergency obstetric services. These centres are also responsible for providing pre-referral emergency care for women who develop complications during delivery. To assist the service providers in imparting knowledge and skill, case sheets were developed, which will help them in providing services to women in labour and obstetric emergencies thereby reducing maternal mortality.

The process of development of the case sheet uncovered areas in which the team needed to reach agreement on the best guidance to provide especially when source guidelines were not specific or in agreement or when guidelines did not comply with the best available international evidence. This deliberation among all those involved helped ensure a detailed and comprehensive tool that was uniquely suited to PHCs (Figure 4.2).

More specifically, the principles and benefits of case sheets especially in the PHCs are as follows:

- The case sheet follows a logical sequence for diagnosis and management of cases and provides readily accessible guidelines for managing complications and referrals. It is hoped that providers will view the tool as a valuable job aid and not a tedious paperwork requirement.
- The inclusion of complication case sheets is especially important since in PHCs providers may not routinely encounter certain complications, making it difficult to readily remember care protocols. The case sheet is also intended to support improving referral practices as assessments indicated that providers did not always know how to detect and manage complications or when to refer.
- The case sheet can be modified to better suit the PHC context. The case sheet should include a simplified partograph based on the WHO partograph and be adapted to be useful at the PHC level.
- The detail included in the case sheet also provided guidance on the type of knowledge and skills providers need to have to be able to manage cases.

If the basic case sheet does not provide necessary knowledge, providers identify markers for complications they are referred to more detailed case sheets that provide guidelines for more accurately diagnosing and treating maternal and newborn complications.

Figure 4.2 *Sample Case Sheet*

Project Sukshema   Department of Health, Government of Karnataka   National Rural Health Mission

COMPLICATION CASE SHEET F

For initial management and referral for women with postpartum haemorrhage

Send a copy of the case sheet along with this sheet to the referral facility

A.BACKGROUND INFORMATION

District _____ Taluka _____ PHC Location _____

Name _____ Thayi card number ☐☐☐☐☐☐☐☐☐

Address _____

B.SPECIFIC DIAGNOSIS AND INITIAL MANAGEMENT

☐ Shout for help. Mobilize all available health personnel

   Record vital signs Pulse ___/min BP ___mmHg Respiration ___breaths/min Temperature ___°C

☐ Insert 16-18 gauge IV and give Normal Saline or Ringer's Lactate or 5 % Dextrose Normal Saline at 30 drops per min

☐ Insert Foley's catheter

   If the woman is in shock (systolic BP <90 mmHg, and/or pulse >110/minute) or she is bleeding heavily (soaking one pad in less than 5 minutes) give the following

   ☐ Give IV Normal Saline or Ringer's Lactate or 5 % Dextrose Normal Saline at 60 drops per min for the first 1 litre (2 bottles)

   ☐ Next 500ml (1 bottle) at 30 drops per min ☐ Repeat if necessary

   ☐ If the systolic BP increases to ≥100 mmHg and pulse slows down to <100/min, slow the IV drip to 3 drops per min

   ☐ Keep the woman warm, keep her feet elevated. ☐ Give oxygen. ☐ Keep the woman NPO

Diagnosis (Tick a, b, c, or d)	Initial management at the PHC (Tick when management done)
a. ☐ Retained placental fragments within first 24 hours postpartum (Tick boxes; both must be present) ☐ Increased bleeding ☐ Placenta not delivered either completely or partially	☐ Give Oxytocin 20 IU in IV infusion in 500 ml of Ringer's Lactate or Dextrose Normal Saline at 60 drops per minute Give the following antibiotics (prophylaxis prior to performing manual removal) ☐ Ampicillin 1g IV ☐ or Orally ☐ and ☐ Metronidazole 500mg IV ☐ or 400 mg Orally ☐ and ☐ Gentamicin 80mg IV ☐ or IM ☐ Reason if not given _____ ☐ Perform manual removal of placenta or fragments Reason if not done _____ If unable to perform manual removal ☐ Call and determine the nearest facility where blood and surgical intervention is available, if necessary ☐ Arrange transport ☐ Continue Oxytocin 20 IU in 500ml of Ringer's Lactate or Normal Saline or 5 % Dextrose Normal Saline at 30 drops per min ☐ Perform bimanual compression of the uterus if bleeding is heavy during transport
b. ☐ Atonic uterus (Tick boxes; all must be present) ☐ Increased bleeding ☐ Placenta expelled ☐ Soft and flabby uterus	☐ Massage the uterus to expel any clots ☐ If not given earlier, give Oxytocin 10 IU IM ☐ Give Oxytocin 20 IU in IV infusion in 500 ml of Ringer's Lactate or Normal Saline or 5% Dextrose Normal Saline at 60 drops per minute ☐ Follow up with Oxytocin 10 IU in IV infusion in 500 ml of Ringer's Lactate or Normal Saline or 5% Dextrose Normal Saline at 40 drops per minute Reason if not given _____ If bleeding continues, give one of the following additional uterotonics, either ☐ Methergine/ Ergotamine 0.2 mg IM per dose ☐ can be repeated every 15 minutes for a total of 5 doses. Do NOT give if high blood pressure is present. Repeat doses given ☐ Number of doses:_____ or ☐ Prostaglandin/ Carboprost 0.25 mg IM per dose ☐ can be repeated every 15 minutes for a total of 8 doses. Do NOT give if patient has asthma. Repeat doses given ☐ Number of doses:_____ or ☐ Misoprostol 600 mcg Orally ☐ or Rectally ☐ Reason if not given _____

1

Disclaimer: This image is for representation purpose only.

Table 4.3	*Case Sheet Elements*

Case Sheet Outline for 24×7 PHCs

Case sheet for normal labour and delivery
    Section 1: Initial assessment
    Section 2: Labour monitoring (including simplified partograph)
    Section 3: Delivery notes
    Section 4: Postpartum period
    Outcomes sheet

Supplemental complication case sheets
    A: Prolonged/obstructed labour
    B: Pre-eclampsia/eclampsia
    C: Antepartum haemorrhage
    D: Infection/sepsis
    E: Premature rupture of membranes
    F: PPH
    G: Newborn complications
    H: Other complications

Supplemental case sheets (each 1–2 pages long) are provided for management of eclampsia, PPH, prolonged or obstructed labour and other complications, as described in Table 4.3.

Block monitoring visits

The RMNCH+A strategic approach for improving maternal health and child survival envisages support from development partners, state and district programme management unit for integrated planning, implementation and monitoring of the RMNCH+A interventions across high priority districts. In order to ensure that districts get timely support to implement the most critical interventions, the development partners are expected to offer need-based, district-level assistance and work alongside district and block-level stakeholders to identify key bottlenecks and address them systemically. It has been observed from the field visits that there exist inter-block variations within the districts in terms of health infrastructure and service delivery. This could be due to clustering of vulnerable and marginalized populations, geographical inaccessibility or security concerns, on account of which these blocks remain relatively underserved. Under the district intensification plan, the block is envisaged as the primary unit for implementation and management of RMNCH + A interventions, the capacities for which are to be developed locally through mentoring support by the district and state management units and the development partner.

Purpose of block monitoring visits

- Make a quick assessment of the infrastructure, human resources and provision of services (both at facility and community level)
- Assess service delivery (quality and coverage) at block level
- Review progress of community outreach and community-/home-based interventions
- Validate the data reported into HMIS
- Gauge the client (beneficiary) satisfaction level with RMNCH + A services

Steps in block monitoring visit

To achieve the aforementioned goals, constitution of appropriate mixed skills team is important. These team members should be able to provide mentoring/hand-holding and supportive supervision. It is proposed that district monitors, assigned by various development partners, visit one block each month in each HPD. They will be joined on these visits by government representatives from district and state, and where directed by the SPMU, experts, RPs from mentoring institutions and NGO representatives may also be part of the team. The dates for block monitoring visits should be informed in advance to all team members. The schedule of visit for three or six months may be drawn up so that the district monitors can schedule it in their monthly work plans and availability of all team members is ensured.

The team should visit delivery points including DH and FRU (if present in the block), 24×7 PHC, CHC and sample of SCs designated and interact with the community. During the visit, the focus should be on:

- Bottleneck hampering quality/effective coverage of essential interventions saving newborn and mother lives, at all level community, outreach, facility level throughout continuum of care
- Implementation of strategies overcoming the bottleneck and addressing inequity and disparity at block level (geographical, gender, social groups)
- Trends/progress of key indicators to follow
- Effective implementation of strategy
- Reduction of bottleneck
- Increase coverage of essential interventions
- Real-time feedback and report to adjust and accelerate implementation and scale up from block to district-wide scale

Reporting format

Following the visit, the district monitors, along with the team members are expected to prepare a visit report that includes:

- Major actionable points and level at which the action is to be taken (i.e., facility, block, district or state).
- Stakeholders (development partners, district programme management [DPMU], SPMU, other experts or RPs, NGOs) responsible for providing technical support along with timelines.
- Actions taken on previously identified bottlenecks and visit reports.

The reporting format provides a broad guidance on the parameters to be assessed during monthly visits to the blocks and to be reported thereafter. Additional components may be included by the District Monitors based on experiences from the field visits so that most relevant and critical issues are reported. It is important that not only is the progress captured but also the bottlenecks for delay are explored and recorded. The actions should focus on addressing these bottlenecks. The reports should be forwarded by the District Monitors to the concerned authorities at district and state level within one week of completing the visit. The SLP agency can compile the reports from different block visited during the month, present the key findings and proposed actions to the SRU/SUT before forwarding it to the National RMNCH+A Unit (NRU) in the following month.

Community behavioural tracking survey

The proposed CBTS is designed to meet the requirements for evidence-based programme planning and review at subdistrict levels that are not being provided by the national surveys. They are meant to be short, focused and semi-annual. The data will facilitate in programme management, tracking outcomes, validating HMIS/MCTS and making mid-course corrections in strategies/service delivery mechanisms.

Objectives of CBTS

1. To support block-, district- and state-level programme managers to monitor and periodically review programme activities based on real-time population-based data on coverage, utilization and outcomes related to RMNCH+A
2. To validate block-level HMIS and MCTS data

The CBTS will be administered to five target groups that represent distinct periods along the RMNCH+A continuum: (1) mothers who delivered in the past 2 months (2) mothers with children aged 3–5 months (3) mothers with children aged 6–11 months (4) mothers with children aged 12–23 months and (5) girls aged 13–19 years. Sample sizes and the questions administered will vary across these survey groups such that we get precise measurement of indicators relevant for each group.

Two types of indicators will be measured in CBTS: output and outcome. Output indicators measure the activities on the part of the FLWs/health facilities, whereas the outcomes measure the behaviour/utilization of services on the part of the mothers/households. A total of 50 indicators will be measured through CBTS—17 output and 33 outcome indicators. The number of indicators is the highest at 36 for the first survey group (mothers delivered in the past two months) and the lowest at five indicators for the girls aged 13–19 years (Table 4.4).

Rolling facility survey

As a part of concurrent monitoring at facility level, the rolling facility survey (RFS) is intended to provide feedback to the managers for planning. Its focus is primarily on outputs and outcomes and on the lines similar to the CBTS. The main purpose is to support block-, district- and state-level managers in periodic review by generating facility-level data on knowledge, practice, skills of the nurses and outcomes related to RMNCH+A. The survey can be conducted at all the levels of the facilities and the periodicity of the survey depends upon the feasibility and should be conducted at least three times a year. The data collection can be carried out at all delivery points if not in selected representative number of blocks. The data collection procedures depend upon whether data is collected on knowledge or practice. If it is knowledge, the questionnaire method should be used and if the data needed is on practice of the nurses, it will be observed during day as well as night-time. As far as skill of the nurses is concerned, it will be assessed during daytime using the demonstration method.

In order to provide the detailed data to be collected for each of the domains such as knowledge, skill and practice, the lists of indicators given in Tables 4.5–4.7 are valuable to develop the questionnaire and/or themes or topics.

Table 4.4 RMNCH+A Indicators Measured in CBTS

Survey Indicator	Type	Survey Group
Reproductive health		
1. Percentage of recently delivered mothers using IUD or TL by 6 months after delivery	Outcome	0–2 m, 3–5 m, 6–11 m
2. Percentage of FP acceptors received FP follow up care within 1 month after acceptance	Output	0–2 m, 3–5 m, 6–11 m, 12–23 m
3. Percentage of recently delivered mothers who received FP counselling during pregnancy and within 6 months of delivery	Output	0–2 m, 3–5 m
4. Percentage of recently delivered mothers who are using IUCD or tubal ligation (TL) for at least 6 months	Outcome	6–11 m
5. Percentage of recently delivered mothers who experienced complications due to FP procedures	Outcome	0–2 m, 3–5 m, 6–11 m, 12–23 m
6. Percentage of women with unmet need for family planning	Outcome	0–2 m, 3–5 m, 6–11 m, 12–23 m
Maternal health		
7. Percentage of recently delivered mothers who received full ANC services[1]	Outcome	0–2 m
8. Percentage of recently delivered mothers who had BP measured and Hb tested during last trimester of pregnancy	Outcome	0–2 m

(Continued)

Table 4.4 Continued

Survey Indicator	Type	Survey Group
9. Percentage of recently delivered mothers who were registered within the first trimester of pregnancy	Output	0–2 m
10. Percentage of recently delivered mothers who received 100 IFA tablets during pregnancy	Output	0–2 m
11. Percentage of recently delivered mothers who consumed 100 IFA tablets during pregnancy	Outcome	0–2 m
12. Percentage of recently delivered mothers who had an emergency birth preparedness plan	Outcome	0–2 m
13. Percentage of recently delivered mothers who had at least 2 contacts with the health system during the last trimester of pregnancy	Output	0–2 m
14. Percentage of recently delivered mothers who had the delivery at a health facility	Outcome	0–2 m
15. Percentage of mothers who recently delivered at home who used misoprostol	Outcome	0–2 m
16. Percentage of recently delivered mothers who were attended by an ANM/LHV/SN/doctor during delivery	Output	0–2 m
17. Percentage of recently delivered mothers with major direct obstetric complications treated at CEmOC facility[2]	Output	0–2 m
18. Percentage of mothers recently delivered (non-Caesarean) at a facility who stayed in the facility for at least 48 hours[3]	Outcome	0–2 m
19. Percentage of recently delivered mothers who received follow-up visit at home within 24 hours after delivery or returning from the facility	Output	0–2 m
20. Percentage of recently delivered mothers contacted at least three times within the first week of delivery	Output	0–2 m

21.	Percentage of recently delivered mothers contacted at least once a month in the first three months after delivery	Output	0–2 m
22.	Percentage of recently delivered mothers contacted at least once between 5–8 months after delivery	Output	3–5 m, 6–11 m
23.	Percentage of recently delivered mothers who received full ANC services, had institutional delivery, and received follow-up visit at home within 24 hours after returning from the facility[4]	Outcome	0–2 m
24.	Percentage of recently delivered mothers who received support to breastfeed immediately after delivery	Output	0–2 m

Newborn health

25.	Percentage of newborns who received initiation of breastfeeding within one hour of delivery	Outcome	0–2 m
26.	Percentage of newborns who were not given any pre-lacteal	Outcome	0–2 m
27.	Percentage of newborns who did not receive any application at the stump of their cord	Outcome	0–2 m
28.	Percentage of weak newborns[5] identified by FLWs	Output	0–2 m
29.	Percentage of identified weak newborns correctly managed as per HBNC and F-IMNCI/NSSK guidelines	Outcome	0–2 m
30.	Percentage of newborns who were not bathed within 3 days of birth	Outcome	0–2 m
31.	Percentage of newborns with fever who were treated with gentamicin	Outcome	0–2 m

Child health

| 32. | Percentage of children aged 0–5 months who are currently exclusively breastfed | Outcome | 0–2 m, 3–5 m |

(Continued)

Table 4.4 Continued

Survey Indicator	Type	Survey Group
33. Percentage of children aged 12–15 months who are currently breastfed	Outcome	12–23 m
34. Percentage of infants aged 6–8 months who currently receive solid, semi-solid or soft foods	Outcome	6–11 m[6]
35. Percentage of children aged 6–23 months currently receiving age-appropriate complementary feeding (in frequency, quantity and variety plus breastfed)	Outcome	6–11 m, 12–23 m
36. Percentage of recently delivered mothers who received counselling from an FLW regarding exclusive breastfeeding in the past 30 days	Output	0–2 m, 3–5 m
37. Percentage of mothers who received counselling from an FLW regarding age-appropriate complementary feeding in the past 30 days	Output	6–11 m, 12–23 m
38. Percentage of children received micronutrient supplementation (Vit. A and IFA) in the past 6 months	Output	6–11 m
39. Percentage of infant aged 6–11 months who received DPT3 vaccine	Outcome	6–11 m
40. Percentage of children aged 12–23 months who received measles vaccine	Outcome	12–23 m
41. Percentage of children aged 12–23 months fully immunized (received BCG + DPT123 + Measles)	Outcome	12–23 m
42. Percentage of children aged 0–24 months with diarrhoea treated with zinc and oral rehydration therapy (ORT)	Outcome	0–2 m, 3–5 m, 6–11 m, 12–23 m
43. Percentage of children aged 0–24 months who had pneumonia treated with appropriate antibiotic	Outcome	0–2 m, 3–5 m, 6–11 m, 12–23 m

44. Percentage of children aged 0–24 months screened for 4Ds (birth defects, development delays, deficiencies and disease) and its management	Outcome	0–2 m, 3–5 m, 6–11 m, 12–23 m

Adolescent health

45. Percentage of births in the past 2 months that are to women under 19 years	Outcome	0–2 m
46. Percentage of girls aged 13–19 years who received weekly dose of IFA	Output	13–15 y
47. Percentage of girls aged 13–19 years who consumed weekly dose of IFA	Outcome	13–19 y
48. Percentage of girls aged 13–19 years screened for anaemia at least once in the past three months	Outcome	13–19 y
49. Percentage of girls aged 13–19 years who consumed albendazole 400 mg in the last six months	Outcome	13–19 y
50. Percentage of girls aged 13–19 years who bought sanitary napkins from FLWs in the past 6 months	Outcome	13–19 y

[1] Three ANC check-ups at a facility/VHND, 2 TT injections and 100 IFA tablets.

[2] This indicator will also be measured at facility level. The major direct complications include obstructed labour, ante/PPH, eclampsia and sepsis. CEmOC facility refers to the DH or an FRU or a private facility with CEmOC services.

[3] This indicator may also be worded as follows: Percentage of recently delivered mothers who received PNC from a doctor/LHV/nurse/ ANM/ other health personnel within 48 hours after delivery. A similar indicator at the facility level will be: Percentage of mothers discharged within 48 hours of delivery to total deliveries at the facility in the month.

[4] Measures continuum of care for mothers.

[5] Underweight and/or premature.

[6] The questions related to this indicator will be addressed to children aged 6–8 months.

Table 4.5	RFS Indicators
S. No.	**Practice Indicators**
1.	Percentage of cases where all the 3 steps of AMTSL were practised correctly
2.	Percentage of cases in which partograph is used to monitor the progress of the labour
3.	Percentage of cases where BP was measured before delivery
4.	Percentage of cases where the placenta was checked for completeness
5.	Percentage of cases where foetal heart rate was measured before delivery
6.	Percentage of mothers who received instruction on newborn danger signs after delivery
7.	Percentage of newborns weighted
8.	Percentage of cases where the weight of the newborn was documented
9.	Percentage of newborn who were LBW
10.	Percentage of cases where the newborn was placed on the mother's abdomen immediately after delivery
11.	Percentage of cases where the newborn was dried up immediately after delivery
12.	Percentage of cases where the newborn was wrapped immediately after delivery
13.	Percentage of cases where the cord was cut between 1 to 3 minutes after delivery
14.	Percentage of cases in which skin-to-skin care for the newborn practised
15.	Percentage of newborn breasted within 30 minutes
16.	Percentage of cases where cord clamped at correct point
17.	Percentage of mother received counselling on any family planning options after delivery
18.	Percentage of mother accepted PPICUD/TL as a family planning options

S. No.	Practice Indicators
19.	Percentage of nurses washed hand before vaginal examination
20.	Percentage of nurses washed hand with correct technique before vaginal examination
21.	Percentage of cases where women given oxytocin (IM or IV) before delivery
22.	Percentage of nurses using personal protective equipment (PPE) during delivery
23.	Percentage of cases where fundal pressure applied during delivery
24.	Percentage of cases in which sterile delivery trays used during delivery
25.	Percentage of cases where routine episiotomy conducted at the time of delivery

Dashboards

A programme management dashboard is a tool to help support programme managers understand performance, take action and make decisions during the programme planning, implementation and review phases. The dashboards will cover all of RMNCH+A to help provide a complete understanding of programme performance (both good and poor service delivery), and the range of intended users includes CM, HM, PSH and DM to district (DM, CMO, DPM) and block (MOIC, BPM) programme managers.

Dashboards support programmatic decision-making within the health system by including all relevant data in a single forum; accessing a range of indicator types (physical resources, human resources, training, services and health outcomes); allowing the user to drill down beyond the district level to individual blocks and facilities and providing a better understanding of performance through comparisons to targets, benchmarks and total

Table 4.6 *Skill Indicator*

S. No.	Skill Indicators
1.	Percentage of nurses able to demonstrate all steps of AMTSL
2.	Percentage of nurses able to demonstrate plotting the partograph correctly
3.	Percentage of nurses able to demonstrate Hb measurement
4.	Percentage of nurses able to demonstrate urine strip test for protein
5.	Percentage of nurses able to demonstrate four grips during an abdominal examination
6.	Percentage of nurses able to demonstrate measurement of BP correctly
7.	Percentage of nurses able to demonstrate measurement of body temperature
8.	Percentage of nurses able to demonstrate measurement foetal heart rate (FHR) correctly
9.	Percentage of nurses able to calculate EDD
10.	Percentage of nurses able to calculate gestational age
11.	Percentage of nurses able to demonstrate family planning counselling skills
12.	Percentage of nurses able to able to demonstrate PPIUCD insertion correctly
13.	Percentage of nurses able to demonstrate resuscitation of newborn with asphyxia

need. Dashboards offer engage visualizations (i.e., maps, graphs, charts) of the most critical indicators to quickly convey performance to the user.

The conceptualization of the dashboard sought to include indicators of all relevant programme components. Critical indicators were selected through a process of outcome mapping whereby outcomes that have the greatest contribution to targeted GoUP

Table 4.7 *Knowledge Indicators*

S. No.	Knowledge Indicators
1.	Percentage of nurses able to describe how to identify of high-risk pregnancy
2.	Percentage of nurses able to describe steps of AMTSL
3.	Percentage of nurses able to interpret partograph
4.	Percentage of nurses able to describe four grips during an abdominal examination
5.	Percentage of nurses able to describe four major maternal danger signs needing referral
6.	Percentage of nurses able to describe management preterm labour
7.	Percentage of nurses able to describe how to identify severe anaemia
8.	Percentage of nurses able to describe pre-referral management of severe anaemia
9.	Percentage of nurses able to describe how to identify pre-eclampsia
10.	Percentage of nurses able to describe how to identify eclampsia
11.	Percentage of nurses able to describe management pre-eclampsia
12.	Percentage of nurses able to describe how to manage eclampsia
13.	Percentage of nurses able to describe loading dose of $MgSO_4$ to manage eclampsia
14.	Percentage of nurses able to describe how to identify PPH
15.	Percentage of nurses able to describe how to manage PPH
16.	Percentage of nurses able to describe how to identify maternal sepsis
17.	Percentage of nurses able to describe how to manage maternal sepsis

(Continued)

Table 4.7	Continued
S. No.	**Knowledge Indicators**
18.	Percentage of nurses able to describe how identify obstructed labour
19.	Percentage of nurses able to describe how to manage obstructed labour
20.	Percentage of nurses able to describe how to identify foetal distress
21.	Percentage of nurses able to describe newborn danger signs needing referrals
22.	Percentage of nurses able to describe immunization for newborn at birth
23.	Percentage of nurses able to describe medicines to be given for normal newborn
24.	Percentage of nurses able to describe how to identify LBW
25.	Percentage of nurses able to describe how to manage LBW
26.	Percentage of nurses able to describe how to identify newborn sepsis
27.	Percentage of nurses able to describe how to manage newborn sepsis
28.	Percentage of nurses able to describe about cord care
29.	Percentage of nurses able to describe what information to give women/families about newborn care

impacts were identified, and then the most critical services, training, staff, infrastructure and EDS were mapped to that outcome(s).

Integrated ICT Solution

The major challenge that current health system is grappling with is the lack of evidence-based approach in identifying major gaps in service delivery, planning, monitoring and provision of efficient solutions. This is primarily due to absence of business intelligence systems that can capture, collate and synthesize data to help take feasible and timely decisions. At present, there are a number of IT solutions to increase the performance of health systems. However, the solutions are implemented by different entities that are domain specific, and there is no system to integrate all existing solutions. Just to give a few examples, at community level, in spite of having an individualized tracking system (MCTS), it is technically complicated and operationally difficult to track pregnant women those are at a risk of mortality. Since the current system could not customize the need for generating high risk pregnant women or tracking women that needs to be followed up. At system level, the human resource management system is unable to identify the pattern, distribution and need of staff deployment at different facilities so that rational deployment of human resources is possible. Similarly, the supply chain management system is unable to guide efficient allocation of drugs and supplies that are essential for life saving interventions.

The ICT-based solutions are expected to make a tangible impact on health systems goals by incorporating existing solutions and accommodating new solutions for improved functioning of health system. The premises of this approach in order to achieve the RMNCH+A target is based on strong requirement for data plan, data for implementing solutions and data for monitoring implemented solutions. ICT system uses an integrated approach that would cater to the requirement of data-driven management systems using data capturing devices such as mobile, tablet, computer and web apps at community level, facility level and system level. This system will be able to accommodate the existing solutions available and also future solutions. The system will have capabilities of setting an efficient management information system (MIS) and be able to guide decision-making processes such as prioritization and alert generation. The proposed system would be able to generate an integrated business analytics (dashboard) that could visualize different dimensions of an opportunity gap by using data elements from cross functions (server) and will help in improvised decision-making. For example, a dashboard monitor on intervention around high-risk pregnancy would be able to visualize opportunity gaps in the following:

- Service utilization and screening of pregnant women for Hb, BP and urine albumin (U/Alb) (data source: individualized tracking system)
- Terms of geographic and other social differentials (data source: common identifier, GIS latitude–longitude)
- Terms of supply chain management for drugs and equipment (data source: LMIS)
- Terms of skilled human resources available (data source: HRIS)
- Planning, monitoring and follow up (data source: PIP tracking)

Such dashboard requires a cloud-based integrated solution, where data elements could easily be used from different server systems across multiple functions. The assumption for this approach is that any ICT-based system cannot be an ultimate solution unless it is backed by strong willingness to adapt new technology and require a continuous support to use the system for improvised planning. The essentials for establishing such integrated solution demands for a platform that is able to meet following requirements:

- **A design frame:** Should be able to articulate the architecture (layout) that can be easily built into existing applications and also future needs.
- **Single data repository:** Have a common repository so that all data from multiple databases are synchronized into a single-server set-up. The system would be able to communicate with different server systems and flexible to accommodate applications developed by different vendors.
- **Common identifier:** Should have predefined common identifier so that data integration would be possible at one or more levels.

- **Strong business analytics:** Should be capable to provide an analytic solution (dashboard, alert system, MIS and the like) and/or able to get similar solutions available in the market (via, IBM, Tableau, SAS, Oracle and the like).

Key elements for ICT implementation

The proposed ICT solutions demand the following requirements—parameters those could be captured (Table 4.8).

Table 4.8		ICT Parameters
Community	Pregnant women	Details of pregnant women along with geographical details
	Child	Details of childbirth along with details as already existing with MCTS and HMIS
	Mother	Details of the outcome of pregnancy and assistance/supported parameters after delivery
	Adolescent women	Details of adolescent women and supported health parameters along with geographical information
	ASHA	Details of ASHA along with status active/non-active and details about job aid and personal data
	ANM	Details of ANM along with status active/non-active and details about job aid and personal data
	AWW	Details of AWW along with status active/non-active and details about job aid and personal data
	CBTS	Details of the survey conducted in all 100 blocks of 25 HPDs and indicator-wise data

(Continued)

Table 4.8	Continued	
Facility	SC	Details of the SC along with geographical information, service availability and human resources
	CHC/FRU	Details of the CHC/FRU along with geographical information, service availability and human resources
	PHC	Details of the PHC along with geographical information, service availability and human resources
	DH	Details of the DH along with geographical information, service availability and human resources
	Case sheet summary	Details of the delivery conducted along with outcome and output of the facility
System	LMIS	Detailed information on the availability of drugs and supplies as per the indenting
	HRIS	Detailed information on the human resources availability and working status along with personal information
	PIP	Detailed microplanning data and tracking of the PIP implementation from the beginning of the execution until the end of the implementation
	MDR	Detailed information on the maternal death system implementation and tracking the indicators based on geographical information

Methodology to capture all the parameters

In order to capture the aforementioned parameters, ICT implementations are required at all levels—community, facility and system (Table 4.9).

Table 4.9 *ICT Interventions Proposed*

S. No.	ICT Solutions	Descriptions
1.	FLW performance monitoring	A tablet-based application having a checklist containing list of 10 parameters to monitor the performance of ASHAs and grade them.
2.	M Health (ETT/ mSwasthya/ CCS/PHFI) [Beneficiary Continuum of Care]	Integrated mobile-based application (job-aids) for ASHA and supervisory application for ANM (tablet). It tracks individual women and helps FLWs in planning outreach service to increase the coverage of health services.
3.	Tracking of high-risk pregnancy	A tablet-based application (job aids) used in VHND by ANM to record Hb, U/Alb and BP to identify, manage and refer pregnant women who are at risk of mortality due to haemorrhage and hypertensive disorder.
4.	Case sheet for nurse mentoring programme	A tablet-based application (job aids) that helps nurses to deliver protocol-based services and generates alters for key lifesaving interventions and actions.
5.	RFS	A survey where the facilities will be evaluated for necessary drugs, equipment and human resources availability and indicators definition based on the collated information.
6.	LMIS/HRIS	Help the government in strengthening existing system.
7.	PIP tracking tool	An online web application which will support the GMs/ JDs/ CMOs/DPMs/MOICs/ BPMs and such others to prepare a micro plan for the execution of each line item from the PIP. This tool will also again help in tracking the progress of each line item and the financial progress from the date of execution until the end of the activity based on the prepared micro plan.

(Continued)

Table 4.9	Continued	
S. No.	**ICT Solutions**	**Descriptions**
8.	MDR	An integrated IVRS, SMS and web-based application to proactively increase the reporting of maternal death and analyse the levels, trends and social and biological causes of mortality.
9.	CBTS	A mobile-based application to capture household survey data and generate key RMNCH+A indicators at block level. The system is already been rolled out and will cover 100 focused blocks in 6 months.
10.	Community gap assessment	A tablet-based application to understand and identify existing gaps in the community in terms of coverage, distribution of FLWs and availability of health service providers. This will be done by CRPs and updated every six months.
11.	Dashboard	Will be hosted in web that has capability of calling data elements from different sources (mentioned earlier) and generate interactive graphs, GIS maps, tables and the like. The main purpose of the dashboard is to identify opportunity gap in the system for corrective actions. The dashboard is a tool that will be used at different levels in review platforms.

Integrating all the parameters captured from the ICT implementations

The integration of all the data sources require creation of a master list of district, block, facility and villages with alphanumeric coding. Since currently the information from various sources such as MCTS, HMIS, KPI, AHS and other ICT implementations

Figure 4.3 *ICT Implementation Architecture*

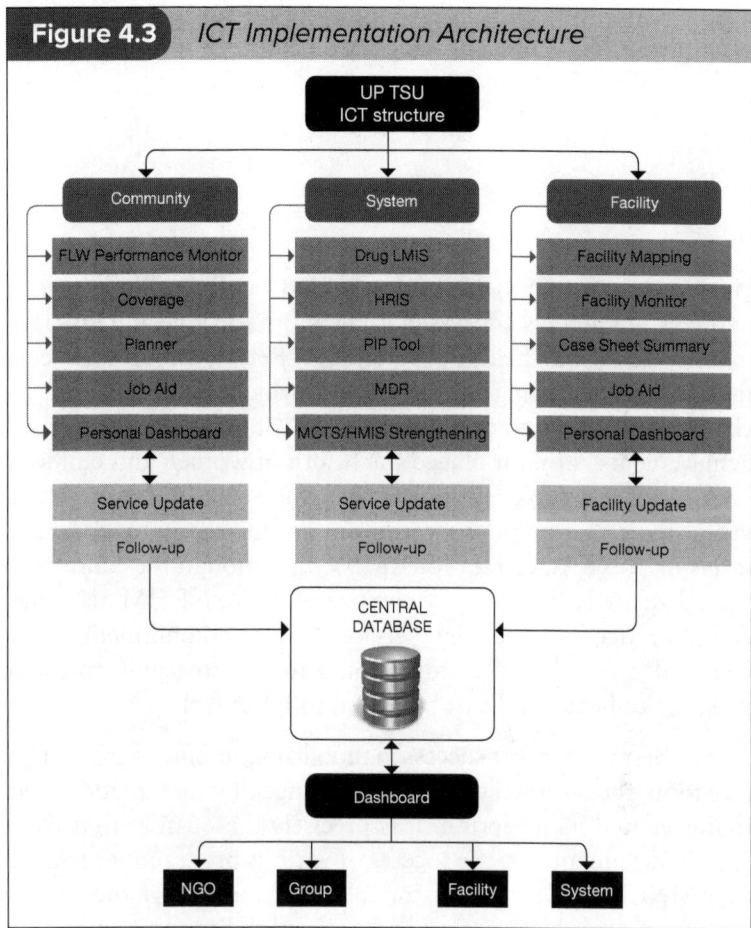

are using different terminologies, these could not be integrated directly. The master list with coding of all the districts, blocks, facilities and villages will be used as a key in integration of the reports from various sources. With the master list in place, any data source from other ICT implementers will also be linked to the central repository and the central dashboard for easily deciphering the status on the field (Figure 4.3).

EPILOGUE: CONCLUSION AND WAY FORWARD

Until recently, RMNCH fell far behind other health priorities and was not always addressed in the most effective and efficient manner in various health programmes. Recent efforts have culminated in the setting up of NRHM, which actively sought to change the status quo on RMNCH. One of the NRHM's biggest achievements is that it placed the health of women and children back at the very top of the public health agenda of India. In recent years, the strategy has succeeded in mobilizing unprecedented levels of public resources for RMNCH, although the funding is not adequate in a country of the size of India. NRHM also triggered a range of policy and service delivery commitments that, being adequately implemented, could contribute significantly to progress of health indicators related to RMNCH.

Yet, despite its great success in mobilizing resources and public attention, the national strategy left a range of issues unaddressed that predated its inception. It is precisely these issues that have proven detrimental to the success of various programmes related to RMNCH. Given the historical shortcomings of the health system, the implementation and accountability mechanisms to ensure that the government's commitments to RMNCH would translate into measurable outcomes at the state and district levels have been called into question. There is a lot that needs to be done to make effective use of resources and to develop high-quality national health plans with strong RMNCH components. Also, there are a number of bilateral, multilateral, national and regional organizations that are providing their assistance in fulfilling the government's commitment to improve mother and child health.

The various options introduced in this book aim to address a few of the shortcomings of the health system and provide viable solutions focused clearly on the aspects that can be addressed in low-resources setting as are many districts in India. The approaches suggested in the book are not mutually exclusive (nor exhaustive), but rather build on each other and become more relevant in rural contexts of India where most of these activities have been implemented. Whereas the experiences vary from state to state, key factors that both promoted and inhibited the work of RMNCH have been identified and addressed in this book.

- For any intervention to be effective, it has to be based on evidence and should address the pressing needs of the community in which it will be implemented. Otherwise, the support to the intervention and the uptake of services will not be noticeable. For evidence to be generated, one has to rely both on primary and secondary data. This book addresses this need by suggesting various assessments and analysis that will help in framing relevant and doable objectives. These objectives, as seen in the chapters that preceded, aim to address the gaps at all levels of the health service delivery, starting from systemic issues to the facility and community levels. Moreover, a series of methods has been provided for the programme implementers to generate enough evidence to customize their interventions in the regions where the programmes will be implemented. If done as intended, these assessments will generate enough evidence to understand what interventions work and what do not work in a given setting, and make case for scaling up of interventions that work.

- Based on the evidence available, the book also proposed a series of technical interventions that address the mother and child health issues in a comprehensive way. The high-impact interventions are prioritized so that with minimum resources maximum benefit can be obtained in fairly quick time. More importantly, innovations are made integral to the designing of RMNCH programmes. These innovations, successful in Karnataka and UP, which were provided as case studies in this book, can be scaled up and taken up and can also be institutionalized for better RMNCH outcomes. Particularly those that relate to the mentoring interventions, FLWs and community involvement need to be given extra attention, as they are sustainable and help in strengthening the various mechanisms initiated by NRHM and other programmes.

- Developing tools that are usable and also user friendly is another important aspect covered in the book. As the FLWs such as ASHAs, ANMs and AWWs are central to the NRHM strategy to reach out to communities, these tools that have been used in programmes in Karnataka and UP and have been described in this book, will decrease the workload and help them undertake their work with ease and facilitate in generating quality data. As the data is backbone for decision-making and policy development, quality data emerging from the field becomes essential; this book tries to fill that particular gap. ASHA Diary, case sheets, ETT and the like lay a solid foundation to gather timely data and reduce the errors in reporting the same.

- Finally, the issues with HMIS and MCTS bring into focus the need for various tools and mechanisms that can be deployed throughout the health system, which can make data accessible for timely decision-making. While the reach of HMIS and MCTS are near universal, the data that is generated and the way it is generated bring a great deal of issues into foreground. The book tries to address these issues by proposing a bouquet of tools that could be used on need basis, which, if used, could generate data at all levels of the health system. These can be used for monitoring and evaluation purposes as well. However, the main need these tools propose to fulfil is to understand the ground reality and help decision-makers and programme implementers to come up with relevant local solutions to immediate problems. An ICT solution, discussed in the previous chapter, although resource intensive and requiring a good deal of planning, could be executed so that all the systems work in unison and any issue in any part of programme implementation could be flagged and addressed from the local level to the national level.

This versatility of strategies proposed in this book was demonstrated through a set of activities that could be implemented by the government as well as implementing partner agencies, using the resources and mechanism already in place, to come up with processes that address RMNCH challenges in the country. Their interventions will generate empirical evidence that could be shared widely and can lead to tools and processes that meet their objective of supporting NHM initiatives to improve mother and child health. Moreover, it is hoped that the priority gaps and challenges identified in this book will inform future advocacy and action, and the evidence from the field will provide evidence for cross-learning and discussion. It is hoped that stakeholders will find these processes to be useful for articulating collective priorities or address a local-level problem or felt need. A clear expectation from this book is that innovations are critical for driving action at the national, state and district levels.

Way Forward

While acknowledging the importance of these initiatives as drivers for effective action and commitment to improving mother and child health in India, there are other critical factors that need to be taken into consideration for effective planning and implementation of these programmes. A few of them are mentioned further as a way forward.

Importance of leadership: At the national level, strong and shared leadership is central to the success of these efforts. A leading body needs to coordinate all partners' efforts and ensure that the progress of the work is measured and shared with all key stakeholders. Technical leads from various key organizations can collectively oversee its quality. These coordinated efforts allow for the identification of additional resources and leadership of this process in the country. One should also ensure that these efforts do not be detracted due to other ongoing activities being undertaken by the government. When the government actively leads the process, it becomes easy to come up with innovations that clearly support and advance government priorities. If the government or other key stakeholders did not lead the process as actively, results will not appear relevant in the overall context, and consequently may not contribute to better health outcomes.

Make continuum of care central to health programming: It is important to recognize that RMNCH cannot be addressed in isolation as each stage is linked to the overall health status of various stages of life. These interventions are essential for the overall well-being of the populations. However, there remains a noticeable gap in programmes that aim to address various aspects of the continuum of care simultaneously. To have a greater impact on improving mother and child health indicators, various RMNCH programmes must be implemented to cover the complete cycle of the continuum of care. Recognizing that this is a huge endeavour, with limited resources at disposal, aligning the programmes to the overall NHM context of RMNCH will produce guidance on how effectively and efficiently resources could be utilized for a common goal.

Community empowerment: Evidence shows that community empowerment should be made a part of all health programming as the community has unique resources in bridging the gap between individuals and the health system. Trained community members can deliver crucial messages related to RMNCH and facilitating access to preventive and curative health care services. They can also, using the mechanisms put in place by NRHM, play the role of monitors to make the health system more accountable. When the recipients of the service become participants in planning and monitoring, then the programme will be sustainable and effective. This in turn will contribute to reducing maternal and child mortality. It is evident that programmes that engage community for health system strengthening will contribute to better access, referral and care. Involving the community with innovative and culturally appropriate ways will ensure that rural communities can access health care services.

Improve access to health care: It is not always possible for rural communities, who are poor and live in remote areas, to access health services. A failure to address the issue of access to health care while encouraging communities to engage with health services might be counter-productive. Simply encouraging communities to access health care systems is not enough to ensure an equitable and affordable health service when issues such as transportation are not taken into account. For a sustainable plan, income generation strategies need to be incorporated into community-related RMNCH projects because poverty is the root cause of many social ills, and if poverty can be address through government programmes, populations will find it easy to lead a healthy lifestyle and access health system easily.

Address issues of gender equality: Gender-related attitudes, especially in rural areas, have a direct impact on the health and well-being of women and girls. The health programmes should promote gender equality by including the empowerment angle for women and adolescent girls. Moreover, engaging men and adolescent boys is essential to improve sexual and reproductive health, including RMNCH outcomes. These programmes should actively engage men and try to change their attitudes and behaviours in areas related to gender and RMNCH. To ensure this, programmes need to have a formal feedback mechanism that can help understand how gender-related attitudes are affecting the health outcomes of a community.

Focus on linkages: Currently, there is inadequate coordination or complementarity among various RMNCH projects in the country, leading to replication of work and neglecting what is working well. To enhance the outcomes of the RMNCH projects, and for scale-up, there is a need to develop supporting mechanism that allows for working with other partners in coordinated efforts. There is a need to develop a common platform to share learnings, analyses and trends. While this book has provided insights into the bottlenecks in information sharing when it comes to monitoring health indicators in order to facilitate information sharing, there is a need to establish a common platform whereby various public health stakeholders can share information and better collaborate in implementing RMNCH initiatives. The initiatives should not be implemented in isolation. Only by linking interventions can we reduce costs and allow for greater efficiency, which in turn will increases uptake of services and provide opportunities for promoting health care.

Building partnerships: In many states, access to health and availability of health care services is decisively influenced by location, funding, access to services or geographical isolation. These disparities have an adverse impact on who can have access to RMNCH services. Collaboration with the government and external partners to identify areas and communities with significant health needs and building capacities on RMNCH at all levels related to the programme activities will result in improved health outcomes. In many cases, programme implementers can collaborate with external partners to increase impact and reach of health services among various communities. There is a need to move from coordination to collaboration with as many actors in the geographic area. This should be done through a formal method of engagement and done in collaboration with the government. Thus, working in health will lead to significant achievements and developing sustainable mechanisms for continuation of RMNCH programmes.

INDEX

ABOUT THE AUTHORS

B.M. Ramesh is an Assistant Professor at the Department of Community Health Sciences, Rady Faculty of Health Sciences, University of Manitoba (UoM), Canada. Prior to this, he was a Director of the Population Research Centre, Dharwad, Karnataka; before that, he was a teaching faculty at the International Institute for Population Sciences (IIPS), Mumbai.

Professor Ramesh has an experience of 30 years of teaching, research and programme implementation, monitoring and evaluation in the field of demography, maternal, newborn and child health, HIV/AIDS and demographic and health surveys. He was a Project Director for the Uttar Pradesh Technical Support Unit (UP TSU) and the Karnataka Health Promotion Trust (KHPT), Bangalore. As a director at the UP TSU, he led the design of the community-, facility- and health system-level technical support strategies, setting up of the TSU (including the recruitment and training of the TSU staff) and mapping of over 9,000 public health facilities in 25 high-priority districts. He was one of the coordinators of the first round of National Family Health Survey (1992–1993).

Professor Ramesh, a demographer by training, earned his PhD in demography from Bombay University in 1986 and was a recipient of the Population Council Postdoctoral Fellowship in 1996.

Shiva S. Halli is a Professor at the Department of Community Health Sciences, Rady Faculty of Health Sciences, UoM. He joined the UoM in 1986 as an Assistant Professor soon after completing his PhD in demography. Based on his exceptional performance in research, within six years he was promoted to the rank of professor in 1992. In his tenure at the UoM during the last 31 years, he has published 9 books and nearly 100 original scientific research papers.

For the last 15 years, he has been working in India on UoM projects such as those on HIV/AIDS and maternal, neonatal and child health. He is a founding member of the university's HIV/AIDS prevention programme team in Karnataka. He was a member of the Evaluation Advisory Group of the Bill & Melinda Gates Foundation for HIV/AIDS programme in India. Currently, he is the coordinator of the Indian programmes of the UoM.

Krishnamurthy Jayanna is currently working as a Senior Technical Advisor, Quality Improvement, for the reproductive, maternal, newborn and child health projects implemented by the UoM in India and Africa. He holds a part-time faculty position as an Assistant Professor in the Department of Community Health Sciences, UoM.

By training, Krishnamurthy is a physician and public health specialist with more than 15 years of experience in various capacities in the developmental field, specifically in the areas of sexual, reproductive, maternal, newborn, child and adolescent health, and communicable and non-communicable diseases.

He received his MBBS degree from Mysore University and MD degree in community medicine from Bangalore Medical College and Research Institute. He has received specialized training in research methods in sexual and reproductive health at WHO, Geneva, and has held a postdoctoral research fellowship from International Infectious Disease and Global Health Training Programme at the UoM.

Mohan H.L. is a social scientist and is currently working as a Senior Technical Advisor for UoM projects in India. He has more than 25 years of working experience in government and non-governmental sectors, especially in the areas of education, health, decentralization, adolescent education and rural development. Currently, he also holds the position of Managing Trustee of the KHPT. He has experience of working as an advisor and a consultant for development projects in India and other countries, including those of UNFPA, UNESCO and UNICEF.

Mohan earned his postgraduate degree in rural and urban community development from the School of Social Work, Roshni Nilaya, Mangalore.